FILM
ENGLAND

*Culturally English Filmmaking
since the 1990s*

Andrew Higson

I.B. TAURIS

LONDON · NEW YORK

Published in 2011 by I.B.Tauris & Co Ltd
6 Salem Road, London W2 4BU
175 Fifth Avenue, New York NY 10010
www.ibtauris.com

Distributed in the United States and Canada
Exclusively by Palgrave Macmillan
175 Fifth Avenue, New York NY 10010

ISBN: 978 1 84885 453 6 (HB)
      978 1 84885 454 3 (PB)

A full CIP record for this book is available from the British Library
A full CIP record is available from the Library of Congress

Library of Congress Catalog Card Number: available

Printed and bound in Great Britain by TJ International Ltd, Padstow, Cornwall

MIX
Paper from
responsible sources
FSC
www.fsc.org FSC® C013056

Contents

Acknowledgements

This book has had a long period of gestation, and I would like to thank those colleagues and students who have over the years and in various ways helped shape the final product. I was also fortunate to receive a grant from the British Academy to enable some of the research to be carried out, and a Research Leave Award from the Arts and Humanities Research Council, which enabled me to complete the writing for the book. Most of the research and much of the writing that appears here was undertaken while I was at the University of East Anglia; I am particularly grateful to my former colleagues and research students in the School of Film and Television Studies there for providing the ideal environment in which to undertake this work. I am also grateful to the university for providing me with a period of study leave. The book was completed after I joined the University of York, and I salute my new colleagues in the Department of Theatre, Film and Television for creating the necessary space for the completion of this project. I would particularly like to thank Ann-Marie Cook, James Caterer, Jon Stubbs, Jane Bryan and Pierluigi Ercole, who all at various times provided superb research assistance, and Marty Zeller, who created the index. I am also grateful to Philippa Brewster and her colleagues at I.B.Tauris for their faith in this project and for their hard work in seeing it through to publication. Finally, this book would not have appeared without the support and encouragement of my wife Val and my daughters Billie and Luisa, who constantly reminded me of the importance of home – and who also watched with me many of the films I discuss here.

Some of the material presented here first saw the light of day in other contexts. Part of chapter 3 is a revised version of papers first delivered at the UCL Mellon Research Seminar *Narrating Nations*, University College London, 17 November 2004; and at the *British Screens Now* conference at Manchester Metropolitan University, 11–13 September 2006. Parts of chapters 3 and 5 draw on material first published in 'Crossing over: exporting indigenous heritage to the USA', in Sylvia Harvey, ed., *Trading*

Culture: Global Traffic and Local Cultures in Film and Television, Eastleigh: John Libbey Publishing, 2006, pp. 203–17. Chapter 4 is a revised version of 'Fiction and the film industry', which appeared in Jim English, ed., *The Concise Companion to Contemporary British Fiction*, Oxford: Blackwell Publishing, 2006, pp. 58–79. Chapter 5 is a revised version of 'English heritage, English literature, English cinema: selling Jane Austen to movie audiences in the 1990s', which appeared in Eckart Voigts-Virchow, ed., *'Janespotting' and Beyond: British Heritage Retrovisions Since the Mid-1990s*, Tübingen: Gunter Narr Verlag, 2004, pp. 35–50. Chapters 7 and 8 draw on papers first presented at *The Middle Ages on Film* conference at University of St Andrews, 7–9 July 2005; *The Tudors and Stuarts on Film* conference at Kingston University/Hampton Court Palace, 7–9 September 2005; the *Collective Memory and the Uses of the Past* conference at the University of East Anglia, 7–10 July 2006; and *Between Science and Myth: The Past in Contemporary Cinema*, a conference organised by the Finnish Society of Film Studies, Helsinki, 7–8 September 2007; some of this material was previously published in '"Medievalism", the period film and the British past in contemporary cinema', in Anke Bernau and Bettina Bildhauer, eds, *Medieval Film*, Manchester: Manchester University Press, 2009, pp. 203–24. I am grateful to the organisers of these various conferences for providing me with the opportunity to present some of the material that now appears here. I am also grateful to the editors and publishers of the books listed above for permission to reuse material here that first appeared in those books.

Introduction

Cinema is one of the means by which national communities are maintained, the people of a nation are reminded of their ties with each other and with their nation's history and traditions, and those people are invited to recognise themselves as national subjects, distinct from people of other nations. Cinema does this by creating particular types of stories that narrate the nation imaginatively, narratives that are capable of generating a sense of national belonging among their audiences. Cinema also establishes a sense of the national through presenting familiar images, images of the mundane, the quotidian, the unremarkable, but which are at the same time steeped in the habitual customs and cultural fabric of a particular nation, signifiers of national identity that are, as Michael Billig puts it, so banal that we take them for granted.[1] Viewed in this way, cinema is then one of the means of narrating nations, telling stories that enable audiences to imagine the nature of particular nations, demonstrating how a nation appears, what its people look like, and how they speak and behave and dress.

Yet at the start of the twenty-first century, it is only too clear that the effects of globalisation are all around us, in the guise of Starbucks and McDonald's, Japanese technology, Chinese consumer goods, Indian call centres, the spread of the English language, and so on. In terms of cinema, there is no doubting Hollywood's global aspirations, its global enterprise, its global reach. In this context, what does it mean to speak of *national* cinema? What space is there for a national cinema or film culture given the scale and scope of global Hollywood? At cinemas in England, as has long been the case, the majority of the most successful films are Hollywood productions, suggesting that Hollywood cinema in some respects constitutes England's national cinema; it is certainly a central part of its national film culture. Does it really make sense in such a climate to speak of 'English cinema', or 'British cinema'? Are there still films that articulate a sense of nationhood and national identity in the way described above? Is there a distinctively English film production business? In fact, of course, there are still a good number of films set in England, that feature English characters, English places, English traditions and English identities, and that draw on English sources. Some but by no means all of them are made in England, some are made by companies based in England, some are funded from English sources. But a good proportion of these culturally English films involve substantial non-English interests.

It would not be unreasonable to identify the following projects as archetypal English films, given their subject matter: *Sense and Sensibility* (1995), an adaptation of Jane Austen's classic English novel, set in England in the early 1800s; *Elizabeth* (1998), about the first Queen Elizabeth, set in England in the late sixteenth century; *Harry Potter and the Prisoner of Azkaban* (2004), one of the series of films adapted from the best-selling novels by the contemporary English writer J.K. Rowling, and set in a semi-mythical Britain; *Match Point* (2005), a contemporary drama set in and around London in the present day; and *Bright Star* (2009), a biographical film, or biopic, about the nineteenth-century English poet John Keats. Described in these ways, all of these films have good reasons for being identified as English films – but all of them were in fact directed by non-English filmmakers, several of them had non-English stars, and several of them benefited from non-English funding. Ang Lee, the director of *Sense and Sensibility*, is Taiwanese, and the film was funded by Sony/Columbia Pictures. *Elizabeth* was directed by an Indian, Shekhar Kapur, and featured an Australian star, Cate Blanchett, as the eponymous English queen. The director of *Harry Potter and the Prisoner of Azkaban* was a Mexican, Alfonso Cuarón, and the production was funded by Warner Bros. *Match Point* was made by the veteran American director Woody Allen, with British, American and European funding, and an American star in Scarlett Johansson. And the New Zealander Jane Campion assembled a cast from Australia, New Zealand and the USA, as well as England, for her production of *Bright Star*, with funding from Australia and the UK.

Looked at from this perspective, it is no longer quite so easy to describe these films as English. There are other issues we might add to the mix as well. *Match Point*, for instance, also belongs to a series of films in which Americans visit England, a strategy clearly designed to broaden the audience appeal of films set there. Other films in this category include *Notting Hill* (1999), in which Julia Roberts plays an

Typical English cinema? *Harry Potter and the Prisoner of Azkaban*, directed by Mexican filmmaker Alfonso Cuarón.

American film star who visits London and falls in love with bumbling Englishman Hugh Grant; and *28 Weeks Later* (2007), in which American armed forces take over Britain to try to control a deadly virus that has wiped out most of the population. To this list, we could add 'English' films, set in England, and dealing with English characters, but with an American actress playing the lead English character – as Renée Zellweger did in the Bridget Jones films (2001, 2004) and *Miss Potter* (2006), Gwyneth Paltrow did in another Jane Austen adaptation, *Emma* (1996), in *Shakespeare in Love* (1998) and in the contemporary London-set drama *Sliding Doors* (1998), Angelina Jolie did in *Lara Croft: Tomb Raider* (2001) and its 2003 sequel, and Johnny Depp did in the London-based period musical *Sweeney Todd* (2007).

We might also note that some of the adaptations of Jane Austen novels were American-led productions, and there were also several Spanish adaptations of Ruth Rendell novels. Meanwhile, global Hollywood, in conjunction with the New Zealand film production business, appropriated J.R.R. Tolkien's *The Lord of the Rings*, and Nick Hornby's London-set novel *High Fidelity* was relocated to Chicago for the film version. Then there are films made by English directors but that do not deal with English subject matter or characters, as with many of the Hollywood films made by Ridley Scott, from *Thelma and Louise* (1991), via *Black Hawk Down* (2001), to *American Gangster* (2007). Then of course there is the whole question of funding and creative control, since there are numerous films that deal with English subject matter or English characters but that are

Hollywood studio projects, such as the Harry Potter films (2001–10). Do they count as English films? Government policies only complicate things further by creating incentives for production to take place in the UK, even when there is no substantive English or British theme or subject matter. *Star Wars: Episode I The Phantom Menace* (1999), for instance, was substantially made in England. Does that make it an English film?

In the context of globalisation, such transnational and intercultural developments are not untypical. Nor are they particularly new: 'English cinema' has for most of its existence been a part of a transnational film culture and film business. In a very useful study of a different national cinema, Mette Hjort has argued that Danish cinema has moved from a nationalist position to that of a hybrid global cinema.[2] By contrast, English cinema has been hybrid from the very start: well before the First World War, film production, distribution and exhibition in England was caught up in a complicated transnational exchange of films and filmmakers. European and American films circulated widely in England, while English films were equally well known in the USA and in several European countries. One of the leading figures in the English film business was an American, Charles Urban, while the French company Pathé had a strong base in England. From at least the 1920s there was a globalising tendency in English filmmaking and the film business, with producers such as Michael Balcon and Herbert Wilcox, and companies such as Stoll, and later British International Pictures, making films designed to work in American, European and Empire markets as much as in the domestic UK market. By the 1920s, Hollywood had already become established as the major force in the English film business, and has remained so ever since.

There has however been an *acceleration* of those transnational tendencies in the contemporary period, in the so-called era of globalisation. This study is in part an attempt to think through national cinema in this era of accelerated globalisation – and to do so by focusing on the possibility of English cinema. It would be difficult to deny that there is still a strong vein of what we might describe as nationalist filmmaking in England today, especially in terms of films exploring the national heritage. But if there is an English cinema or an English film industry, it is very difficult to identify or to demarcate, and it is rarely spoken of. Anglophone film historians conventionally speak of British cinema, as do contemporary professional English-speaking film critics and reviewers – although the film business is now regulated through the

UK Film Council. It is commonplace now to speak of the Scottish film industry and the Irish film industry (north and south of the border) – and even occasionally of the Welsh film industry. It's very rare however to speak of the English film industry, even if the majority of film-related activity in the UK takes place in England. Even then, much of the activity in England involves foreign and especially American films, much of it is sponsored by companies based elsewhere and much of it is undertaken in conjunction with filmmakers who are not English. Englishness in cinema is thus profoundly caught up in the changing circumstances of nationalism, transnationalism and globalisation.

Indeed, most national cinemas are now a complex amalgam of often competing local, national and international forces. What is variously called English cinema, British cinema, or the UK film industry is equally complex, and in many ways difficult to pin down or define precisely. That complexity and imprecision is the product of the diversity of indigenous English and broader British cultural traditions and identities and the marked social and cultural changes that have taken place since the Second World War; but it is also the product of industrial development, market aspirations and government policy. This study is an exploration of the ways in which this complex thing, English cinema, has taken shape in the 1990s and 2000s. I will examine some of the industrial and political forces that have impinged upon the making of films that might lay claim to being in one way or another English films; I will also examine a variety of trends in filmmaking in those years, and how they might be seen as providing representations of England and Englishness. My focus is not limited to films made in England, or made by English directors, however, since there are many representations of England and Englishness that are generated outside England or shaped by non-English directors.

It has not proved easy to adhere to the adjective 'English'. Indeed, when dealing with the film industry and with government policy, it has proved almost impossible. There are now several film organisations whose national remit is writ large in their nomenclature, but that national remit is usually defined in terms that move beyond England: hence the *UK* Film Council, the *British* Film Institute, the *National* Film and Television School. To invoke bodies such as these is also to acknowledge that what we might think of as a national cinema is always much more than the films produced within a particular well-defined geopolitical space. Most of the films watched by audiences in England and the most powerful film companies in England derive of course from Hollywood, so a full account of film culture and the film business within the national borders of England has to take account of this international presence. This means looking at the full spectrum of the film business, from the ways that films are funded, the types of distribution, marketing and exhibition they receive, the debates that are generated around them, and the ways in which different audiences engage with them. It is also important to look at the manner in which these various activities are treated politically and legislatively, for tax purposes and in terms of subsidies, and to examine the role of organisations such as the UK Film Council. I'm certainly not going to be able to deal with all these issues in detail here, but I will in various ways be addressing a good many of them.

In the first chapter, I will focus on the industrial circumstances of filmmaking in England, exploring some of the means by which films get made there, and the economic context that defines to a great extent what is possible. One of the things that will emerge from my discussion of the film industry is the different types of films that have been produced, in terms of budgeting, marketing and box-office performance. In the second part of the chapter, I will look at some other ways of categorising English films, in terms of genre and the sorts of representations of the nation and national identity that they offer. One of the distinctions often made in public debates about cinema in the UK is between *industrially* British films and *culturally* British films. Industrially British films are those made in the UK, drawing on UK production and post-production resources, locations and personnel, but without necessarily engaging with identifiably British subject matter. Culturally British films are those that explicitly engage with British subject matter, characters and stories. Within the context of the global film business, it has to be accepted that films that exploit the UK film industrial infrastructure will often prove financially attractive to those in the business. Equally, it has to be accepted that culturally British films are very much a niche brand. One of the things that I explore in this chapter is the strategies adopted by filmmakers in order to maintain and renew an even more specific version of that brand, namely culturally *English* films.

In the second chapter, I will extend my discussion of the business of filmmaking in England by examining the development of government policy, the tension between economic and cultural interests, and the debate about the cultural value of the film industry. This debate resulted in a new Cultural Test being introduced in 2007 to determine the Britishness of films for official purposes. Ironically, the nationalist dimensions of this test were significantly enhanced by the intervention of the European Commission, a transnational body. Despite devolution, film policy for England has only really been developed in the context of film policy for the UK as a whole. Likewise, statistics about film production and exhibition in the UK are rarely broken down in such a way that specifically English industrial activity can be demarcated. Inevitably, then, I will need to resort to terms such as the *British* film industry and *UK* film production, rather than English cinema, in these first two chapters.

One of the developments that emerges from these chapters is the extent of transnational production activity relating to what might on the face of it be identified as English films. In chapter 3, I explore the impact of such transnational arrangements – and the potentially global distribution that often ensues – on the way that films work at the level of representation. How is Englishness negotiated in such films? How do the local and the national play out in the context of globalisation? I explore these issues in relation to three films set in the present. The first is *Notting Hill*, written by Richard Curtis, one of the most influential figures in the development of filmic representations of Englishness in the 1990s and 2000s; in this film, he endeavours to establish a sense of local community and ordinary Englishness in contemporary London, but also plays on the differences between Englishness and Americanness. The second film is *Bride and Prejudice* (2004), by the British-Asian director Gurinder Chadha, who adopts as her themes the very processes of transnationalism, interculturalism and globalisation, as the film journeys between India, England and the USA, and as characters from different cultural, national and ethnic backgrounds become involved with one another. The third case study is *The Constant Gardener* (2005), a film whose transnational production arrangements are writ large, and whose characters again journey across national borders in a political thriller about the operations of the global pharmaceutical business and the involvement of the UK government.

The film business operates in a cultural economy marked by increasingly intense relationships between different media, best demonstrated by the emergence of the Time Warner conglomerate, which brought together substantial global interests in film, television, publishing, the internet and telecommunications. One of the ways in which this intermedial activity manifests itself in the case of English cinema is in the relationship between filmmaking and book publishing. The adaptation of fiction and drama with a proven market presence has been one of the most important production strategies for filmmakers in the 1990s and 2000s. Cinema's interaction with literary culture and the world of book publishing, however, extends well beyond adaptation as a production strategy. A certain category of middlebrow filmmaking endeavours to engage with audiences attached to a more traditional literary culture by producing biopics of prominent literary figures, but also by making films that appear 'literate' by comparison with most action-led blockbusters – that is, films that draw on some of the same values as so-called quality literature.

In chapters 4, 5 and 6, I explore this intermedial activity and the various ways in which English cinema, in its broadest sense, draws on literary culture. In chapter 4, I identify the range of adaptations of English fiction that appeared in the 1990s and 2000s, from mass-market novels to self-consciously literary publishing, from long-dead canonical authors to those still writing, and from English-language productions from English companies to foreign-language productions by foreign companies. I then survey adaptations of novels by contemporary English writers and consider what is involved in the process of adaptation.

In chapters 5 and 6 I move on to look at the Jane Austen franchise, including adaptations of the novels of this most canonical of English

English cinema's obsession with Jane Austen and American stars: Renée Zellweger in *Bridget Jones's Diary*.

writers, but also various spin-off texts, such as the biopic *Becoming Jane* (2007), which depicts a purported romantic adventure in Austen's early life. Austen was one of the most adapted of English authors in this period, and these chapters demonstrate some of the ways in which classic literature and its authors are taken up by the film business, and how they are pitched to particular markets and audiences, through both apparently more authentic period adaptations and contemporary dramas that rework the material in more radical ways. Chapter 5 focuses on the Austenmania of the mid-1990s, when four film adaptations and two television series appeared in the space of a couple of years. Chapter 6 looks at developments in the 2000s, from the Bridget Jones films, via the Working Title version of *Pride and Prejudice* (2005), to *Becoming Jane*.

Period Austen films such as *Sense and Sensibility* and *Becoming Jane* belong to the heritage costume drama production trend, which gained a great deal of critical attention and secured dedicated audiences, especially in the 1990s, but also to a lesser extent in the next decade. As one commentator noted, 'big heritage films are what the British do best. At least that's the view from across the pond'.[3] Such films certainly found a dedicated audience, and indeed financial backing, in the USA, and this inevitably shaped the production of those films, even if there was usually a strong English involvement at some level. There were also a great many other filmic representations of the English past to which the epithet 'heritage costume drama' is much less easy to apply, ranging from action-adventure epics about the pre-modern period, with major Hollywood studio backing, such as *King Arthur* (2004), to more modest representations of the very recent past, such as *24 Hour Party People* (2002), about the music scene in Manchester in the late 1970s and 1980s.

There are two issues worth noting here. First, if novels have provided one of the key source materials of English films, another key source has been the English past, and events and characters associated with English history. This is one of the main reasons for dedicating chapters 7 and 8 to a survey and analysis of representations of the English past, developing the analysis that I provided in my previous book, *English Heritage, English Cinema*, but also going beyond it in various ways.[4] It is worth noting that the Cultural Test introduced by the government in 2007 to determine the extent to which a film might be identified as British laid great emphasis on films that dealt thematically with the national cultural heritage.

The second issue of note about such films, and the issue that provides the structure for the analysis in chapters 7 and 8, is that the English past is represented in different ways in different types of film. My focus in these chapters is therefore in part on how the pre-modern past, the modern past and the very recent past are represented differently; but it is also in part about how substantial Hollywood investment tends to find its way into action-adventure films and other historical epics, often dealing with the pre-modern past, constructing the English past as a dirty, dangerous and distant time and place, leaving the way for more modest, intimate and refined productions about the modern past and the very recent past. One of the questions that I ask here is about the different visions of England and English identity that emerge in and around these different filmic versions of the past, and the ways in which they are addressed to different audiences. In effect, different aesthetic and ideological traits and cultural traditions are adopted to represent different periods, and to appeal to different audiences.

In chapter 7, I survey the wide range of films made in the 1990s and 2000s that depict the English past, and draw some broad distinctions between pre-modern films and films that depict the modern past. In chapter 8, I examine some of the ways in which those distinctions break down and the differences between historical periods are blurred. However much some films about the past are designed as mainstream entertainment, there is almost always some effort made in publicity and promotional material to establish what is presented as an authentic, realistic representation of the past. I discuss both these claims, and the strategies adopted by filmmakers to establish a sense of verisimilitude. At the end of chapter 8, I come back to the question of how the English past is represented in different types of films, and the extent to which these films can be seen as engaging in debates about Englishness and the national heritage.

The period of English filmmaking on which I focus, the 1990s and 2000s, is one defined by widespread cultural exchange, border-crossing, and the representation of new, hybrid identities alongside more familiar and surprisingly resilient national stereotypes. The chapters that follow provide a variety of ways of looking at the development of English cinema and filmic representations of England and Englishness in this period. While most of the chapters involve some sort of survey, I have not set out to produce an exhaustive taxonomy of English cinema; instead, I provide an indicative examination of films about England and Englishness in the period, which depends as much on case studies as on comprehensive overviews. One of the advantages of the selective, case study approach is that it allows a far more in-depth analysis of the issues at stake and the ways in which they are manifested in particular cases. The range of genres to which English films have contributed in this period is extensive, as I demonstrate in chapter 1. The case studies I develop here are organised less around genres than around themes, production categories and critical debates. Even so, at various times, and in various ways, I will deal with films that can be classified as costume drama, horror, exploitation, contemporary drama, political thriller, biopic, historical epic and romantic comedy, among others. Some of those films are big-budget blockbusters, some are middlebrow films that move between the art-house and the mainstream, and some are quirky, low-budget, niche products.

This approach has enabled me to ask a range of questions. For instance, what sorts of narratives and dramas get made, and why? How are films addressed to different markets, including the popular, multiplex market, the middlebrow market, and the specialist or niche markets? How are cultural distinctions and divisions, and specific tastes, handled within this economy? But equally, how are films designed to embrace different tastes and interests and to cross over from one market to another? And how do the transnational circumstances of so many apparently English films inflect the representations of Englishness on offer?

The approach I adopt draws on the perspectives of cultural history to investigate developments that come right up to the present. On the one hand, this involves drawing on archival, empirical research into the production, distribution, marketing, exhibition, box-office performance and critical reception of a range of 'English' and other films. On the other hand, I analyse a wide range of films, focusing on their stylistic, thematic and ideological characteristics. This combination of contextual and textual approaches has enabled me to build up a comprehensive picture of a range of films, how they came to be made, how they work as films, what representations, attractions and pleasures they offer, and how they have been promoted and taken up by audiences and cultural commentators.

There has been a wealth of filmic representations of England and Englishness in the 1990s and 2000s. Most of those representations have been in films in which English personnel or companies have played an important role, but equally people from other backgrounds and financial input from companies based elsewhere have been vital to the development of this English cinema. The film production business in England in the 1990s and 2000s has perhaps been far more stable and substantial than many might have imagined in the mid-1980s, at a time when government support for the film industry seemed to have disappeared altogether, when cinema-going as a cultural practice and a profitable enterprise seemed to be dying out, and when the global media entertainment business seemed to leave little room for small-scale national production.

From one perspective, then, English cinema has, against all the odds, looked relatively strong and stable in the 1990s and 2000s, generating a range of well-received films, many of them award-winning, and some of them major box-office successes. A more detailed examination of the film production business in the UK suggests a much more precarious and unstable identity, with the business lurching uncertainly from one crisis to the next. It has of course long been considered undercapitalised, highly fragmented, without a large enough domestic market to allow it to develop substantially, and lacking the scale of infrastructure that characterises Hollywood. Writing in 1997, Ian Christie suggested that 'British cinema, with the best will in the world, is more a carefully contrived illusion than a serious industry.'[5] Yet it is an illusion that has a powerful allure, partly because cinema is more than an industry: it is a cultural practice that engages in complex ways with the world in which its audiences live. It is also of course closely bound up with celebrity culture, so that debates about cinema are often framed within debates about stardom and glamour. The glamour of English (or British) cinema and its stars may pall by comparison with Hollywood, but it is still strong enough to create an allure around the film business. It is that business on which I focus in chapter 1.

1 Film production in the UK in the 1990s and 2000s

This chapter provides an overview of film production in the UK in the 1990s and 2000s; wherever possible, I focus on what might reasonably be identified as English filmmaking, but the film business is at certain levels regulated across the UK as a whole, which makes it difficult to sustain a distinction between specifically English developments and those that apply to the UK as a whole. In the first two sections of the chapter, I explore the context in which films got made in England, and especially the financial, organisational and political arrangements that both made production possible and limited its scope. There were many different types of films produced, and one of the key things that distinguished films from one another was budget, which itself had an impact on marketing, box-office performance and cultural presence. The size of a production budget depended to a great extent on whether or not one of the Hollywood studio-distributors was involved – which inevitably had an impact on the 'national' status of the film thereby developed. Of course, there were occasionally low-budget films that performed much better than Hollywood-funded blockbusters and, in examining the market position of films, I will take this sort of performance into account.

In the first section of the chapter, I focus on film production in England in the 1990s; in the second section, I focus on the 2000s. Categorising historical developments by decades in this way inevitably oversimplifies the complex nature of things, but it also makes the process of categorisation manageable. In this case, there was in fact a key development in the year 2000, the establishment of the Film Council (later the UK Film Council), which played a key role in shaping the UK film business in subsequent years. The division of my account into a section on the 1990s and another on the 2000s does therefore have some substantive basis. In the final section of the chapter, I will look at some other ways of categorising

English films besides budget and scale, focusing on genres or production trends, and the sorts of representations of the nation and national identity that they offer.[1]

The UK film business in the 1990s

For a film to reach audiences, a funding package has to be in place to ensure the film can be made – and film funding is by any standards an extremely complex business. Most productions today are in some way or other transnational – which is to say that in order to establish a large enough budget, funding has to be sought from a variety of sources both domestic and foreign. Funding in the UK will come in the form of investment from a range of public and private organisations, companies and individuals, including American-based studios, broadcasting companies, large equity funds and smaller independent financiers, as well as the government-supported British Screen (in the 1990s); public subsidies and grants, notably the National Lottery scheme, which from 2000 was administered by the Film Council, but also various more modest European Union funds; tax breaks and other financial incentives; presale deals with distributors, and so on. Although the National Lottery funding invested in film production has probably attracted the most media attention over the years since it was introduced in 1995, the most significant source of public financial support was, perhaps surprisingly, the various tax breaks, and the related loopholes exploited by film financiers.[2]

As Margaret Dickinson and Sylvia Harvey note, the central problem for UK film producers, the production business as a whole and the film policy that regulates that business has long been and remains 'how to coexist with Hollywood'.[3] A brand name for a series of large and extremely powerful corporations with a global reach and involvement in film financing, production and distribution, Hollywood is a presence that the UK film business cannot ignore. Many UK film productions are in some way dependent on Hollywood finance – and if they are not, they must still find a way of working within a distribution system and an exhibition market that is dominated by the Hollywood companies. Outright competition with Hollywood is not really feasible, although occasionally very large companies without ties to the Hollywood studios will attempt that; most forms of coexistence with Hollywood depend on collusion in some guise or other, however, rather than competition. Some 'British' films are made self-consciously to be different from 'Hollywood' films, a form of product differentiation that is generally designed to exploit niche markets – but many of the films that might be seen as distinctive in this sense are in fact funded by Hollywood companies keen to have a stake in those niche markets.

The smallest films, with no apparent Hollywood involvement, still have to coexist with Hollywood, in the sense that they must jostle for space alongside films that clearly do have Hollywood support. And even the most self-consciously indigenous film will usually still operate in some way transnationally, by securing funding from a foreign source, for instance, or by being shown at film festivals and independent or art-house cinemas in various markets around the world. In this context, putting together a budget for a film production was always a very complex business, involving tapping into a variety of funding sources that often left little scope for profit that could be invested in subsequent productions. Most UK productions in the 1990s and 2000s were put together as one-off packages, therefore, rather than as part of a carefully planned production slate, and companies came into being simply for the purpose of that particular project.

Having established some broad parameters for the period as a whole, the rest of this section will focus on developments in the 1990s, up to the establishment of the Film Council. Taking into account all films produced in the UK and all others shot elsewhere but with a UK financial involvement, an average of 83 UK films was produced each year between 1990 and 1999 – with the average higher in the second half of the decade than the first half, reflecting the positive impact of both tax relief and Lottery funding as sources of production finance. It is also worth noting that more UK films were made in the 1990s than in either of the two previous decades, an impressive turnaround for the UK film business. But it is important to put these figures into perspective. For a start, the majority of funding for these films was inward investment from the USA. Most of the films funded in this way enjoyed a higher budget, and sometimes a significantly higher budget, than the average UK films without US funding. Thus the average budget for films where the majority of funding came from the UK was never *more* than £2.5m; while the average budget for American-financed or part-financed films made in the UK was never *less* than £10m – and went as high as £18.5m in 1997.[4]

It is also important to look at the box-office performance of these various films. Nearly half the UK films made in the 1990s were still unreleased a year after being completed, while only a quarter of them

The Full Monty: a major box-office hit in 1997.

enjoyed a wide release, playing on 30 or more screens around the country. UK films where the majority of funding was from the UK rarely managed to secure more than 4 per cent of the total box-office revenue generated at UK cinemas. The figure of 8 per cent in 1997, for instance, was mainly due to the unexpectedly stellar performance of *The Full Monty* (1997). US/UK co-productions improved their box-office performance dramatically across the decade, reflecting the fact that inward investment in such productions was going up at the same time. This meant that the proportion of box-office revenue generated each year by Hollywood films with no UK involvement went down by a quarter across the decade – but even in 1999, such films were still taking a massive 60 per cent of the UK box-office revenue. In other words, across the decade as a whole the great majority of box-office revenue was generated by Hollywood films with no UK funding.[5]

There was a big gap between the low-budget UK-financed films destined for art-house-type distribution, and the crossover films designed to work in both the art houses and the new multiplexes, many of which benefited from funding from American companies, either the studios or mini-majors like Miramax. There was an even bigger gap between those mid-budget crossover films and those that were primarily about inward investment: big-budget, Hollywood-sponsored films that happened to be produced in the UK. Among films in production during 1997, for instance, *Babymother*, a musical about poor black youths in London, was a low-budget, £2m film funded by Channel 4 and the Arts Council. At the other end of the scale, *Star Wars: Episode I The Phantom Menace* also counted as a British film because it was an inward investment film made in the UK, for a budget initially registered as £25m, though generally estimated to be closer to $115m. It went on to take £51m at the UK box office, where *Babymother* took just £62,000.[6]

Somewhere in between these two poles were rare productions like *Notting Hill* (1999), a film with strongly British (mainly English) subject matter, made by a prominent UK company, Working Title; at the time, Working Title enjoyed backing from a much larger European media corporation, PolyGram, which itself had strong links with an American studio, Universal. *Notting Hill* was made for £15m, which was a major budget for a UK film. It went on to take £31m at the UK box office, and an enormous £113m at the US box office, a figure that was well beyond the reach of the great majority of UK films. Such films ensured that the British film business and British filmmakers maintained a high profile, but also proved the worth of the companies involved in the production and the value of strong connections with the major American distributors, without which it was extremely difficult for UK films to make a mark in the global box-office stakes.[7]

Working Title had established a name for itself in the mid-1980s with risky, innovative projects like *My Beautiful Laundrette* (1985). It remained a vibrant and very successful company throughout the 1990s, with a keen eye for modestly budgeted, UK-focused films that might yet be major commercial successes; it also became the American Coen brothers' production company. On the UK front, Working Title's first major box-office success was *Four Weddings and a Funeral* (1994), which was made for £2m and went on to take £28m at the UK box office alone, and $245m worldwide.[8] Other important films included the Rowan Atkinson comedy vehicle *Bean* (1997), the East London gangster film *Lock, Stock and Two Smoking Barrels* (1998), and the lavish and thrilling costume drama *Elizabeth* (1998). Such films operated in the middle ground of the UK market, somewhere between the niche art-house film and the US-led blockbuster. It is unlikely that Working Title would have been able to notch up so many successes had it not been for the support of PolyGram Filmed Entertainment, which was part of the European group Phillips – but which at the end of the decade was sold to the Canadian giant Seagram's, which also owned Universal.

Another key production company and source of funding in the 1990s was the public service broadcaster Channel 4, and its various subsidiaries, including Channel Four Films, Film Four International and Film Four Ltd. Channel Four was able to operate variously as a funder, a production company, a distributor and a broadcaster of films in which it had invested. At the end of the decade, in 1998, it combined its production, sales and distribution activities under the umbrella of Film Four Ltd, whose launch signalled a new departure in their production and funding policy, away from the innovative and often risky low-budget fare with which they had made their name and towards more expensive international co-productions.

For the bulk of the 1990s, however, it was their support of some of the key English auteur filmmakers of the period that is telling. Thus they funded films by Mike Leigh (*Life Is Sweet*, 1991, *Career Girls*, 1997), Ken Loach (*Raining Stones*, 1993, *My Name is Joe*, 1998), Terence Davies (*The Long Day Closes*, 1992, *The House of Mirth*, 2000) and Peter Greenaway (*The Baby of Mâcon*, 1993, *The Pillow Book*, 1996). They also helped launch the careers of a new generation of filmmakers such as Gurinder Chadha (*Bhaji on the Beach*, 1993), Danny Boyle (*Shallow Grave*, 1994) and Michael Winterbottom (*Welcome to Sarajevo*, 1997). They had a hand in some of the most commercially successful UK films of the period too, in *Four Weddings and a Funeral*, *Trainspotting* (1996) and *East Is East* (1999).

The UK Film Council and the film business in the 2000s

In 2000, the UK government created the Film Council as a body tasked with the maintenance, development and promotion of the UK film industry, including production activity. I discuss the Council in more detail in the next chapter. Suffice it to say here that by the late 2000s, in order to achieve its purposes, the Council was distributing around £27m of National Lottery funding and a further £27m grant-in-aid from the government to film-related activities each year.[9] On the production front, the two key schemes were the Premiere Fund, which provided £8 million a year 'to finance production of popular, mainstream films', and the New Cinema Fund, which provided £5 million a year 'to innovative film-makers'.[10] The Premiere Fund has been used over the years to award grants of up to £2.5m per project, with its largest grant – £2.58m – awarded to the animated film *Valiant* in 2002. In fact, there have only been six other awards of £2m or above: *Mike Bassett: England Manager* (2001), *Gosford Park* (2001), *Sylvia* (2003), *Five Children and It* (2004), *Stormbreaker*

(2006) and *Closing the Ring* (2007). Other films supported by the Premiere Fund in the latter part of the 2000s included *Miss Potter* (2006), *Becoming Jane* (2007), *St Trinian's* (2007) and *Happy-Go-Lucky* (2008).[11]

At the other end of the scale is the New Cinema Fund, used to support riskier and more experimental low-budget work, such as *Once Upon a Time in the Midlands* (2002), *Touching the Void* (2003), *Bullet Boy* (2004), *This Is England* (2006), *Brick Lane* (2007) and *London to Brighton* (2006), which all received between £185,000 and £750,000. Somewhere in between the extremes of the Premiere Fund and the New Cinema Fund was *Bend It Like Beckham* (2002), which received just under £1m, and went on to record a box-office gross 35 times the size of its Lottery grant, which makes it in this sense the most successful Lottery-funded film to date.[12]

For all the work of the UK Film Council, the film business in the UK in the 2000s, as in the 1990s, was dominated by large companies that were either foreign-owned or had little involvement in film production. The large distributors and exhibitors were thus much larger and more powerful than any of the UK-based production companies. The production business in the UK remained, in the words of the Film Council, 'corporately-dispersed', with numerous companies still set up simply for the purpose of making one film.[13] In 2008, for instance, the Film Council recorded 202 companies as being involved with UK film production activity, of which 185 were associated with single projects.[14] Among UK-based production companies, the most successful in the 2000s included Working Title again; Pathé Productions, the UK arm of a French multinational producer and distributor; Aardman, the makers of the *Wallace and Gromit* animated films, *Chicken Run* (2000) and *Flushed Away* (2006); two television company spin-offs, BBC Films and Film Four; and various other companies such as Future Films, Vertigo, Revolution, Ingenious and Heyday Films, the UK company behind the Harry Potter series. BBC Films was involved in more than 50 productions, more than any other UK-based company in the 2000s, while Working Title was again probably the most successful, in terms of the number of films it produced, their combined budgets, and their critical and box-office success.[15]

Working Title, by now affiliated with Universal, had a slate of 44 films between 2000 and 2008, including five entries in the top 20 UK films of the period in terms of box-office gross: the two Bridget Jones films (2001, 2004), *Love Actually* (2003), *Mr Bean's Holiday* (2007) and *Hot Fuzz* (2007).

There were numerous other films acclaimed for one reason or another: from populist fare such as *Ali G Indahouse* (2002), *Johnny English* (2003) and *Shaun of the Dead* (2004), to more middlebrow productions such as *Pride and Prejudice* (2005) and *Atonement* (2007). Pathé was one of three companies to win a six-year franchise from the Film Council in 1997, securing funding that was designed to enable the sort of continuity of production and producer–distributor link-ups that were so often lacking in the UK film business. Its continuing strength as a company lay in its distribution activities; as a producer, projects it was involved with ranged from *Love's Labours Lost* (2000) and *The Claim* (2002), via *The Girl with a Pearl Earring* (2003) and *Bride and Prejudice* (2004), to *The Queen* (2006) and *Slumdog Millionaire* (2008). The BBC tended to back smaller films, and therefore had fewer genre pieces or box-office winners than Working Title or Pathé. Productions they supported included *The Mother* (2003), *Sylvia, My Summer of Love* (2004), *Bullet Boy* (2004), *Match Point* (2005), *Miss Potter, Becoming Jane* and *The Other Boleyn Girl* (2008). Channel 4 started with expansive ambitions for their FilmFour subsidiary, with a deal with Warner Bros. and comparatively lavish investment in two films that turned out to be box-office and critical disasters, *Charlotte Gray* (2001) and *Death to Smoochy* (2002). The broadcaster quickly withdrew from international production, cutting its annual film production budget from around £30m in 2001 to £10m in 2003, and denting the hopes of many in the UK film business.[16]

It is difficult to compare the number of UK films produced annually in the 2000s with those produced in the 1990s because there are no consistent statistics that run across the whole period. The figures given above for 1990s productions are drawn from statistics compiled and presented by the British Film Institute (BFI). To access statistics across the 2000s, it is necessary to go to the Film Council, whose criteria differed from the BFI's. It is still, however, possible to draw some conclusions about broad trends. One very noticeable trend is that UK productions rose gradually in the early 1990s, but then experienced a spurt in 1996 and 1997, as Lottery funding made its initial impact. For the next few years, domestic productions decreased, but co-productions increased, but it was not until 2003 that overall numbers reached – and exceeded – the levels of 1996 and 1997. The overall numbers of UK productions again fell off slightly from 2005, as new regulations came in regarding tax relief, which made it more difficult for co-productions to secure funding. Film Council statistics reveal that, on average, 124 UK feature films were made each year in the 2000s, around twice as many as were made in the early 1990s. These figures include films funded substantially by inward investment, co-productions and 'domestic' UK productions, made with little or no co-production or inward investment money.[17]

According to the Film Council's statistics,[18] around 40 per cent of the films released in the UK each year originated from the USA or had substantial American involvement – and that figure goes up to 45 per cent if UK/USA collaborations are taken into account. The top 20 films at the UK box office account for around 50 per cent of revenues each year, and the top 50 films account for around 80 per cent of revenues. With an average of around 480 films released in the UK each year in the 2000s, that means a great many films make very little money. USA-originated films captured an average of 73 per cent of UK market share each year – with UK-originated films capturing just 24 per cent of the market share. All of the top 20 best-performing films in the UK for the period 2000–2008 had some American studio involvement, and only two of those films were neither sequels nor part of a franchise. Thus the list was dominated by the Harry Potter films, the *Lord of the Rings* trilogy, and one or more entries from the James Bond, *Star Wars*, *Shrek* and Batman franchises. Their box-office takings were far higher than the most successful independent UK films – that is, UK films with no major American studio involvement; indeed the combined total UK box office for the ten most successful independent UK films was less than the total for the two most successful films of any origin in that period (*Mamma Mia!*, 2008, and *Harry Potter and the Philosopher's Stone*, 2001). Then again, the UK box office is only a very small part of the global box office, and the biggest Hollywood films will now open with a simultaneous worldwide release, on around 22,000 screens. By comparison, a good release in the UK will go onto around 550 screens.

The most successful films with a strong UK involvement also performed very well in global markets, with the Film Council eager to draw our attention to the fact that 'of the top 200 global box office successes of 2001–2007, 30 films are based on stories and characters created by British writers'. The key writers in this respect were J.K. Rowling (the Harry Potter films), J.R.R. Tolkien (*The Lord of the Rings* trilogy), C.S. Lewis (the *Chronicles of Narnia* films) and Ian Fleming (the James Bond films). The Film Council went on to note that 'nine of the top 20 global box office successes … are based on novels by British writers', while 'more than half of the top 200 films … have featured UK actors in lead or prominent roles. British directors made 20 of the top 200 biggest films of the last seven years with David Yates and Ridley Scott topping the league.' The Film Council concluded that 'these talents play an important role in projecting the UK's national identity – and creative abilities – across the globe'.[19] The Film Council was also keen to celebrate the fact that the amount of money spent in the UK on film production, including inward investment, reached record levels in 2003 and 2006.[20]

These are interesting and valid statements and statistics, and indicate the role that a certain version of British culture and certain British creative workers are able to play in the contemporary global creative industries and contemporary popular culture. This section is not the place to consider the particular versions of national identity promoted through such films. For the moment, what is important to note is that the particular films under discussion here are major investments, blockbusters with substantial Hollywood input, films that are for the most part too big to be initiated from the UK. The exceptions here are some of the Working Title films, including the Bridget Jones films and *Love Actually* – but even here, it is important to remember that Working Title had close links with the Hollywood company Universal. Once again, the difficulty of drawing clear lines around something that might be called the 'British film production business' becomes evident. Films whose subject matter might be described as British or where there is some British creative involvement embrace a much wider spectrum of activity than what could reasonably be described as the UK film production business. On the one hand, this is typical of the globalisation of culture and business in the contemporary period. On the other hand, there is nothing terribly new about the situation, since American filmmakers have been making British-related films since the early silent period.

At the other end of the scale from the transnational and global blockbusters are the independent UK films, with no major US studio involvement. Even here, though, it is very unlikely that all the funding for such films or all the creative talent involved is from the UK. The most successful films in this category between 2000 and 2007 were *Gosford Park*, *St Trinian's* and *Bend It Like Beckham*, all three of which received Lottery funding from the UK Film Council. *Run, Fat Boy, Run* (2007), *Kevin and Perry Go Large* (2000), *East Is East* and *The Queen* were not far behind, with all these films grossing between £10m and £12m at the UK box office. In the middle range, between the Hollywood-led blockbusters

The Football Factory: a low-budget film that made money when released on DVD.

and the independent UK films, were films with some American studio involvement, like the Working Title films cited above (the two Bridget Jones films and *Love Actually*), and other Working Title projects such as *Mr Bean's Holiday* and *Hot Fuzz*, which each earned between £20m and £42m. By comparison, the six Harry Potter films, *Casino Royale* (2006) and *Quantum of Solace* (2008) all earned between £46m and £66m at the UK box office, and a lot more internationally – nearly a billion pounds, in the case of the most successful Harry Potter films.[21]

A thorough account of the extent to which a film circulates publicly would of course require a careful examination of the video and more recently the DVD and Blu-ray markets. Total DVD sales are enormous. In 2004, for instance, the number of DVDs legally bought in the UK passed the number of admissions in cinemas for the first time.[22] Inevitably, the vast majority of DVD sales are for the same blockbuster movies that dominate the cinema box office, although rental statistics suggest a wider repertoire of films.[23] Indeed the proliferation of DVD titles, and the ease of distribution, mean that some small films are able to improve their prospects in the DVD market, even if they have been squeezed out of the theatrical exhibition market. *The Football Factory* (2004), for instance, a violent, low-budget film about football hooliganism, was made for £600,000, and cost another £600,000 to release in cinemas. The cinema release generated a box-office gross of just £750,000, of which less than a third would have found its way back to the producers. However, when the film was subsequently released on DVD, the revenue shot up to £4.5m. As Rupert Preston, the executive producer of the film, noted, 'the cinema release ... was just a marketing exercise for the DVD'.[24]

There are of course no hard and fast lines drawn between these different categories of film – and how those categories are defined tends to differ from one context to the next. For the purposes of applying tax breaks and the like, for instance, the Treasury makes a distinction between what it calls 'limited-budget' films and higher-budget films. Section 48 of the 1985 Films Act defined limited-budget films as those with a budget of less than £15m; by 2007, and the introduction of a new tax credit system, the cut-off point for limited-budget films had risen to £20m. But as should already be clear, the majority of British-made films in fact cost significantly less than £20m or even £15m.[25] Another loose categorisation was provided by the British Film Institute's magazine, *Sight and Sound*, which ran a regular column in the late 2000s on art-house box-office performance. In this context, it seemed, art-house could mean films such as *Sweeney Todd* (2007), *The Duchess* (2008) and *The Other Boleyn Girl*, all of which featured international stars and played in both art houses and mainstream multiplexes. An examination of the exhibition of these films reveals that their theatrical release was in fact much wider than a conventional art-house release. The 2008 Bond film *Quantum of Solace*, a blockbuster by any criteria, opened on 540 screens, for instance, but *The Duchess* also played on 426 screens at its widest and *Sweeney Todd* on 437.[26] In the UK market at least, it is difficult to distinguish between a blockbuster and what *Sight and Sound* calls an art-house film on the basis of exhibition alone.

The Film Council meanwhile operates with a working definition of 'specialised film' for the purposes of intervening in distribution and exhibition in the UK, defining specialised films as anything other than 'mainstream, US studio-originated material' – although the category does include some films handled by mainstream studio-based distributors. This broad definition enables the specialised category to embrace almost all foreign-language films with subtitles, documentaries and archive/ classic films, as well as indie and art-house films and others that don't sit easily within mainstream, highly commercial genres. Most of the small UK-made films fall into this category too.[27]

Culturally English filmmaking: exploiting a niche

The production sector in the UK in the 1990s and 2000s has remained precarious, even if it has at the same time proved relatively prolific, with enough films achieving box-office success or critical acclaim for the sector to seem viable. English and other filmmakers, working in conjunction with bodies such as the Film Council, and often drawing on foreign and especially American investment, have developed a variety of strategies for getting films made. One of those strategies has involved creating films about England, English characters and English history. This might be regarded as a specialist topic within the global film industry, although as we have seen Hollywood has occasionally seen it as worthwhile to develop its own English-oriented productions, as well as to invest in UK-initiated productions. From a business point of view, there are sufficient financial and market incentives for exploiting this particular topic, from box-office success to the ability to raise production funds to tax relief. Selling Englishness thus works as a reasonable business strategy, even if it is a specialist one.

But of course English filmmakers do not make films about England simply because there is a market niche to be exploited and financial incentives to follow up: many are genuinely committed for ideological reasons to making films about their own country and culture. They still have to find the commercial wherewithal to make such activity possible – and some have found it easier to work within the terms of industrially British cinema, in effect as an outpost of Hollywood, than to engage with the production of culturally English films. Film policy in the UK, as will become clear in the next chapter, has been developed at different times and in different ways; in some cases, the purpose of such policy was to encourage investment in film-related industrial activity, almost regardless of the films being made; in other cases, there was a clear cultural motivation, designed to encourage culturally British – and within that, culturally English – films, films that are in some way self-consciously engaging with English culture. The business incentives for making culturally English films certainly improved in the late 2000s. But filmmakers also developed other strategies designed to attract sufficient funding for culturally English films to be made.

One such strategy is to mine English settings, characters and cultural texts, but to market them internationally by employing American and other Hollywood stars to put on English accents and add a level of box-office appeal that can't always be achieved by English stars. Another strategy is to build on the box-office success of one film by reworking its various attractions and ingredients in subsequent films – thus if a particular type of English romantic comedy or English costume drama proves successful, it will be followed up by others in the same vein. Sometimes, of course, this will be done overtly in the guise of the sequel, from *Bridget Jones: The Edge of Reason* (2004) to *Elizabeth: The Golden Age* (2007). Other strategies include meeting the criteria for tax breaks or for public funding, or securing co-production funds or developing other sorts of international partners in one guise or another – although of course such strategies are themselves often dependent on the casting or the script for the film. What is at stake is finding appropriate means of exploiting a specific local brand on a transnational or global scale, since the English market alone is not big enough to support all but the very lowest-budgeted films.

In various ways, then, filmmakers and production companies have sought the means to secure and maintain an English-oriented niche in the global marketplace. If the English production sector thus exhibits some globalising tendencies, they are based on an industrial infrastructure and operational model that is quite different in kind from that of global Hollywood.[28] While PolyGram in the 1990s operated with considerable capital and economies of scale, the English production business at the end of the twentieth century and the beginning of the twenty-first century was not about controlling huge corporations operating on a global scale. Such companies may have invested in the English production sector in various ways, but that sector in itself was not made up of such companies. While some England-based producers have formal, ongoing links with major international distributors, with the exception of the Working Title/ Universal relationship, they are not in themselves integral parts of global distribution outfits, as the Hollywood studios are. In this respect, once again, the production of culturally English films remains a specialised, niche business, especially when the number of low-budget UK productions is taken into account. The effort to secure global or at least transnational distribution for UK-made films involves tapping into a variety of often piecemeal and ad hoc funding initiatives, and liaising with either a global distribution partner or a series of region-specific distributors. This is more about putting together a production–distribution package on a film-by-film basis, rather than operating as a global distributor from the outset.

One thing that should be clear from the foregoing discussion is that the range of films that are in various ways about England, English characters or English history can be categorised according to where the creative and financial control lies, the size of the production budget, and therefore the type of production, the mode of address and the audience aimed at. Inward investment films where the bulk of the funding is coming from non-English sources will therefore be controlled by non-English interests, and will often be medium- to high-budgeted films that require blockbuster treatment at the point of distribution and exhibition, as with the Harry Potter franchise. A lot of the independent or domestic UK productions, on the other hand, where there is very little in the way of co-production funding or inward investment, and where the creative control is UK-based, will tend to be low-budget films that require a more specialised art-house or crossover distribution and exhibition strategy, films such as *Bhaji on the Beach*, *Bullet Boy* or *London to Brighton*.

Somewhere in between the inward investment blockbusters and the domestic low-budget productions are what by UK standards are medium-budgeted films, where the financial input, creative control and the mode of address is more hybrid. Most will occupy middlebrow territory, with some veering towards what might be classed as mainstream popular genres, and others towards the so-called quality end of the market. On the one hand, then, there are the romantic comedies that followed in the wake of *Four Weddings and a Funeral*, films such as *Notting Hill* and *Bridget Jones's Diary* (2001); on the other hand, there are polished literary adaptations, from *Sense and Sensibility* (1995) to *Atonement*.

Versions of national identity

It is worth reflecting on the different regimes of national identity promoted by these various categories of film, and asking to what extent the ideological perspective of a film is determined by its intended position in the market and the type of creative control exerted over it. At the big-budget end of the market, where inward investment in well-established franchises is the order of the day, films such as the James Bond espionage thrillers, the Harry Potter adaptations of best-selling children's books and the *Tomb Raider* computer game spin-offs, the dominant version of Englishness on offer tends to draw on upper-class English traditions of aristocratic wealth, Establishment politics and private school education. Given the success of these films, this is evidently an eminently bankable version of Englishness. The process by which these traditional, class-specific identities are further defined through their contrasts with various categories of otherness leads to an emphasis on archetypal white, 'English' characters, pitted against other stereotypical national characters. At the same time, such films are designed for global distribution, and therefore to appeal to a variety of national and transnational audiences, hence Bond's globetrotting.

When Warner Bros. first took an interest in buying the film rights to the Harry Potter novels, there was no guarantee that the films would reproduce the implicit Englishness of J.K. Rowling's fictional world. However, as a newspaper report records, 'British film mandarins went to extraordinary lengths to secure the work and the money that the Harry Potter movie franchise could bring to the country'; the result was that the majority of the money spent on the production of the films was spent in England, with Leavesden Studios near London being used as the long-term production base for the series.[29] As the then head of the British Film Commission explained, 'Harry Potter is something that is weirdly about us ... It's culturally British and the thought of it being made anywhere but here sent shudders down everyone's spine.'[30] Creating an English base for this particular blockbuster franchise was thus about both generating substantial business and securing a sense of national identity, an identity that was at the same time both fictional and familiar, its class-bound world reproducing the mores of a traditional, privileged private school education and the solidity of ancient institutional buildings.

The middlebrow films tend to focus on a similar class and ethnic milieu to the blockbusters, with many of the films exploring the identities and traits of the white, English, London-oriented middle and upper classes. What gross generalisations such as these overlook, of course, is the complexity of the representations on offer, and their ability to be read in different ways by different audiences. The potential for feminist readings of the (white, upper-middle-class and upper-class, English) female protagonists of the *Tomb Raider* films and Austen adaptations like *Sense and Sensibility*, for instance, means that adherence to national traditions cannot be taken for granted or treated simplistically. Some of the other mainstream genres besides the post-*Four Weddings* romantic comedies – the gangster films such as *Lock, Stock and Two Smoking Barrels*, for instance – offer more varied representations of Englishness too. Even so, the contrast between the national identities on offer in the big- and medium-budgeted films and those in the low-budget, more independently made English films is telling.

As I have already noted, many of the small, indigenous films concentrate much more on local places, characters and identities, rather than on metropolitan centres or the traditional sites of middle- and upper-class Englishness. Such films may still circulate globally, through film festivals, art-house circuits and the like, but they are more likely to challenge traditional representations of national identity and explore hybrid and/or local identities. It has been in this category of film that ethnic minority communities and stories have been most carefully examined, in films like *Bhaji on the Beach, Bend It Like Beckham* and *Bullet Boy*. The working classes and the post-industrial underclasses are also more likely to figure in such films, from *Riff-Raff* (1991) to *Nil by Mouth* (1997) to *This Is England*. Whereas the blockbuster and middlebrow films have often appealed to the tourist business because of the way that the UK is represented, the small, indigenous films, because they rarely focus on the familiar and because their narratives are often bleak and uncompromising, have proved less appealing in this way. Arguably, such films denationalise their representations, or at least they often provocatively refigure the national as complex, hybrid and changing.

In broad terms, then, it is possible to see a correlation between budget size and the locus of creative control on the one hand and mode of representation on the other. The bigger the budget, in broad terms, the more conventional and conservative the ideologies of Englishness on display; smaller budgets by contrast tended to lend themselves much more readily to innovative representations of a more extensive range of social types. England looked different, and so did the people who inhabited it. Selling variants of Englishness on film may then be a specialist activity, but it can still run the gamut from blockbuster to low-budget in terms of the scale and type of production – and that scale and type can have a profound effect on the types of representations on offer even if the above picture is necessarily highly generalised.

Genres and Englishness

Culturally English films can also be categorised by genre. Different gen-res can be used to engage with and explore national identity in different ways; they are means of packaging Englishness and its many variants in particular ways for particular audiences. Or to put it another way, film-makers have identified a small number of generic models for presenting culturally English stories, themes and issues, models that have proved commercially and/or critically successful, financially efficient and man-ageable, and amenable to repetition with variations. Occasionally, genre is closely related to the market position and budget of a film, and in some cases it perhaps makes more sense to think in terms of production cycles rather than retrospectively applied generic models. Even so, an examination of the field of culturally English films in terms of genres will be useful and will give a slightly different picture from the one painted so far.

Genres are not hard and fast categories with clear rules; rather they are best understood as loose bundles of attractions and ingredients that can be mobilised by filmmakers in different ways. Their visibility as something that might be identified as a genre emerges only over time and by comparison with other films deemed to be similar. Nor are there clear lines between genres; on the contrary, there are always going to be plenty of overlaps between one genre and another. The decisions made by filmmakers will depend to some extent on what has proved successful on previous occasions; in this way, production cycles, and eventually genres, will emerge; but filmmakers working in the highly fragmented and precarious UK film production sector will rarely make conscious decisions on the basis of what come to be regarded as genres. Franchises and sequels obviously work in similar ways to genres, but they are much more bound to the reappearance of particular characters and the continuation of storylines than most generic models, which tend to be looser. Even so, and despite all the caveats, it is still possible to identify a series of dominant genres in culturally English filmmaking of the 1990s and 2000s.

One of the genres that has proved most commercially and critically successful for filmmakers seeking to produce culturally English films is the romantic comedy. There are really two versions of the rom-com – the rom-com in period costume and the contemporary rom-com. Both versions have been widely exploited since 1990. The success of the contemporary English romantic comedy was kick-started by the achievement of *Four Weddings and a Funeral* in 1994, and was mined most thoroughly by that film's scriptwriter, Richard Curtis, who also wrote or co-wrote the scripts for *Notting Hill* and the Bridget Jones films, and wrote and directed *Love Actually*. All of these films were made by Working Title, all but one featured the English star Hugh Grant, and all proved incredibly successful at the UK box office. Other films that might be placed in this category include *Sliding Doors* (1998) and *Wimbledon* (2004). The frequency with which American actors and characters appear in such films – with Andie MacDowell in *Four Weddings*, Julia Roberts in *Notting Hill*, and Renée Zellweger playing the English lead character of the Bridget Jones films, for instance – demonstrates the extent to which these films were conceived as vehicles for selling a niche brand, Englishness, in the international marketplace.[31]

Four Weddings and a Funeral: the opening gambit in Richard Curtis's romantic comedy cycle.

Perhaps the most prominent and successful examples of the romantic comedy in period costume were the Jane Austen adaptations, from *Sense and Sensibility* and *Emma* (1996) in the mid-1990s to *Pride and Prejudice* in the mid-2000s, films that I discuss in detail in chapters 5 and 6. The period rom-com is also part of another much broader generic model, the costume drama, films that deal in various ways with the English past, heritage and tradition. Following on from the success of films such as *Chariots of Fire* (1981) and *A Room with a View* (1985) in the 1980s, films about the English past have proved particularly popular with English and other filmmakers. Given the number of such films, and the various ways in which they work as texts, it makes sense to divide them into those that deal with what we can call the distant past, those that deal with the modern past, which in terms of English films seems to start around the turn of the nineteenth century, and those about the very recent, post-Second World War past.

Romantic comedy and drama tend to dominate those films that deal with the modern English past; besides the Austen adaptations, other important examples include *Howards End* (1992), *The Remains of the Day* (1993), *Mrs Brown* (1997), *The Wings of the Dove* (1997), *Gosford Park* and *Miss Potter*. I have argued elsewhere that such films may often seem to work very conservatively to reproduce notions of established national heritage and partly invented tradition, but they also in various ways expand and renew ideas of Englishness (and its constituent elements), challenge certain traditions and reimagine certain national myths.[32] *Orlando* (1992) and *Mansfield Park* (1999), for instance, engage in different ways with the legacies of English imperialism, and like many other heritage films of this ilk explore the plight of women in national history.

Whereas romantic comedy and drama dominate the films about the modern English past, those about the more distant past tend to present it as a much more dangerous space, and one that is therefore amenable to treatment in terms of action and adventure rather than or as well as romance. Films that work in these terms include *Robin Hood: Prince of Thieves* (1991), *Rob Roy* (1995), *King Arthur* (2004) and *Plunkett & Macleane* (1999); another group of films allow the romance to come to the foreground, as in *Elizabeth* and its sequel, *Elizabeth: The Golden Age*, *The Other Boleyn Girl*, and most successfully, *Shakespeare in Love* (1998). Whereas the films about the more modern past work with a generic model associated more with European cinema than Hollywood, the films about the more distant past tend to work with a generic model honed over the decades in Hollywood's studios. Even when Hollywood studios moved into the former territory, as in the Sony/Columbia version of *Sense and Sensibility*, the films looked more like quality European packages, albeit ones that were in various ways Americanised and treated as products with global marketability (Ang Lee, the director of *Sense and Sensibility*, for instance, is, as I noted above, Taiwanese).

Both the films about the modern past and those about the distant past tend to deal with familiar and well-documented historical and/or fictional figures, and with the monarchy, the aristocracy and the upper classes. In costume dramas about the very recent past – the latter half of the twentieth century – the emphasis is more likely to be on ordinary people or the beneficiaries of meritocratic rather than aristocratic status and the consequent vagaries of celebrity culture. Films that fall into this category include *The Long Day Closes*, *Shadowlands* (1993), *The Land Girls* (1998), *Enigma* (2002), *Vera Drake* (2004) and *Control* (2007). *The Queen* was unusual since it dealt with the monarchy in the very recent past. The line drawn between films about the very recent past and contemporary drama can occasionally be very thin and is easily blurred. For instance, a cycle of films about troubled working-class communities – including *East Is East*, *Billy Elliot* (2000) and *This Is England* – shares much with contemporary social drama, but is actually set in the 1970s and 1980s. I discuss all of these various filmic versions of the English past, from the medieval to the very recent past, in much more detail in chapters 7 and 8.

The contemporary social drama is another major generic model for culturally English films. As already noted, many such films tend to be small-scale and independently made, dealing with ordinary people in local, urban settings. Various films about ethnic minority and working-class communities have already been cited; others would include much of the work of Ken Loach (including *Ladybird, Ladybird*, 1994, *My Name is Joe* and *Looking for Eric*, 2009), *My Son the Fanatic* (1997), *Dirty Pretty Things* (2002) and *Somers Town* (2008). If one strand of this genre bleeds into films about the very recent past, another bleeds into comedy-drama, with films such as *The Full Monty*, and much of the work of Mike Leigh (from *Life Is Sweet* via *Career Girls* to *Happy-Go-Lucky*), or even the musical, as with *Bollywood Queen* (2003). Drama or comedy, these films are characterised by the often sharply cutting ways in which they explore contemporary social problems and concerns.

Other contemporary comedies shun both the critical edge of these films and the romantic focus of the rom-coms. They work more obviously as popular genre films, although they still negotiate Englishness in interesting ways. Several such comedies are vehicles for stars who made their names on TV, including Rowan Atkinson (*Bean, Johnny English* and *Mr Bean's Holiday*), Harry Enfield (*Kevin and Perry Go Large*) and Sacha Baron Cohen (*Ali G Indahouse*). Along with other films such as *St Trinian's*, such productions in various ways satirise established English identities and traditions. Another very successful series of comic dramas in the mid-2000s was as much about satirising film and television genres as the English characters that inhabit them – the horror film in *Shaun of the Dead*, the television police series and action films in *Hot Fuzz* – or simply comically expanding the genre, and the figure of the loser, as in the rom-com *Run, Fat Boy, Run*.

Most of the films discussed above in terms of genre presented widely recognisable English characters, identities and traditions for consumption and scrutiny to both domestic and global audiences. Some of the characters and identities may be played straight, as in costume dramas from *Howards End* to *Gosford Park* to *The Other Boleyn Girl*, but those characters are often larger than life, thereby aiding their recognition as national types. Others are played parodically, as in the *Bean* films or the Bridget Jones films – but of course parody depends upon both playing

Casino Royale: reinvigorating the James Bond thriller franchise.

out a recognisable character and identity and then ridiculing it, so that
the object of mirth still has a certain resilience as a social type. Low-
budget contemporary social dramas worked much less frequently with
character types that might be familiar on the international stage; indeed,
by exploring local contexts, even within the UK, the characters in such
films might appear unfamiliar to many. In various ways, then, once
again it can be observed that such films extended the range of social
types represented in culturally English films.

Another strand of popular genre films, contemporary dramas played
as thrillers or gangster films, tends to populate its stories with more
readily recognisable social types. Some of the thrillers are big-budget,
inward investment projects, including the *Tomb Raider* and James Bond
franchises – in some of which the larger-than-life heroes become almost
self-parodic. The English gangsters of *The Krays* (1990), *Lock, Stock and Two
Smoking Barrels*, *Snatch* (2000) and *Layer Cake* (2004) also relied heavily on
stereotypical characters, some of which again came close to self-parody.
Such populist genre films were more about playing out generic or series
conventions than about exploring social, cultural or political contexts,
and were very much aimed at mainstream – for which read youthful,
Hollywood-oriented – cinema-going audiences. Other more modestly
budgeted thrillers also played out the figure of the Englishman at large,

confronting a variety of national, ethnic and class others, in films as diverse as *The Constant Gardener* (2005), *Match Point*, *Enduring Love* (2004) and *28 Days Later* (2007).

There is one more genre that has proved important in the creation of culturally English films in the 1990s and 2000s, and that is the children's film, or perhaps better, the family film, since these are films designed to work both for parents/carers and the children they take to see them. In the 1990s, there were several subtle adaptations of classic English children's novels, including *The Secret Garden* (1993), *Black Beauty* (1994) and *The Borrowers* (1997). In the 2000s, the animation company Aardman produced a series of feature-length films: *Chicken Run*, *Wallace and Gromit: The Curse of the Were-Rabbit* (2005) and *Flushed Away*. But the most prominent entries in this genre were big-budget, Hollywood-led productions that were treated as franchises, with sequels planned from the outset: the Harry Potter films, the *Chronicles of Narnia* films, and *The Golden Compass* (2007), from Philip Pullman's *His Dark Materials* trilogy. All of these films were again adaptations; all were made as major global products, some as inward investment UK productions, but others with no formal UK interests. There was often little in such films to challenge hegemonic constructions of Englishness: white skin and well-spoken Southern English middle-class accents prevailed, although the regional accents of *Wallace and Gromit* provided welcome relief, as did the 'ordinary people' that appeared centrally or marginally in *The Borrowers*, *The Secret Garden*, *Black Beauty* and the Harry Potter films.

One thing that emerges from surveying the production of culturally English films is the number of times that the narrative source is a literary property. There are a number of reasons for this. First, the author of the novel or play has already created a world peopled with believable characters and a ready-made narrative framework for making sense of that world. Second, that world and those characters – and their author – are already defined in terms of Englishness: national identity is thus a given. Third, many of the literary properties are pre-sold, in the sense that they have already proved their market worth and to some extent guarantee audience interest in their adaptations.

Literary adaptation is not a genre, although it is a production strategy. Most of the culturally English children's films or family films are adaptations, for instance – and to the list above it is possible to add *Charlie and the Chocolate Factory* (2005), as well as films aimed at young teens, including *Stormbreaker* (2006) and *Angus, Thongs and Perfect*

Snogging (2008). Many of the middlebrow period romantic comedies and dramas are adaptations, of work by authors as diverse as Jane Austen, E.M. Forster and Ian McEwan. Kenneth Branagh has specialised in Shakespeare adaptations, including *Much Ado About Nothing* (1993), *Hamlet* (1996), *Love's Labours Lost* and *As You Like It* (2006). Several of the thrillers were also adaptations – the Bond films, for a start, but also *The Constant Gardener* and *Enduring Love*. Given the cultural status and/or the commercial success of so many of the literary properties on which these films were based, it makes a great deal of sense for filmmakers to work with such properties. While they might not have quite the pulling power of an international star – although the Harry Potter films might challenge such a statement – English literary properties still represent an important way in for filmmakers seeking to create culturally English films that might be fundable and marketable. I consider this particular strategy for creating culturally English films in chapters 4, 5 and 6.

National themes, international audiences

In the sense that many of the films included in this generic survey thematise Englishness and its variants, feature English places, characters and traditions and draw on English literary properties, they can be thought of as elements in a national cinema. In the sense too that many of these films proved successful at the UK box office and therefore presumably engaged English audiences, they can again be thought of as elements in a national cinema. Clearly, however, the production and distribution of many of these films depended upon inward investment from Hollywood companies, or upon co-production partnerships with companies from other national bases – while some ostensibly 'English' films had no formal UK involvement at all. In this sense, what is being described is a transnational cinema – suggesting that there is no longer, if there ever was, a distinctively English cinema. The representation of England and Englishness is not unique to English filmmakers or production companies; England, it seems, cannot claim ownership of such representations.

Even so, there is no denying that a large number of films, some of them quite successful, explicitly thematise a sense of English nationhood, exploring a series of usually well-established and well-defined identities, traditions and customs, and an equally well-established and well-defined territory. Other films do less to explicitly thematise Englishness, even if at a relatively banal level they adopt English settings. That is to say, they adopt national characteristics or iconographies that are so much part of everyday life, so seemingly trivial or habitual, that they are taken for granted by many people – but they can still establish a sense of a distinctive national space and reinforce ideas of English identity. With the introduction of a Cultural Test for determining the Britishness of film projects, government policy in the late 2000s sought to encourage the production of films that were explicitly *about* England in a thematic sense, as well as adopting a banal English setting. Does that make a national cinema?

In part, this can only really be answered by looking at how audiences engage with such films. As will become clear in the next chapter, there is some evidence that culturally English or indigenous films will do better with English audiences than other films, at least in a relative sense; but that does not mean that such films are necessarily capable of generating a national sense of shared belonging, or a national self-consciousness, among English audiences.[33] Part of the problem here is that the audiences for many of these films are by no means solely English: the films circulate in many other territories, so the question arises of how other audiences respond to and engage with films that to others may appear as their own national cinema. And English audiences also routinely watch Hollywood films that in no sense thematise Englishness or adopt banal English settings. How does such activity shape how English audiences view the world, the space they live in, and their sense of belonging and allegiance?

As a report commissioned by the UK Film Council notes, the reception abroad of films that in the UK might be thought of as English films is complex. On the one hand, the evidence of the report is that contemporary social dramas with a realist bent will often be recognised and appreciated as specifically English or British films. On the other hand, as many of these films are relatively low-budget and devoid of major stars, they are only likely to be seen by minority audiences in foreign markets. The films that do reach mainstream audiences are likely to be those with high budgets and recognisable stars – and most of those films will have Hollywood studio involvement, and will as a result be experienced as American films, or as global films that have no evident national markers. As the report notes:

> The majority of the films accounting for the strong commercial per-
> formance of British cinema in [foreign markets] are not seen by audiences
> as specifically British artefacts – this is the case with many US-financed

blockbusters made in UK studios. While the Harry Potter films may be effortlessly experienced as British by Anglo-Saxon audiences attuned to their cultural signals and the cadences of British English, non-Anglo audiences focus instead on the scale and production values and identify them more readily as American. The trend is compounded in countries where these films are dubbed in the national language.[34]

In effect, as high-budget films circulate abroad, two sets of cultural markers compete for attention: on the one hand, there are those markers that, for some audiences at least, identify the characters, settings and concerns as English; on the other hand, the presentation of the films as relatively spectacular cultural products marks them as American. Once again, the perception of cultural identity becomes a highly problematic issue, as different audiences engage with or prioritise different aspects of the films as texts, and rework them within their own frames of reference.

Against the odds, filmmakers in the 1990s and 2000s identified a variety of means of exploiting the niche brand of culturally English filmmaking in the increasingly globalised film business. Budgets and the locus of creative control have in many ways shaped the ways in which that brand has appeared on screen, as too have the conventions of different genres – although how things appear on the screen and how different audiences actually attend to them are different matters. In the next chapter, I examine how public debate and government policy responded to the challenges of maintaining a viable UK film business and sought to establish a framework within which culturally English filmmaking might develop.

2 Film policy and national cinema: cultural value and economic value

Film production in the UK developed in the ways that it did in the 1990s and 2000s for a variety of reasons. For some, film production was a small aspect of one of the most important businesses of the period, whether it was defined as an entertainment business or a media business. For others, it was less about business and more about cultural and social engagement, whether this was conceived in terms of entertaining audiences, or developing ideas and views of the world in which we live. Public interest in and debate about cinema was considerable, with much of it framed in terms of a fascination with celebrity culture. Such a high-profile cultural industry also attracted the attention of government policy-makers and regulators. Again, this attention has taken different forms and been generated by often competing interests. During the 1990s and 2000s, the government was committed to the development of the UK production sector because of both its economic and its cultural dimensions. In part, this was about ensuring the well-being of the national economy; in part it was a recognition of the cultural or ideological role that cinema can play in national terms. As such, the government sought to regulate the sorts of film production activities that took place in the UK, and that regulation depended in part on how film was defined in national terms.

In this chapter, I look at the historical development of official film policy in the UK, and at the various definitions of 'British' film that have emerged in this context. I focus in particular on the debate about the economic and cultural value of film production in the UK that developed from the late 1990s onwards. Finally, I examine the complex terms of an official 'Cultural Test' that emerged in 2007, as a means of defining UK film production in an increasingly global arena, and the competing interests of national, transnational and global forces in that arena.

The development of official UK film policy

To understand the nature of government policy and regulation in the 1990s and 2000s, it is necessary to fill in some of the historical back-story, from the 1920s to the 1980s. In the 1920s there was a growing debate in Establishment circles about the pervasiveness and popularity of Hollywood films in the UK, and the perceived threat of Americanisation and the erosion of British culture – but also about the more general sense in which cinema functioned as a key element of contemporary popular culture. There were also deep-rooted industrial concerns about the precariousness of the national production sector. The combination of these cultural and industrial concerns eventually moved the government to establish a protectionist framework to support British film producers. Such concerns continued to play a key role in persuading successive governments to adopt industrial measures to protect British film production.

From the late 1920s until the Thatcher government unravelled it in the 1980s in the name of free-market economics, there was then a system of government support designed to bolster the production sector and to protect and nurture the filmmaking business in the UK. This system may have been primarily economic or industrial in nature, but the debates that led to the introduction of the system and that ensured its continuation for more than half a century primarily revolved around cultural concerns. Cultural policy also determined government support for the British Film Institute from 1933 onwards, while social policy shaped the development of both state-supported documentary and informational filmmaking and a film censorship system in the UK.

As John Hill points out, film policy in the UK has thus always involved a mix of industrial, cultural and social motivations, not least because of cinema's dual status as both an industry and a cultural practice, both an entertainment business and an art form. There was also a well-established perception in governmental and other decision-making circles that film was a different kind of cultural activity from more established and traditional art forms. In terms of support for mainstream film production, however, until recently it was the industrial motivation that dominated. Government film policy was thus different from government policy about the other arts. As Hill explains:

> Unlike the traditional arts, the cultural value or aesthetic worth of cinema has not been a given and film has therefore not automatically fallen within

the domain of 'arts policy' (or, following its establishment, the Arts Council). ... Historically, government film policy has been pre-eminently an industrial policy concerned with the preservation and support of commercial film making.[1]

From the late 1940s until the 1980s, this industrial policy was founded upon a system of public subsidy from the Exchequer, coupled with a protectionist mechanism for ensuring a minimum percentage of screen time in UK cinemas for British-produced films. In the 1980s this public support was dismantled, to be replaced in the early 1990s by measures designed to encourage private investment in film production, notably in the form of a tax-relief scheme that provided financial incentives to British film producers from 1992, but also through loans provided by British Screen. Public funds were reintroduced in 1995 with the decision to use National Lottery funding to support film production. The new Labour government elected in 1997 built on these modest foundations, expanding the tax-relief system in 1997, creating a Films Minister in the government in 1998, and establishing a Film Policy Review Group the same year. The recommendations of this group paved the way for the founding of the Film Council in 2000, renamed the UK Film Council in 2003. This body took over much of the responsibility for developing and implementing government film policy and funding, using money received direct from government as well as a sizeable amount from the Lottery, and absorbing some of the responsibilities of British Screen, which was dissolved, and the British Film Institute, which was now funded through the Film Council.[2]

The UK Film Council became a key institution in the organisation and development of British cinema in the 2000s. Its mission was 'to stimulate a competitive, successful and vibrant UK film industry and culture, and to promote the widest possible enjoyment and understanding of cinema throughout the nations and regions of the UK'.[3] As such, it brought together the various strands of government film policy and practice, industrial, social and cultural. Given its commitment to a commercially viable industry, many of its policy directives were designed to encourage avowedly populist, commercial filmmaking of a kind that would win wide audiences. It promoted the UK as an international centre for film production, lobbied the government for tax relief and other fiscal incentives that might make the UK an attractive base for film production, and dispensed public funds – primarily Lottery funds – to productions with a degree of UK involvement. It also promoted UK films at home and abroad and supported training for the film business. As such, it played a vital role in building capacity and generating a greater sense of economic and financial stability and focus in the production sector. It worked closely with government to develop policy that enabled public and private funds to flow productively into UK-based filmmaking, whether through grant in aid, Lottery funds, tax relief or other financial incentives, and helped establish a customised and more logical public financing system.

While all these measures were designed to secure the sustainability and commercial viability of UK-based film production, other measures had purposes that were more about social, cultural or educational commitment. Thus it funded the British Film Institute, various schemes to promote new filmmakers, innovative filmmaking and regional activity, and schemes to encourage the distribution and exhibition of as wide a range as possible of UK and other films, including what it calls specialised (i.e. non-mainstream) cinema. It also had an access policy designed to encourage a more socially inclusive workforce in the film business. To some extent, these various aims can be seen as internally contradictory, with commercial enterprise set against public service responsibility. As Hill points out, some of the Film Council's policies and practices were pro-market and industry-focused, and designed to support mainstream, populist commercial filmmaking in the UK – which in part meant encouraging Hollywood majors to invest in UK production activity; but some of its other policies and practices were designed to skew the market in favour of social inclusion, cultural diversity and specialised cinema.[4]

What is an 'English' film? What is a 'British' film?

In this context, it was important for both the government and the UK Film Council that they were able to operate with appropriate definitions of what constituted British cinema or British films (*English* cinema was not an issue at this level). Critics and historians will occasionally devise their own means for establishing what does and does not count as a British film, often focusing on the extent to which the subject matter or characters are perceived as British, and/or taking account of films directed by British citizens. That of course is by no means a foolproof set of definitions. There has also over the years been a series of official definitions of British cinema. The Cinematograph Films Act of 1927, for instance, involved a clear definition of what could count as a British film, and since then most of the official definitions have been overwhelmingly economic in nature, and were designed to identify those films that might benefit from the various financial incentives provided by the government for indigenous production. In the 1990s and the early 2000s, the key piece of legislation was Schedule 1 of the 1985 Films Act, which sought to identify those 'British' films that might qualify for tax relief, and later Lottery funding. According to the Films Act, in broad terms, a British film was one made by a company registered or controlled in the UK or in the European Union, where the proportion of money spent on the production in the UK was at least 70 per cent, and the proportion of money spent on employing citizens of the UK, the Commonwealth or the European Union was also at least 70 per cent. But films could also qualify as British by meeting the conditions of an official co-production with one of the few countries recognised for these purposes. In such cases, the qualifying terms were slightly different.[5]

As with all previous such official definitions of British film, dating back to 1927, cultural criteria were conspicuous by their absence from this definition. As with previous formulations, what were being defined were industrially British films, rather than those that might be considered culturally British. This was because the purpose of the definition was primarily economic, in that it was designed to identify the type of film production activity that might be eligible for some form of governmental support. On the one hand, it was about enabling producers to access public funding and/or tax relief. On the other hand, it was about encouraging investment in the UK film production business, not just by UK companies but by foreign companies as well. The definition did also seek to ensure that not only investment but also creative control was framed in national terms – but as with all such definitions, there were many loopholes open to exploitation. It is also noteworthy that membership of two transnational bodies, the European Union and the British Commonwealth, skewed the nationalist aspect of the definition, so that a 'British' film could be made by a company registered in, say, France, with the majority of the creative team from Canada!

This particular definition of British film remained in force until 2007. From the early 1990s, dissatisfied with the official formulation, the British Film Institute (BFI) sought to establish a more refined set of definitions about what might and might not reasonably count as British films, taking

note of both economic input and cultural identity. These definitions provided the BFI with a framework for a series of annual statistical overviews of the British film business, which were adopted as a reference tool
by both those working in the film business and those commenting on
British film, from professional reviewers to academics. The grounds on
which the distinctions between films were made were inevitably to some
extent both tentative and subjective, and they were modified slightly
from year to year. In the BFI's 1994 *Handbook*, it was suggested that while
the Films Act of 1985 'is the basis for all attempts to define British films, it
isn't much of a starting point. We therefore have to come up with a definition of our own.'[6] The resulting definition involved identifying whether
'the financial *or the creative* impulse came from Britain. The guiding principle is to identify films which directly contribute to British film culture
or to the culture of the British film industry.'[7]

Gradually, the BFI devised four different categories of 'British'
filmmaking – or rather, of UK film production. First, there were those
films where 'the cultural and financial impetus was from the UK, and
the majority of the personnel were British'; second, there were 'majority
UK co-productions', 'films in which, although there are foreign partners,
there is a UK cultural content and a significant amount of British finance
and personnel'; third, there were 'minority UK co-productions', 'foreign
(non-US) films in which there is a small UK involvement'; and finally
there were 'American films with a UK creative and/or part financial
involvement'.[8] These are useful distinctions, which take due account of
the globalisation of the film business, and the extent of transnational co-
productions, but which also take into account the cultural as well as the
economic dimensions of filmmaking. Inevitably there is a certain degree
of creative thinking behind the apparently objective gathering of statistics, but it is more the process of defining and acknowledging different
types of 'British' film that interests me here than their precise objective
veracity.

When the Film Council was established in 2000, it generated a similar range of statistics, but sought to move towards a more economically
objective set of distinctions, working primarily with official categories of
British filmmaking initially based on the definitions embodied in the 1985
Films Act. However, they still made some effort to distinguish between
different types of films. Thus there were inward investment films,
where a significant proportion of the funding came from foreign, usually American, companies, even if British creative talent, infrastructure

The Golden Compass benefited from significant inward investment.

and locations were involved; there were official co-productions, which were further subdivided into majority co-productions, where UK investment is the highest among the co-production partners, and minority co-productions; and there were what it called 'independent UK films', which it defined as those made without major US studio involvement.[9] These categories were by no means mutually exclusive, and again they acknowledge the complicated business of film funding in what is now so clearly a global business; they also reflect the Film Council's policy of encouraging foreign investment in the UK film business, recognising that the British film production business would be minimal if there was no such investment.

At the same time, as noted in chapter 1 above, the Film Council also presented statistics that were designed to demonstrate the extent of what might be called British cultural content in a range of different types of film. Thus the Harry Potter films (2001–10), *The Bourne Ultimatum* (2007) and *The Golden Compass* (2007), for instance, were all classified as inward investment films, with substantial input from major Hollywood studios, but they also all had strong British connections, in terms of their source material, their subject matter or key members of the cast and crew – and they were all wholly or substantially made in Britain. What this suggests is that definitions of 'British' film need to remain flexible in order to be sensitive to the vagaries of the film business and the thoroughly transnational processes of film funding and film production; and they need to allow for different permutations of funding sources, production companies, creative workers and subject matter.

The process of gathering statistics that might be of use to the industry and to policy-makers is clearly led by economic motives, even if cultural criteria come into play in various ways. Filmmakers have however played a key role in another set of debates about the nature of British identity. Definitions of Britishness and of the purpose of UK institutions have been in flux for some time, with long-standing ideas of a unique and homogeneous national identity increasingly giving way to ideas of cultural diversity, and an acknowledgement of the differences of the various nations and regions that make up the UK, but also the various cultural and ethnic identities that have developed in those spaces. As John Hill has argued, already in the 1980s UK films were beginning to express

> a much more fluid, hybrid and plural sense of 'Britishness' than earlier British cinema generally did. In this respect, while the British cinema of the 1980s failed to assert the myths of 'nation' with its earlier confidence it was nevertheless a cinema that could be regarded as representing the complexities of 'national' life more fully than before.[10]

In various ways, and through various types of film, this tendency has continued through the 1990s and 2000s. For instance, numerous small British films, from *Bhaji on the Beach* (1993), via *Babymother* (1998) and *Bend It Like Beckham* (2002), to *Brick Lane* (2007) and beyond, have explored in often quite subtle ways the contribution of ethnic minority groups to contemporary British economic, cultural and social life.

Acknowledgement of these broader cultural shifts became enshrined in the film policy created by successive Labour governments between 1997 and 2010, when they lost power to the Conservatives. Thus one of the goals of the Film Council was to 'support and encourage cultural diversity and social inclusiveness'[11] – and Lottery funding was invested in both *Bend It Like Beckham* and *Brick Lane*. Filmmakers and the Film Council have thus generated a body of films that promote new ideas about British cultural and social identity, although the statistics produced by the Film Council and the primarily economically motivated definitions of British film that lie behind them hardly attend to these ideas and identities.

To some extent, this is the result of the tension within the Film Council between its cultural and social policy on the one hand and its

Brick Lane: putting the British-Asian community on screen, thanks to Lottery funding.

commitment to an economically viable UK film business on the other. That tension can be seen in the Council's statement of its purpose as 'to help make the UK a hub and natural home for film in the digital age, a place with a diverse and vibrant film culture and a flourishing, competitive film industry'.[12] On the one hand, then, cultural diversity; on the other hand, economic competitiveness. According to statements such as this, it was as important to attract inward investment from foreign companies and to nurture a skilled film industry workforce in regular demand as it was to produce 'successful and distinctive British films'.[13] And even then, the films were to be simply distinctive, rather than distinctively British. Cultural diversity may have been one of the Council's goals, but cultural Britishness did not seem to be high on the agenda. The national appears in such statements as a relatively neutral space, which is to be filled with a dynamic range of film-related activities, both economic and cultural – with no particular obligation to a strongly defined cultural Britishness. Clearly, then, even in this era of intensely transnational and at times global cultural and economic activity, the national still has some purchase; but it is too often an empty signifier, a brand name for a particular type of commodity or a particular economic space, rather than a clear exposition of values and identities.

Cultural value and economic value

Does it matter that it is difficult to devise an adequate definition of a British film, let alone an English film? After all, we live in a period where old national ties and cultural boundaries are constantly being stretched, challenged and overridden. Transnational production arrangements are enabling all sorts of films to be made that might not otherwise be made, while the globalisation of film culture potentially creates access to a much wider range of world films for a much wider range of world audiences. Is the apparent erosion of traditional national cultures – and national cinemas – necessarily a bad thing? One response is to note that the new global cultural economy is of course dominated by a few very large corporations, and a few highly successful commodities and wider franchises handled by those corporations. In terms of cinema, this is what is now often called global Hollywood. And while global Hollywood is in part about investing in products that have local appeal, the resulting cultural hegemony will still squeeze out certain voices, values and identities. In this context, vibrant national production bases and innovative, independent filmmakers do still have an important role to play in terms of articulating voices, values and identities that may otherwise fall by the wayside.

If much of the official policy around film in the UK has been dominated by economic concerns, from 1997 to 2010, successive Labour government also endeavoured to find space for the cultural dimensions of 'British' cinema. In 1998, the first Minister for Culture, Media and Sport, Chris Smith, wrote of his department's work that 'we have recognised a very simple fact about movie-making: that is it *both* a cultural and an economic activity'.[14] Six years later, his successor, Tessa Jowell, called for an intelligent public debate about the value of culture. She began that debate by arguing that 'our culture is critical to the type of country we are', that 'without culture we are not complete citizens', and that subsidising culture is an important 'bulwark against the homogeneity of globalisation'.[15]

These are important arguments, and they begin to underline the value of cultural activity – and the value of national governments intervening in such activity. The problem for the Film Council, whose task it is to follow through on the government's film policy directives, is that a debate about culture that doesn't engage with questions of economic as well as cultural value is a debate that is not going to be taken seriously by the Treasury. Chris Smith was after all in no doubt that cinema was both a cultural and an economic activity, and that inward investment was vital to its well-being; elsewhere, for instance, he explained that he wanted to 'ensure that film making in the UK remains a pleasurable and profitable experience for overseas companies'.[16] The Film Council is in effect constantly obliged to speak to two masters, both the Treasury and the Department of Culture, Media and Sport, hence the tensions at the level of policy and practice between economic principles and cultural principles. Its goal has therefore been to convince its masters that, as a creative industry, film has both cultural and economic benefits.

As Stephen Pratten and Simon Deakin note, the Film Council thus emerged in a context in which 'cultural justifications for film policy' were increasingly viewed as part of the wider policy of encouraging the economic competitiveness of UK businesses, and especially the creative industries.[17] Government policy in the late 1990s, they argued, assumed that 'the preservation of an active and independent British film industry can simultaneously meet two goals: the production of cultural goods which are, in some way, distinctively British; and the fostering of competitive advantage in ... the cultural industries'.[18] As will become clear, the commitment to distinctively British filmmaking was gradually enhanced in the mid-2000s. The fostering of competitive economic advantage on the part of the film industry meanwhile took a particular line, and was by no means as straightforward as fostering a UK production sector that was strong enough to compete with Hollywood. Competitive advantage also involved creating a production infrastructure and a tax regime that might attract foreign, and especially Hollywood, producers to make their films in the UK – and these were not necessarily films that had any British cultural content.

Emerging in this context, the Film Council lobbied hard on behalf of the UK film industry, seeking to create a sustainable business, and one that found favour both in official and especially governmental circles and with the news media and the general public. It endeavoured to make as strong a case as it could for the economic and cultural benefits of the film industry, the value that the industry added to both economic and cultural well-being in the UK. It regularly cited both direct and indirect economic benefits, demonstrating that the film industry made a substantial contribution to gross domestic product and the balance of payments, and directly employed significant numbers of people, while also making an indirect contribution to a range of service industries and to the tourism industry.

The Council also argued that the film business played a major role in maintaining and promoting a sense of national cultural identity, a brand that could be sold both domestically and worldwide. That UK brand was also perceived as vital in creating and maintaining demand for exports of other British goods and services.[19] This was less an argument about the competitive advantage of the UK film production business, and more an argument about the value of the film business in terms of its contribution to the UK balance of payments and to the Exchequer, and the number of jobs it supported. It was about demonstrating that there were clear economic benefits to be derived from investing public money in film production or otherwise promoting film production in the UK.

In 2007, the Film Council commissioned a report from Oxford Economics, which examined in detail the economic benefits and impact of the UK film industry. The tone of this report is indicative of much of the current debate about film policy. The report concluded that the industry directly employed 33,500 people, and indirectly supported another 95,000 jobs in service industries, tourism, trade and merchandise sales. It produced careful estimates on the considerable contribution of the film industry to the UK economy, and the importance of inward investment in film production activity in the UK. It also argued that 'films depicting the UK are responsible for attracting about 1 in 10 overseas tourists' (and therefore their spend in the UK) and that UK businesses exporting goods benefited from 'the part UK films play in establishing and reinforcing the country's image and brand'.[20]

The report also went to some length to tie these more obviously economic benefits to what may be seen as the cultural benefits of UK films, concluding that 'UK films contribute substantially to the cultural life of the country' and 'are a key means of expression of UK identity'.[21] Drawing on such arguments, the report suggested that 'the overall social value of [a] UK film may well exceed the price that consumers pay to see it at the cinema', and went on to attempt to establish what it called 'a monetary estimate of the cultural value of UK film'.[22] In so doing, it provided econometric evidence that suggested that UK film audiences, given a choice, preferred to watch UK-made films, and especially what could be described as 'indigenous films': 'our estimates suggest that, other things [being] equal, a film shown in the UK can expect its box office revenue to be up to 30% higher if it is indigenous'.[23] As will already be clear, the concept of indigenous film is always going to be loose – and in this respect, is probably best understood as meaning those films that are strongly marketed as British, and where the 'UK brand' is therefore well established.

The Oxford Economics report, not surprisingly, was primarily a document about the economic situation of the film business, so it is interesting to note the extent to which cultural factors and explanations were played out in the report. For instance, the enhanced box-office success of 'British' films was explained in cultural or ideological terms: the appeal of what the report calls indigenous films, it was argued, was that they

> may help inform British people about who they are, how they fit in the world and what they share with other nationalities. Successful UK films therefore play an important role in defining our nationality, identity and self-confidence. Moreover, they also influence how the nation is perceived abroad.[24]

The report also suggested that 'the full cultural value' of UK films to UK audiences exceeded what could be demonstrated solely through box-office statistics, and had to take into account 'such things as national self-esteem and identity'.[25] Stated in these terms, this was a speculative argument, although it was also of course an argument that was widely accepted; the authors of the report, however, sought to substantiate the argument with further statistical evidence. To this end, various studies were cited that suggested that 'people value the cultural content of indigenous audio-visual content highly, and often significantly more than the price they pay for it'.[26] The statistics are compelling, although no account was taken of the fact that so-called indigenous films may have been marketed more extensively in the UK than elsewhere. The more general argument is occasionally crude and tautological, more effective rhetorically than logically, and there is little in the way of analysis of the sorts of images of national identity on offer in so-called indigenous film. To that extent, questions of nationality are taken as given, rather than understood as open to debate and negotiation, with little attention being paid to the cultural and social differences lived out by the inhabitants of the UK and other British subjects.

Just occasionally, the report did touch on such issues in passing. For instance, it cited a series of small-budget indigenous films that it argued addressed challenging contemporary social issues, from drug addiction in *Trainspotting* and prejudice in *Billy Elliot*, to race relations in *Bend It Like Beckham* and immigration in *In This World* (2002). Such films, it was argued,

Billy Elliot: addressing contemporary social issues.

played an important role in exploring aspects of 'UK identity', 'address[ing] issues of diversity that are critical to meeting the challenges of the 21st century'.[27] Overall, such arguments played only a very small part in the report. Even so, the report amply demonstrated the efforts being made both to identify and then to bind together the perceived economic and cultural value of UK film production, and the demands it made on the pub-lic purse. The real purpose of the report was not to get into a debate about the ideological role of film and the nature of cultural identity, but to attempt to quantify cultural value, to set an economic value on the cultural ben-efits of indigenous films to British people, to establish how much audiences were prepared to pay for the perceived public good of those films.

As such, the tenor of the report is indicative of efforts being made to articulate a sense of cultural value around film production activity and to link it to the perceived economic value of the business. Even the Treasury had acknowledged the cultural benefits of film when it stated that its purpose in reforming the UK tax incentive system in 2005 was to ensure that it promoted the 'sustainable production of culturally British films in more effective ways': in other words, cultural identity was at the heart of the proposals, implying that the Treasury saw value in supporting *culturally* British films, rather than simply *industrially* British films.[28] Indeed, the opening statement in the document outlining the Treasury's proposals reads:

> The Government recognises the important role that the British film industry plays in the representation and expression of British culture and national identity, and is committed to encouraging the enjoyment of film and promoting film production in the UK.[29]

But was this any different from the long-standing process, stretching back to the 1920s, whereby cultural motivations were used to bolster what were in the end economic goals? The Treasury insisted there was a difference, arguing that the goal of achieving economic sustainability 'underpins the primary objective of ensuring the flow of cultural benefits from film production'.[30]

Indeed, this particular Treasury document is littered with statements about the cultural value of British films: 'the framework of Government support for the UK film industry', it was argued, 'reflects both the economic and cultural benefits that British films bring to the UK',[31] while it is 'the important role that film plays in British cultural life [that] provides Government with a specific case for the forms of intervention that are made … to support the industry'.[32] The document even allowed for the production of films that may be commercial failures but that still add cultural value or play a culturally significant role.[33]

The need for government intervention was explained in detail in an appendix to the document, which is worth quoting at length for the insight it gives into government thinking about film as a creative industry:

> Cinematic film provides a universal and readily accessible medium for the expression and representation of British culture and national identity. Where cultural contribution goes beyond providing entertainment in this sense, the social benefits often fail to be captured in the transactions that people undertake in the market. In this regard culturally British films can be regarded as merit goods that the market often fails to provide at the optimum level. The social benefits that attach to cultural production suggest that there is a public interest in ensuring greater supply than the market would otherwise provide.[34]

This is a very interesting argument, in effect about the ideological role of film in the articulation of national identity, and the potential for the government to intervene in what is undoubtedly a global film market to create space for that articulation of national identity: in Tessa Jowell's words, to create a 'bulwark against the homogeneity of globalisation'.[35] But what exactly did cultural Britishness mean in such contexts? Did such statements not simply reproduce traditional conservative definitions of British national identity as homogenous and unchanging, definitions that are unable to take on board the social and cultural diversity of contemporary Britain? It is all very well making statements that 'British films are an important part of our cultural heritage and a significant channel for the continuing expression and dissemination of British culture.'[36] But what exactly is to be expressed and disseminated in the name of British culture? There are once again important questions here about ideology and the power to define or impose identities.

In fact, somewhat surprisingly – but then these statements were being made under the auspices of a Labour government – the Treasury document did go on to articulate a sense of cultural diversity:

> Without Government intervention, a richer, more diverse and more representative range of voices may not emerge, resulting in a more impoverished and limited range of choices for the public. The aim of support is to address the market failure in the supply of culturally British films by way of an incentive for specific behaviour – the production of culturally British films.[37]

But it is important to note that the Treasury document did not attempt to define what a British film was, and more specifically, what a *culturally* British film was, beyond this open sense of creating space for a range of diverse and representative voices. Nor is it clear whether those voices were envisaged as national, where the goal is to ensure that a univocal British voice could be heard alongside other national voices from around the world. Or is the document inviting its readers to consider a range of voices *within* Britain: internal cultural diversity rather than international diversity?

In order to answer these questions, it is necessary to look beyond statements from the Treasury, which was not the only institution seeking to provide an official understanding of the cultural value of film. At the same time that the Treasury was establishing the rationale for its tax incentive reforms, the Department of Culture, Media and Sport and the Film Council were devising a new Cultural Test to determine which films might now qualify as British for tax purposes and for purposes of public funding. The debate around this test in fact drew greater attention to questions of cultural diversity, as will become clear in the next section. Through such developments, a new, official sense of a diverse British culture was emerging, one that could be enhanced by a publicly supported UK-based film industry.

How did this tally with developments elsewhere? Mette Hjort and Duncan Petrie have argued that, around the world,

> national film policy has [in recent years] become less concerned with protecting local production or culture perceived as being under threat from Americanisation, and instead is embracing the putative benefits of the new international division of cultural labour, most notably the substantial levels of inward investment that major Hollywood-funded productions bring in terms of local employment and the purchase of goods and services. This shift from a cultural to an economic imperative may chime with the neo-liberal turn in world trade but it has also generated a great deal of anxiety about the erosion of cultural difference and non-commercial filmmaking practices that might be entailed by acquiescence to a Hollywood/American agenda.[38]

While some of these developments clearly apply to the UK film industry, they by no means all map on in anything like a straightforward manner. It was certainly the case that early British film policy was dominated by the discourse of protectionism and involved imposing restrictions to free trade in an attempt to curb what was perceived by many as the threat of Americanisation. But if cultural anxieties about the erosion of national culture in Britain lay behind the system of state protection for the film industry from the late 1920s to the 1980s, the measures introduced were, as already noted, much more about economic rather than cultural protection. Domestic production was to be encouraged, but no cultural principles were set to determine the content of British films. It is well established too that American producers and distributors exploited loopholes in the system that enabled them to benefit from the measures introduced by the government. There was also a long-standing concern about the balance of payments, which effectively encouraged what would now be called inward investment – and there was plenty of such investment in both the late 1930s and the 1960s, for instance. The discourse of protectionism may no longer feature heavily in the debate about national film policy in the UK, and inward investment may have become a key concept; even so, it is clear that much of what applies in the 1990s and 2000s was already the case in previous decades.

The various official and officially commissioned documents discussed above also suggest that, in the British context, there is no simple shift from a cultural imperative to an economic imperative. Rather, the cultural and the economic continue to interact at the level of both policy and practice, but perhaps in a rather different way from how they interacted in the 1930s or the 1960s. The encouragement of inward investment and the development of an industrial and fiscal infrastructure that might be attractive to foreign producers were certainly policy priorities, but there was still an official commitment to fostering cultural Britishness, which, at least in Jowell's statement, was about resisting hegemonic global forces. The introduction in 2007 of a Cultural Test to determine which films might count as British simply reinforced that commitment.

The Cultural Test for British films

In the early 2000s, UK-based film production had benefited from various creative accounting arrangements, including sale-and-leaseback deals and tax avoidance schemes – variously referred to as sole trader operations, sideways loss relief and GAAP equity funding – along with the officially sanctioned Enterprise Investment Schemes and tax-relief system. Much was made of the fact that several of these funding opportunities benefited from unintended tax loopholes, and that specialist investment companies were doing better out of these various schemes than filmmakers themselves. The government was understandably keen to streamline the system and to ensure that filmmakers and audiences were the real beneficiaries. Following an extensive review, a dedicated tax-relief scheme for British film production was introduced in 2007. One of the key features of this new scheme was a rigorous Cultural Test for determining the 'Britishness' of a film production and therefore its eligibility for public funding and/or tax relief. This test radically overhauled the official definition of a 'British' film, moving beyond the economic principles that had been the guiding force for the previous 80 years and finding space for the acknowledgement of cultural value.

This was the first time that an official film industry scheme had adopted any form of cultural criteria and is therefore a landmark of sorts, since it explicitly sets out to encourage the production of culturally British films. At the same time, the scheme was not intended to make inward investment unattractive, since this was still seen as one of the lynchpins of UK film policy. The new scheme thus endeavoured to strike a balance between inward investment and cultural Britishness – with the two brought together in the form of investment in a UK industrial infrastructure and labour force. The Cultural Test was designed to offer a means of quantifying the cultural benefit a film might generate for the UK, to identify and then quantify cultural value, alongside economic value. Implicit in the test was an assumption that non-UK economic, financial or creative interests in a film would have an effect on the types of representation of UK life, traditions and people that the film might provide – and that therefore UK interests should be encouraged. While foreign economic interests were also still encouraged, their involvement in films that might be designated UK productions was to be limited.

Meanwhile the criteria that made up the Cultural Test assigned a positive value to certain types of creative practice and at the same time adopted an impressively broad-ranging assessment of how British culture might be defined. The Cultural Test was speculative, however, in that it endeavoured to predict the cultural (and economic) value of a film prior to its release – or indeed its production – in order to provide financial incentives up front. Through a system of tax credits, tax relief could be granted in advance of production, relief that might amount to up to 20 per cent of the total production budget – and up to 25 per cent for films costing under £20m. Given the continuing role envisaged for inward investment, the scheme was typical of government initiatives around the world, with countries competing with each other to attract foreign investment in film production, primarily from the big Hollywood companies.

In terms of the upfront support the tax-relief system provided for production activity, it made sense that the scheme was predictive in its assessment of the 'Britishness' of a film, but it is also worth thinking about how one might identify the cultural value of a film once it has been released. Here reception studies would come into play, so that one might examine box-office statistics, measuring the size and make-up of the audience in various ways, but one might also try to establish the ways in which a film has been taken up in the contemporary culture, the cultural presence and impact it has, its critical reception, and so on, as well as undertaking detailed qualitative research with actual audiences. Clearly, such assessments were beyond the new Cultural Test.

When the test was introduced in 2007, it was just one part of a larger set of schemes for identifying films that might be eligible for official support. As with previous schemes of this nature, various criteria had to be met before tax relief would be granted, to ensure that the British production business was the prime beneficiary. Films and film production companies could qualify for tax relief by meeting the requirements of one of three different schemes: a film could be made according to the regulations for one of the UK's official bilateral co-production treaties; it could be made under the auspices of the European Convention on Cinematographic Co-production; or it could qualify by passing the official Cultural Test to determine its 'Britishness'. The test did not therefore apply to films made under one of the two co-production arrangements. To qualify for tax relief, a film also had to be made for theatrical release, and at least 25 per cent of the core expenditure had to be spent on goods or services used or consumed in the UK.[39] The production companies of films qualifying under any of these schemes were also eligible to apply for UK Film Council funding.

In 2009, there were co-production treaties with seven countries (Australia, Canada, France, India, Jamaica, New Zealand and South Africa), while further treaties were being negotiated with Morocco and China. The European Convention meanwhile was designed to enable co-productions between at least three companies in separate European Community countries, and 'to safeguard creation and freedom of expression and defend the cultural diversity of the various European countries'.[40] Each of these co-production arrangements was designed 'to encourage international co-operation between filmmakers', and to share 'the skills and resources of more than one country'.[41] They also enabled production companies to benefit from the financial incentives, tax break schemes and subsidies available in more than one country. Thus alongside the promotion of cultural Britishness was a commitment to transnational cooperation, in part as a means again of encouraging cultural diversity at a different level.

Films that did not meet the terms of one of these official co-production arrangements had to pass the Cultural Test to qualify as British in order to be eligible for UK Film Council funding and to secure tax relief. The Cultural Test had four broad categories, covering 'cultural content', 'cultural contribution', 'cultural hubs' and 'cultural practitioners'. The category of 'cultural content' tested whether a film was set in the UK, whether its lead characters were British citizens or residents, whether it depicted British subject matter or was adapted from 'underlying material' created by a British citizen or resident, and whether the original dialogue was recorded mainly in English (or one of the UK's six officially recognised indigenous minority languages).[42]

The 'cultural contribution' category sought to determine whether a film made a significant cultural contribution over and above the more banal aspects of cultural content measured under the first category. What the test rewarded under the category of 'cultural contribution' was what it defined as a significant representation or reflection of either British cultural heritage or British cultural diversity, and/or a representation of British culture that might be seen as involving 'a novel and creative approach to filmmaking'.[43] The 'cultural hub' category rewarded films where location and/or studio shooting and/or post-production work took place in the UK. Finally, the 'cultural practitioners' category rewarded films where one or more of the director, scriptwriter, producer or composer, or the lead actors or the majority of the cast and/or crew were British or from another state within the European Economic Area.

A scoring system was devised by which film production companies had to achieve at least 16 points out of a maximum 31 points to qualify as British. The scoring was heavily weighted towards cultural content and cultural contribution, which between them had a maximum yield of 20 points, with the other two categories yielding only 11 points. Points had to be accrued from all four categories, and further stipulations ensured that only films with a clear British content, according to the guidelines, could pass the test. The allocation of points in each category depended on the degree to which each particular criterion was fulfilled. Thus, 4 would be awarded if at least 75 per cent of a film was set in the UK, 3 points for 66 per cent, 2 points for 50 per cent, and so on, with the percentages based on the number of pages in the script that are set in the UK (regardless of where a scene is actually shot). In other cases, producers were asked to make the case for the centrality of a particular character, or the extent to which their film 'depicts a British story', for instance.[44]

Historical idiosyncrasies were also taken into account. Thus, 'a character who was a subject of England, Scotland, Wales or Northern Ireland prior to those countries becoming part of Britain or the United Kingdom will...be considered to be British for the purposes of the test', as too would be 'any character who, at the time the film was set, was a British subject in the UK's colonial territories'.[45] Cultural practitioners, however, were not required to be British for the purposes of the Cultural Test, but to be citizens of any state within the European Economic Area. The Cultural Test was thus a curious mixture of the national and the transnational.

The emphasis of the test, however, was very much on culturally British films rather than merely industrially British films – and it represented a very bold attempt to quantify cultural value. Somewhat surprisingly, this emphasis on cultural criteria was in fact the result of a last-minute amendment to the regulations, following the intervention of the European Commission (EC), in light of its regulations about state aid. Prior to this intervention, and following consultation with the UK film trade, the plan had been for a much reduced weighting for cultural content, with cultural hubs and cultural practitioners attracting the most points.

The initial Cultural Test proposals failed to meet EC requirements about ensuring open competition between member states; under these requirements, the British government was only able to subsidise or otherwise provide state aid to film production if that aid was strictly designed with cultural purposes in mind.[46] The effect of the intervention of the EC was really quite dramatic, since it beefed up the cultural content section considerably and introduced the new category of cultural contribution. It was also in some ways ironic that a transnational body committed to a neo-liberal economic policy, the EC, acted to ensure the furtherance of a particular national culture.

The guidelines for the Cultural Test contain some very elaborate and sophisticated justifications for the various elements of the cultural contribution category; indeed, they read more like essays in cultural studies than guidelines for an official funding mechanism. It is in these essays that the innovative nature of the legislation becomes most apparent: this is very much a piece of cultural policy, and not merely economic policy. In the preamble to the section on cultural heritage, for instance, the guidelines to film producers state:

> Britain's cultural heritage is an important determinant of the British national identity. It is therefore important to preserve British cultural heritage on screen for audiences of the present and the future. British cultural heritage shapes a common understanding of representation of British people and their contemporary and historical culture. ... Preserving cultural heritage builds the collective memory of the nation, establishing a sense of citizenship and the individual's place in the community. A Cultural Test which values 'heritage' and which values British cultural perspectives, modern and ancient history and the interpretation of the past and the future is therefore a more accurate arbiter of culturally British filmmaking.[47]

Where many of the other criteria identified by the Cultural Test could be taken for granted, it was evidently felt that the ideological role of filmic representation, and especially representations of the past, in the maintenance of national identity had to be explained in detail. But if 'the portrayal of heritage on screen' can be seen as 'a key determinant of a culturally British film', little effort is made to identify or define Britishness itself: it is assumed to be 'unique', and it is assumed that films should play a role in ensuring that British heritage remains relevant to modern society, but it is taken for granted that producers and others will know what Britishness is.[48] In some ways, this is worrying, since it potentially allows the most dominant, established and conservative definitions of Britishness to creep to the fore. But in other ways this element of the guidelines can be seen as positive: Britishness is left open, so that it can in principle be anything to do with the citizens of what is now the UK or set in what is now the UK or in some way related to the output or affairs of the UK or its citizens.

There is then potentially much to value in this seemingly non-prescriptive sense of British heritage, especially when it is combined with the other two criteria in the 'cultural contribution' category of the Cultural Test, which respectively foreground cultural diversity and a creative or innovative approach to representation. On the one hand, 'heritage', it is suggested, 'has the potential to be a catalyst for creativity in allowing unique interpretations of stories of British cultural heritage'.[49] On the other hand, 'the diversity of Britain is a celebrated feature of British culture and a key determinant of a culturally "British" film is the communication of this element of our society'.[50]

The identification of diversity as a 'celebrated feature of British culture' and as a feature of films that might be rewarded with valuable points under the Cultural Test is clearly more prescriptive in its efforts 'to reflect our position as a culturally diverse nation'.[51] Little is left to chance here:

> When we refer to 'diversity', we are recognising and attaching value to those aspects or dimensions of self and/or community identity relating to gender, ethnicity or national origins, religion or belief, age, sexuality, disability, [or] social and economic background, for example...An approach which values 'diversity' therefore values and encourages differences in attitudes, cultural perspective, beliefs, ethnic [identity], ability, skills, knowledge and life experiences of people of diverse backgrounds living in Britain.[52]

It is further proposed that 'the treatment of such diversity on screen is ... an important determinant of a culturally British film'.[53] But it is also argued that diversity can

> stimulat[e] cultural value by enhancing the range of stories to be told, the way they are told on screen, and levels of access and engagement in film culture for audiences. Cultural diversity can directly influence the content and tone of a film; its sensibility and authority. Much has, for example, been written on the issue of the lack of women as directors, and the differing perspectives and sensibilities that women as directors bring to film.[54]

The encouragement of diversity is thus not just about what appears on the screen but about who creates the film:

> Encouraging cultural diversity implies challenging preconceptions, assumptions and ways of working. It goes beyond simple equal opportunities and a recognition of difference and emphasises the potential creative connections that can be forged across different perspectives through access, inclusion, and collaboration – and the direct impact of these on the film as a cultural product.[55]

It is perhaps not surprising to find *Bend It Like Beckham* cited in the document as an example of a film that embraces diversity, given the

Bend It Like Beckham: embracing diversity.

way that its story challenges gender stereotypes, explores race relations and ethnic identities and embraces diverse sexualities. That it was also directed by a British-Asian woman makes it even more significant as an example of a film that captures cultural diversity in a dynamic way. It can also stand as a good example of the creativity that is encouraged by the Cultural Test, and the proclamation that 'the impact of a film and its success in communicating British culture can in large part be dictated by its creative approach'.[56] While the section on cultural heritage might potentially be seen as encouraging a relatively conservative approach to representations of what is now the UK, the invitation to filmmakers to embrace cultural diversity and to adopt a novel and creative point of view takes things in the opposite direction, with the Cultural Test explicitly rewarding filmmakers who produce 'creative, new interpretation[s] of British culture'.[57]

The Cultural Test in effect represents a renationalisation of British film policy, since 'British films' did not previously have to be *about* Britain or to engage with British heritage, and so on, to be eligible for official support. Some aspects of the test worked at the level of what Michael Billig calls *banal* nationalism;[58] this would apply to the criterion that rewarded productions whose story is set in the UK. But some aspects worked at a much more self-conscious and self-reflective level, where national identity and the nature of Britishness is explored rather than merely asserted or assumed. In this respect, the Cultural Test implicitly challenged traditional outmoded perceptions of British national identity as homogenous by promoting a sense of cultural diversity under the umbrella of Britishness. In a report produced by the Department of Culture, Media and Sport on the proposed framework for the Cultural Test, the department had stated that it was not its intention 'to dictate the content, or style' of films, but the final version of the test clearly did encourage filmmakers to move in a particular direction.[59] Thus where much state policy is about nation-formation or nation-maintenance, the purpose of the Cultural Test is effectively about national renewal or rebranding, encouraging a recognition of Britain as a multicultural space and society, marked by diversity and heterogeneity. Rather than simply seeking to affirm a traditional, homogenous sense of national identity and national culture, the Cultural Test was thus more about expanding and renewing identities and cultures, plural.

At the same time, co-production and inward investment were also positively encouraged by the government and the Film Council, and both stretched British film policy in transnational directions, thereby challenging the more nationalist project of the Cultural Test and the commitment to the sustainable production of culturally British films. Some saw this as a worrying threat, while others argued that it was necessary to avoid what they saw as a parochialism at work in the terms of the test. There were also those who argued that the sustainable production of culturally British films depended upon the further development of the industrial infrastructure and a large skilled workforce in regular employment, which could only be achieved if there were more substantial levels of inward investment than the test allowed for.

The trade union BECTU, for instance, which represents technical, craft and creative workers in the film industry, was anxious that the new tax-relief system might act as a disincentive to inward investment, and to industrial activity in the UK that might be film-related, but was not necessarily British in content or theme. While the union accepted that 'British cultural content is obviously and self-evidently a desirable element within the range of British production', they also argued that 'without ... a strong, locally-based industrial infrastructure, aspirations to the production of culturally-British films will be worthless'. They were also concerned that the proposed Cultural Test might work well for low-budget British productions, but not for larger inward investment productions – that is, big Hollywood studio projects that might be shot in the UK, regardless of whether they dealt with British content or British characters.[60] What this underlines once again is the close interrelationship of economic and cultural factors in the debate, with some parties emphasising one side rather than the other.

According to those who designed it, the tax-relief system and the Cultural Test were intended both to incentivise inward investment and to encourage and support indigenous production, and the government was at pains to reassure stakeholders that the new system would benefit the industry as a whole. The minister responsible for the film industry when the Cultural Test was announced, for instance, declared that it would ensure 'a successful, stable and sustainable film industry', and would be good for both small, independent films and large studio productions, and indeed for the development of the film industrial infrastructure in the UK. But he could not avoid underscoring the cultural dimension of the new tax arrangements, which would ensure 'that every film qualifying for tax relief either reflects or contributes to furthering British culture'.[61] Again, there was a nod towards both films that reproduced existing cultural traditions and identities, and those that moved in novel directions, while still offering some sort of commentary on Britain or Britishness.

Despite reassurances, there remained concerns that both bigger-budgeted films funded from outside the UK and official co-productions gained little from the new tax credit system and were therefore going elsewhere, thus affecting inward investment and potential UK production output. Others argued that the system actually favoured the Hollywood studios but disenfranchised other foreign producers or funders. There was also a concern that British productions shot abroad were unable to benefit from the tax credit system – even though the salary of a foreign star in a film shot in the UK with significant funding from a Hollywood studio might qualify for tax credit. As the journalist Geoffrey Macnab put it, 'it is no longer possible for films to qualify as British – and take advantage of UK fiscal incentives – by dint of some clever paperwork.... The downside is that Britain isn't [any more] an attractive place for foreign producers.'[62]

Others argued that the Cultural Test was encouraging an unnecessarily parochial film industry that would be wary of or unable to collaborate with foreign producers and investors. In the words of one producer, 'film is an international business, and British companies have to build alliances with international producers and financiers in order to get our films made'.[63] The problem with the new tax credit system, according to a report commissioned by the UK Film Council, was that 'incentivising a film to be produced wholly in the UK risks parochialising the types of stories that can be told which may have detrimental consequences for the value of the film in the international market'.[64]

In the debate about film policy that took place in the UK from the late 1990s onwards, two issues were paramount. First, there was the tension between those who valued the film business for its economic benefits and achievements, and those who valued the cultural contribution that films made to national life. Second, there was the tension between the national and the international in an increasingly global business. On the one hand, as a Treasury spokesperson put it, tax policy was designed to 'strengthen... the British film industry and encourag[e] the production of high quality homegrown films'.[65] On the other hand, some in the film industry were arguing that transnational arrangements were absolutely vital to the financial well-being of film productions, and that film content needed to look beyond national boundaries if films were to be marketable and profitable in global markets. Of course it is by no means necessarily the case that self-consciously nationalist or locally specific films will fail to do well in the global marketplace, as the niche success of the 'British' films of a Mike Leigh or a Ken Loach suggests, or as the box-office achievement of *Bend It Like Beckham* suggests. The picture is only complicated by the fact that it was a transnational body, the European Commission, that ensured that the British tax credit system adopted a relatively inward-looking Cultural Test designed to encourage the production of films that in some way explore or comment on British cultural identity.

In the next chapter, I will consider some of the implications for British and especially English cinema engendered by such transnational developments. First, however, a postscript to this chapter is in order. The year 2010 marked the tenth anniversary of the Film Council, by which time it had invested £160m of Lottery funding in more than 900 films, generating over £700m at the international box office. But 2010 also marked the end of the Labour government that had created the Film Council and, as this book went to press, the new Conservative government announced its intention to abolish the Council as part of the draconian cuts it was making to public spending. The immediate response from many in the business was one of shock. Screenwriter Ronan Bennett commented that 'every single writer, director and producer I know in this country considers the Film Council essential to film-making in the UK. Along with BBC Films and Film Four, the Film Council was the main port of call for those of us trying to get feature films off the ground, especially if those films tended ... to be outside the mainstream.' But the Council's commitment to encouraging inward investment and aligning UK production with Hollywood's global players meant others responded differently to its proposed abolition. Director Alex Cox, for instance, argued that the proposal was 'very good news for anyone involved in independent film. The Film Council became a means by which lottery money was transferred to the Hollywood studios. It pursued this phoney idea that James Bond and Harry Potter were British films. But, of course, those films were all American – and their profits were repatriated to the studios in Los Angeles.'[66] Either way, it seems that 2010 marked the end of an era for UK film production.

3 English cinema, transnatio and globalisation

Transnationalism and globalisation

The film *The Constant Gardener* was released in 2005. An adaptation of a novel by the English author John le Carré, it is a contemporary drama-cum-thriller, about British involvement in present-day Kenya, focusing on an English diplomat working in the country, and his English wife, a healthcare activist, with some scenes set in London. The project was initiated by an English producer, Simon Channing-Williams, who was best known for his work with Mike Leigh. Channing-Williams lined up an English director, Mike Newell, of *Four Weddings and a Funeral* (1994) fame, to shoot the film – although he subsequently dropped out, in order to make *Harry Potter and the Goblet of Fire* (2005). Channing-Williams also lined up funding from the UK Film Council, and from an English film financing company, Scion Films.

So far, then, this looks like an English film, but further inspection reveals a much more thorough-going transnational dimension. Thus a large part of the funding came from Focus Features, the specialty or art-house division of Universal Pictures, with further funding from Germany and Canada. Much of the film takes place in Kenya and in Germany, and was shot on location in those countries. And in the end, a multinational production team was assembled, including the Brazilian director Fernando Meirelles and the Uruguayan cinematographer César Charlone, best known for their work on the Brazilian film *City of God* (*Cidade de Deus*, 2002). As a result, different sources describe the 'nationality' of the film in different ways, with the British Film Institute's magazine *Sight and Sound* attempting to be definitive, describing it as a USA/UK/Canada/Germany co-production.

This sort of transnational production arrangement is by no means untypical in present-day filmmaking: films, especially films like *The*

Transnational filmmaking: location shooting in Kenya in *The Constant Gardener*.

Constant Gardener, rarely respect national boundaries. At the level of funding and production, they draw money, actors and creative personnel from different national contexts. At the level of representation, their narratives deal with characters from different places interacting with each other in a variety of settings, as they journey between different countries and cultures.

Some films go out of their way to renegotiate identities and traditions on a transnational and intercultural basis. *Bride and Prejudice* (2004), for instance, Gurinder Chadha's loose, modern-day Bollywood-style reworking of Jane Austen's *Pride and Prejudice*, has the Bennets of eighteenth-century England become the Bakshis of twenty-first-century India, while Darcy becomes an American businessman. The film moves between Amritsar and Goa in India, the British-Asian community in and around London, and Los Angeles. Chadha thus uses Austen's plot and characters to confront us with a narrative about diasporic and hybrid cultural identities in a globalised cultural space. At the level of exhibition and reception, too, such films are shown at film festivals and in cinemas around the world. Another of the Harry Potter films, *Harry Potter and the Prisoner of Azkaban* (2004), for instance, a USA/UK co-production, with a

Mexican director in Alfonso Cuarón, was released in 46 countries in the space of two weeks. *The Constant Gardener* may have been a much more modest production, but it won prizes at awards ceremonies and festivals in Britain, France, USA, Brazil, Spain and Italy, showed at festivals in Canada, Finland, and Yugoslavia as well, and eventually screened in at least 39 countries worldwide.

As examples such as this demonstrate, the globalisation of the entertainment business means that English cinema cannot be understood in isolation. From the mid-2000s, while UK film policy focused on the possibility of creating a sustainable industry for the production of culturally British films, the policies that were developed also took careful account of the forces of globalisation. Thus the government and the Film Council encouraged co-production arrangements and inward investment as means of expanding the capacity and capability of the UK production sector. The paradox that film policy is designed to negotiate is that a strong film production business in the UK is dependent in so many ways on attracting foreign capital. In this context, tensions inevitably rise up between the national, the transnational and the global. Inward investment is primarily about global Hollywood operating in the national space of the UK, while co-productions are by definition transnational in scope. The Cultural Test meanwhile encouraged producers to focus on the national, and on internal diversity and difference – but effectively discouraged cross-border mixing, by making it unattractive to spend production money abroad.

As I have already noted, there is nothing new about this tension between the cultural dynamics of national cinema and the global economy of film production, distribution and exhibition, even if the particular forms it takes now are different from those in previous periods. Film culture, cultural production and the cinema business do not map easily onto the nation state, even if nation states still attempt to regulate those cultural and business practices. Indeed, this tension is a defining characteristic of what I am exploring in this book. Culturally English filmmaking has to be grasped from two different perspectives. On the one hand, there are films made in England, with English funding, by English filmmakers, and which deal with English subject matter, characters and themes; on the other hand, there are a great many representations of England, Englishness and English culture and identity produced beyond the borders of the nation, sometimes through co-productions and sometimes not.

It is in fact a rare occurrence for a film to be funded solely from UK sources, to feature English characters, settings and subject matter, and to show only to English audiences. National film production in such an extreme form can't really work for English film producers, since the costs of film production cannot be recouped by distribution in the UK alone, let alone England; even low-budget independent films rely on international festivals, and/or international art-house distribution and/or international DVD sales. Such films may not benefit from global Hollywood's current practice of simultaneous worldwide releases, but they will often tap into other cross-border networks of distribution and exhibition, for instance through European initiatives such as Eurimages, Europa Cinemas and MEDIA – self-consciously transnational operations which are at the same time designed to counter Hollywood's globalising tendencies.

Transnationalism, in the guise of the co-production, may be simply an economic arrangement, although the terms of that arrangement are likely to encourage at the very least the movement of the resulting commodities across national borders. The globalisation of the creative industries also means that for certain categories of creative worker, employment is no longer nationally based, and key members of production crews and casts will move around the world as employment demands: hence the Indian director and Australian stars of the *Elizabeth* films (1998, 2007), the Taiwanese director of the Jane Austen adaptation *Sense and Sensibility* (1995), and the Brazilian director and Uruguayan cinematographer of *The Constant Gardener* – all apparently English films, but all in various ways transnational productions.

In various ways, all these filmic developments are the products of transnational cultural exchange, and all of them challenge the concept of national cinema. The cross-border flow of cultural commodities, personnel, ideas and creative practices necessarily challenges the idea of discrete, distinctive and unique national economies, cultures, audiences and public spheres. When transnationalism is not simply a form of economic cooperation but also enables a cultural and representational practice that mixes elements from different sources, whether characters, languages, themes or settings, it thus potentially challenges traditional ideas of the nation and national identity.

In this chapter, I will consider what happens to filmic images of England and English people when they are produced for consumption beyond the national borders, what happens to national identities when they circulate in the global marketplace. For some, the fear is that all cultural products will end up looking the same. If all production and all market outlets are owned or controlled by a few very powerful global corporations, surely global culture will become excessively homogenised: this is what we might call the McDonald's version of global capitalism.

As national boundaries become blurred and transnational or even global cultures form, we might expect the cinematic projection of a self-consciously national identity to be markedly weakened. I would suggest, however, that very often the most traditional and stereotypical manifestations of English national identity are reproduced as novel and meaningful in films intended for transnational circulation. The most banal images of England and Englishness are underlined, exaggerated and foregrounded; banal markers of national identity thus become exotic signifiers of difference in the global marketplace. On the one hand, this might allay the fears of those who see national cultures being eroded by the forces of globalisation: national identities and traditions are still presented on screen. On the other hand, it is often the least complex and the most familiar, the most stereotypical 'national' representations that prevail in such circumstances. To what extent, then, can transnational creative endeavour encourage and enable new forms of cultural diversity, exchange and interpenetration?

I want to examine this phenomenon by looking at three films that are each in some way about contemporary England or Englishness: *Notting Hill* (1999), *Bride and Prejudice* and *The Constant Gardener*. All are at one level English films, but all of them were also international co-productions, with *Notting Hill* receiving both European and American backing, as well as English funding, and *Bride and Prejudice* funding from England and Germany, as well as the support of the American distributor Miramax. They were all also carefully designed for international circulation – hence the major Hollywood star Julia Roberts in *Notting Hill*, playing an American film star who visits England; hence the Brazilian director of *The Constant Gardener*, with its international thriller narrative roaming between England, Kenya, Sudan and Germany; hence the Indian star of *Bride and Prejudice*, Aishwarya Rai, and the Indian, English and American settings; hence too *Balle Balle – Amritsar to LA!*, the dubbed Hindi-language version of *Bride and Prejudice*, released simultaneously with the English-language version of the film in India.

These three films each emerge from particular production trends that have proved significant within the development of English cinema in the 1990s and 2000s. The significance of *Notting Hill* can be demonstrated by a statement in a report commissioned by the UK Film Council, commenting on the role that films play in reproducing a sense of British national identity:

> in recent times probably the highest profile stream of screen products to perform this function has come from writer Richard Curtis, including *Four Weddings and a Funeral*, *Notting Hill*, *Love Actually* and the *Bridget Jones* films. By reaching a global audience with a positive, humorous and endearing view of the UK and Britishness, these films have possibly done more to promote the UK in general as a tourist destination than any other screen products. Furthermore, they have created an awareness of British culture which other films and programmes have been able to build on, presenting an alternative, sometimes grittier or darker side of the UK.[1]

Notting Hill belonged to a production trend that owed a great deal both to the scriptwriting talents of Curtis and to the production company Working Title; that these films were all romantic comedies with English settings that brought together American and British stars further consolidates the sense of a coherent trend. Each of the Curtis films cited in the report was a major box-office success, with all of them appearing in the list of the top 20 highest-grossing UK films of all time. *Notting Hill* itself took a massive £31m at the UK box office, and $364m worldwide.[2]

Bride and Prejudice and *The Constant Gardener* were both much more modest productions that inevitably fared less well at the box office, but they still showed decent returns on the money invested in their production. *Bride and Prejudice* brought in $24m worldwide, against a budget of $7m; *The Constant Gardener* brought in $82m, against a budget of $25m.[3] Both were in part romantic dramas, with the former mixing drama with comedy, but in terms of production trends, they are perhaps best characterised as modestly budgeted literary adaptations, a key type of film-making in the UK sector in the 1990s and 2000s, with *Bride and Prejudice* milking the Jane Austen franchise and *The Constant Gardener* reworking le Carré's best-selling political thriller.

How do films like *Notting Hill*, *Bride and Prejudice* and *The Constant Gardener* imagine the nation at the level of narrative and image? How do they narrate the nation? How do they mobilise certain familiar and therefore banal *mises-en-scène* of England and Englishness? And how do audiences respond to such narratives and images? Certain narrative strategies seem capable of generating a sense of national belonging in their audiences – but since so many films enjoy international distribution and thus speak to a range of local, national and transnational audiences, they are also capable in various ways of generating a sense of '*not-belonging*'. That is, these same films can speak to foreign audiences, who can still imagine and recognise England and Englishness, but as something precisely other, not something to which they belong. In that process, they may also perceive as exotic that which national audiences experience as banal.

Nationhood is always in part defined in a system of differences from other nations and national identities, and films like *Notting Hill*, *Bride and Prejudice* and *The Constant Gardener* play quite self-consciously within their narratives on such a system of familiar differences, as they seek to address a range of international audiences with different allegiances. But nationhood is also defined internally, not simply by reference to others.[4] There are perhaps five vital components of nationhood, in this sense.[5] First, a nation exists as a body of people, a distinctive ethnic community, which may all the same be ethnically diverse or ethnically pure. Second, nationhood has a spatial dimension; it insists on a geography; a nation occupies, whether literally or metaphorically, a particular place, a territory, a homeland. Third, nationhood assumes a distinctive culture and customised models of morality and behaviour. Fourth, nationhood assumes a collective memory, a shared history; to that extent, a nation has a temporal dimension, it has a past, a present and a future, it exists in and through time. Fifth, a nation depends on a means of regulating its inhabitants in space and time, maintaining their relationships with one another, distinguishing them from others, demarcating and policing the boundaries of the nation and thereby asserting the sovereignty of the nation; to this extent, nationhood depends on a system of governance.

Defined in these terms, nationhood is ripe for narrative development, since nations consist of a community of protagonists, well-defined characters who move through time and space in a rule-governed way. Except that the dominant narrative traditions with which we are familiar today, drawing on the traditions of the mythic quest and the picaresque, very often deal not with a community of protagonists, but with a single central protagonist. Thus the most widely accepted definition of the classical Hollywood narrative focuses on the goal-directed actions of the central protagonist; thus it's an *individualistic* narrative rather than a narrative of community.[6] The question then arises, can an individualistic narrative of this sort 'narrate' a large-scale collective body such as a nation? One response to this question would be to note the centrality of individual wish-fulfilment to the American Dream, the centrality of an entrepreneurial drive, to which end one might argue that in fact such a narrative can certainly engender a national mythology.

There is another sort of narrative structure, however, which is organised around a community of protagonists, and which involves multiple interweaving narrative lines threading across a carefully delineated space. A classic example of this narrative in contemporary moving image culture might be the English soap opera. *EastEnders* for instance represents a small, tightly interlocking community, and develops distinct but overlapping and interconnected narratives around a multiplicity of characters, who operate in a claustrophobically defined neighbourhood, a carefully delimited territory, a homeland. Metaphorically, that community and that neighbourhood may be read as standing in for the nation; it may both narrate the nation and pictorialise it. That same strategy of imagining the community of the nation was also a feature of certain English films of the 1940s, feature-length fiction films that drew on the documentary traditions developed in Britain over the previous decade, films that self-consciously addressed a nation at war.[7]

A good example of this type of film is *The Bells Go Down*, an Ealing film made in 1943, and the way in which the narrative works is laid bare in its opening sequence. The film begins with a series of high-angle shots, offering a bird's-eye view of an area of London, then moving into the detail of a street market. Various characters are subsequently presented, with the camera picking up and following different characters as they literally pass each other on the screen: this becomes the basis for weaving together a series of narratives that interlock, and collectively form a vision of a community of people at work and play. Through this strategy, we are presented with a vision of a consensual community made up of different classes and ethnicities – the upper-middle-class vicar, the lower-middle-class courting couple, the working-class characters around the fish and chips shop, and alongside these Anglo-Saxon characters, a Jewish furniture salesman, and so on. As the *Daily Mail* described it at the time, 'it is a picture of the people and for the people'.[8]

There are also a series of further, banal signifiers of nationhood: the reference to the *'National* Fire Service' in an opening title, the Anglican church, the fish and chips shop, a discussion about greyhound racing, the accents and character types, the reference in a voice-over to memories etched in the national consciousness – the date of the start of the war in the summer of 1939, the Blitz, and concepts like 'the people', 'the folk', 'the community'. Through these further devices, the narrative of community is effectively mapped onto a discourse of nationhood.

The documentary-style voice-over that accompanies this sequence plays an important role in this mapping process, and in the establishment of community. At one point, it is stated that 'London isn't a town, it's a group of villages. This is the story of one of those villages, a community bounded by a few streets...' Using devices like this to address its wartime British audiences, *Bells* develops a narrative of recognition and belonging for those audiences, metaphorically narrating a unified nation at war, and suggesting a role for national subjects to play in the grander narrative of that nation.

Notting Hill

More than half a century later, *Notting Hill* has a remarkably similar sequence at the start of its narrative, with a similar set of high-angle shots of a street market in London, and a similar set of characters introduced, partly in voice-over. *Notting Hill* might be described as the idealised fantasy of an 'ordinary', repressed, middle-class Englishman, William Thacker, played by Hugh Grant, in which against all the odds he becomes romantically entwined with a fabulous female Hollywood star, Anna Scott, played by Julia Roberts. The film works in the middlebrow English tradition of *The Bells Go Down*, except that its version of Middle England has shifted up a notch or two in class terms. Thus, like *Bells*, *Notting Hill* too can be read as a relatively self-conscious attempt to project an image of the nation, to represent the nation metaphorically, by focusing on a small, tightly knit community of people who in their very ordinariness can stand in for the nation. Whether that nation is Britain or England is a moot point. But there is certainly no denying that the vision of ordinariness with which we are presented is a particularly white, privileged and middle-class version.

Even so, the film depends on the idea of 'ordinariness', on the idea that Hugh Grant/William Thacker embodies 'ordinary Englishness', which is then played against the extraordinariness of Julia Roberts' incarnation

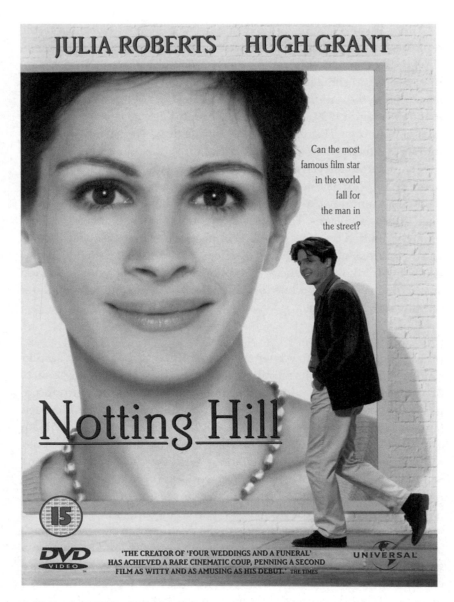

Publicity for *Notting Hill*: Hugh Grant's English everyman walks in front of Julia Roberts's Hollywood star image.

of Anna Scott, Hollywood star. Indeed this contrast between the ordinary man in the street and the glamorous Hollywood star was central to the publicity for the film, whose key image showed a casually, even sloppily dressed Grant/Thacker shuffling past a giant billboard featuring a close-up of an impeccably styled Roberts/Scott. The film's title sequence provides a marvellously evocative celebration of Hollywood stardom in a montage of publicity images of Roberts/Scott. The unreality of Hollywood stardom, however, rapidly gives way to the very down-to-earth reality of Hugh Grant striding around the street market in Notting Hill, introducing us to the local village community, which metaphorically I want to suggest once again stands in for the nation.

As in *The Bells Go Down*, local London is presented as a small, tight-knit community – 'this village in the middle of the city', as Hugh Grant/ William Thacker has it in his voice-over. Again, the community and the neighbourhood are captured in a montage sequence, including the same high-angle bird's-eye view of the locality. Again, there is the street market and a crowd, from which a few individuals are singled out. Again, there is a series of interacting characters – and one gets the sense that the film has been cut down from something much bigger, where all these other characters would have much larger lives of their own. To this extent, the narrative strategy of the film is very similar to the one in *Bells*, picking up characters as they pass across the screen. In another indication of the class aspirations of the film, however, the fish and chips shop of *Bells* has become an upmarket fish restaurant, albeit one that is not very successful.

There are other important differences between the two films, especially in the way in which the relations between community and the individual, and between realism and fiction, are played out. This is not least because *Notting Hill* is primarily a romantic comedy or a date movie, not the overtly propagandist product of heightened patriotism and a wartime crisis of nationhood. The violent disruption that initiates the narrative drive of *Bells* is the outbreak of the Second World War; the equivalent in *Notting Hill* is the moment when Grant/Thacker bumps into Roberts/Scott and spills a cup of orange juice on her bright white T-shirt. If a sense of a community is established in *Notting Hill*, the narrative initiated by this 'violent' coincidence is at the same time much more clearly individualised. Thacker, the protagonist, may be decidedly non-heroic and inactive, but the point is that we stay resolutely with this character as he moves hesitantly through the limited space of his neighbourhood on his dreamlike quest to maintain a relationship with a Hollywood star.

If *Bells* can usefully be understood as an Ealing film, then *Notting Hill* can be understood as a Richard Curtis film, since as scriptwriter he played a major role in determining its shape. In a later film not only written but also directed by Curtis, *Love, Actually* (2003), there is a much more concerted effort to articulate a sense of community, with no single protagonist dominating the narrative, no single character at the centre of the community, and numerous interweaving narrative lines. *Notting Hill*, however, resists the temptation to flesh out the lives of its other characters in anything more than a very cursory way. It also adopts a realist mode of representation, especially in the opening section of the film, with the montage sequence of the street market, the real locations and the documentary device of the voice-over. The tone of the voice-over is now heavily ironic, however, and has become *part* of the diegesis, delivered in autobiographical mode by Grant/Thacker, whereas in *Bells* it was delivered from outside the diegesis, an anonymous official voice commenting on the community from the outside.

The narrative strategy of *Notting Hill* is not just about imagining a self-contained, self-sufficient community, however; nor is it just about one particular character moving through his own particular locality. It is also about pitting one national identity – a version of middle-class, white Englishness – against another – the glamorous American ideal of the Hollywood star, the exotic outsider who visits the locale and confronts the group of friends that inhabit it. Englishness is in part then defined in a system of differences, or at least of binary oppositions; Englishness is in part defined by what it is not, Americanness, and the differences might be laid out as follows:

Englishness	*Americanness*
Hugh Grant/William Thacker	Julia Roberts/Anna Scott
The man in the street	The megastar
Ordinary	Extraordinary
Mundane, domestic	Jet-setting, in the public eye
Underachieving	Successful
Inferior(ity)	Superior(ity)
Reality	Glamour
Realism	Fantasy

This is of course in part a marketing strategy, a means of stretching the market appeal of the film through casting stars with particular national, and indeed international, images and reputations. But how do international audiences respond to such narratives, images and characters? Is it sufficient to suggest that through such strategies as those described above, films can generate a sense of national belonging in their audiences? After all, *Notting Hill* was designed for international distribution, to address a range of audiences with a range of national and other allegiances in a range of markets. For such audiences, as noted above, it is important to recognise that the same film might generate a sense of 'not-belonging'. The American academic Diane Negra, for instance, in an article written when she was based in the USA, discusses *Notting Hill* as an example of 'recent *American* cinema' (my emphasis),[9] in which a transnational romance takes place after the protagonist, the heroine, has left America for Europe; she calls this 'the tourist romance'.

In this reading of the film, Thacker/Grant, the mundane Englishman, becomes an exotic figure of desire, a 'creature of his environment', who 'take[s] life at a slower pace' and lives 'in just the right place';[10] he is further perceived as a representative of 'social harmony' and stability,[11] who inhabits a 'European urban paradise',[12] an ideal, utopian homeland. This is rather different from the reading above of Thacker as mundane, albeit 'posh mundane', an inept and incompetent loser, compared to the exotic high achievements of Anna Scott, the American film star. In other words, the binary oppositions identified above have been turned around:

Englishness	*Americanness*
Grant/Thacker	Roberts/Scott
Exotic otherness	Ordinary American
Utopian figure, object of desire	Embodiment of neuroses of modern America
Settled, stable	Incomplete, in search of stability
Social harmony	Social chaos

What does this different reading of *Notting Hill* tells us? Well, first of all it still depends on a stereotype of Englishness. This may be the era of globalisation, films like *Notting Hill* may circulate across national borders, and are indeed designed to do so – but this does not necessarily mean that the projection of national identity is weakened. On the contrary, stereotypical Englishmen such as Hugh Grant's Thacker still exist on film – and indeed such films will often depend on the solidity and the familiarity of their representations of traditional English identities. As I suggested at the outset of this chapter, traditional national identities are thus reproduced as novel and meaningful in global cultural products. The banal and the commonplace is underlined, but as such can also function as an exotic signifier of difference – as it does when Anna Scott and William Thacker confront each other in *Notting Hill*. On the one hand, Hugh Grant/William Thacker's version of Englishness is so familiar and so underplayed as to be unremarkable; on the other hand, it is so thoroughly overdetermined and overstated that it becomes exotic. There is thus a perverse exaggeration of the national in order for it to signify easily in a range of international markets. In other words, the transnational or global context of distribution actually *reinforces* a particular if reductive vision of Englishness in such films.

The problem here is that this dominant stereotype of middle-class, male, Southern Englishness squeezes out other versions of Englishness and makes it very difficult to embrace the diverse communities of modern England. Imagining a national community on the basis of this dominant version of Englishness makes it very difficult for other classes and other ethnicities to feel that they belong in this image of collectivity. Like the English films of the Second World War, *Notting Hill* presents its audiences with a vision of an overwhelmingly white middle-class community, despite the post-war history of Notting Hill as an area associated with black Britons. As such, its vision of England is very different from those provided by the white working-class communities of *The Full Monty* (1997) or *Billy Elliot* (2000), or the British-Asian communities of *East Is East* (1999) or *Bend It Like Beckham* (2002), or the black British communities of *Babymother* (1998) or *Bullet Boy* (2004).

If in part *Notting Hill* generates a sense of community and belonging through its narrative strategy of providing a network of background plotlines and characters, the hard-to-avoid impression that this is a decidedly Southern, metropolitan English community is achieved as much through its banal *mise-en-scène* of middle-class, middlebrow Middle England. Narrative events always need a space in which to unfold, a territory for the protagonists to move through. Indeed, it would be difficult to argue that a narrative strategy in itself could narrate a specific nation, rather than either a more generalised and abstract sense of community, or a very local sense of community. *Mise-en-scène* is thus needed to make that narrative concrete, to give the community a recognisable homeland.

Consider for example another state-of-a-certain-portion-of-the-nation narrative in the Stephen Frears film *High Fidelity* (2000). The Nick Hornby novel from which the film was adapted is set in another London neighbourhood, Holloway rather than Notting Hill. But in the film, a broadly similar plot and broadly similar characters are transposed to Chicago. Narratively, novel and film are pretty much the same; it is the unremarkable, banal *mise-en-scène* and the particular but equally banal way in which the dialogue is accented that locate the film in national terms. Images and sounds create a narrative setting in films, they lend the narrative a meaningful space, a diegetic space, in which to unfold – but as *High Fidelity* shows, they can also radically transform the narrative's meaning and suggest a very different national context.

Iconographies of Englishness: *Bride and Prejudice*

Within English cinema, it is possible to identify three dominant icon-ographies of Englishness, three dominant *mises-en-scène* of Englishness. Each impresses by its familiarity, its banality – but also of course by its difference from other iconographies. First, there is what we might call traditional heritage England; that is, a pre-industrial, semi-rural version of England, a nation of small villages and grand houses scattered about a green and pleasant land. There is both a pastoral landscape version of this *mise-en-scène*, in films such as *Black Beauty* (1994) and *Miss Potter* (2006), and a stately home version, as in films such as *The Remains of the Day* (1993) and *Brideshead Revisited* (2008). The success of a film like *Sense and Sensibility* (1995) is in part that it manages to combine the two ver-sions of traditional heritage England.

Second, there is what we might call mundane urban modernity, or perhaps the urban village. This has a working-class version (in films like *The Bells Go Down*, but also more recent films such as *Last Orders*, 2001, and *The Full Monty*); it has a more suburban, lower-middle-class and solidly middlebrow version (in films such as *Enduring Love*, 2004, or *Happy-Go-Lucky*, 2008, and parts of *Four Weddings and a Funeral*); and it has a dark and dirty version, what Andy Medhurst calls the teeming metropolis, and Charlotte Brunsdon the infernal metropolis.[13] The teem-ing metropolis itself has both a Dickensian period variant, as in *The Fool* (1990) or *Oliver Twist* (2005), both set in the mid-nineteenth century, and a contemporary variant, as in *Lock, Stock and Two Smoking Barrels* (1998) or *Dirty Pretty Things* (2002). In each version of this mundane urban modernity, we rarely see the upper classes, while on the edge of this urban modern space is generally traditional heritage England, to which the urban dwellers so often want to escape. There is also an earlier, pre-modern version of the infernal metropolis, in films like *Restoration* (1995) or *Plunkett & Macleane* (1999), its difference from mundane urban modernity signalled in part by the presence of the aristocracy.

Finally, there is what we might call a monumental metropolitan modernity, which is perhaps exclusively about an internationally recognisable version of London, rather than anywhere else in England. Monumental metropolitan modernity thus embraces public London, official London, the civic London of Big Ben, Trafalgar Square, Tower Bridge, and red London buses, what Brunsdon calls landmark London.[14] This is the London that is often glimpsed in the James Bond films, the London that the characters occasionally walk past in *Match Point* (2005). London, among English cities, is perhaps unique, in that it is both a global city, whose monumental landmarks are known the world over, and a series of local spaces, the urban villages of *The Bells Go Down* and *Notting Hill*.

Monumental metropolitan modernity and traditional heritage England have become in part tourist iconographies, consumerist spectacles of Englishness. *Notting Hill* in a sense gentrifies and glamourises the iconography of mundane urban modernity, transforming the real Notting Hill into another tourist spectacle. Tourism invokes the international, and reminds us again that films circulate internationally and reach international audiences. Gurinder Chadha's *Bride and Prejudice* was specifically made to address both Western audiences and Indian audiences. Like *Notting Hill*, *Bride and Prejudice* also adopts familiar but exaggerated national identities to enable it to function in a range of international markets; like *Notting Hill* it trades on more or less subtle versions of some very familiar English stereotypes. But where *Notting Hill* feels like a celebratory assertion of a particular type of English identity, and an attempt to affirm a sense of national cohesion, Gurinder Chadha wants to move beyond the nation and its established traditions. As such, *Bride and Prejudice* is probably best understood as a self-consciously *post*-national or *trans*national film, in which the traditional *mises-en-scène* of England and Englishness themselves remain both oddly secure yet subtly transformed.

Thus as the Bakshi family travel from India to England, the film provides a montage of images of London, another bird's-eye view of a cleverly revised version of monumental metropolitan modernity. On the one hand, London looks banally familiar, with images of Big Ben, Tower Bridge and St Paul's Cathedral; on the other hand, it looks subtly different, with the London skyline now including the hypermodernity of the London Eye, Canary Wharf and the Swiss Re Building (the 'giant gherkin'), and finally a key icon of multicultural London, the Sikh temple in Southall. In a similar way, the mundane middle-class suburban *mise-en-scène* is now presented as a hybrid British-Asian mix. And the *mise-en-scène* of heritage wealth, the grand house with its view of traditional England – Windsor Castle, seen across the Thames and framed by green trees – is now the property of a wealthy British-Asian family, rather than the inheritance of the white aristocracy.

Bride and Prejudice still trades on the idea of a knowable community – but it is no longer a community rooted in the traditional, pre-modern village England of Jane Austen; nor is it the modern urban village of *The Bells Go Down* and *Notting Hill*. Rather, it is a new postmodern global village, where friends and acquaintances run across each other at international airports, and where diasporic communities, extended families and romantic liaisons stretch across continents. This global village is decidedly complex, transcultural and ethnically hybrid – but arguably the community of the English nation has always been complex,

The Sikh temple in Southall: part of the London montage sequence in *Bride and Prejudice*.

transcultural and hybrid. What is perhaps novel here is that the focus is now on a self-consciously transnational and transcontinental community, a much broader geography of community that exceeds the national but still manages to absorb particular flavours of the local.

With *Notting Hill*, we are confronted with an assertion of the national in face of the global – and indeed, in order to exploit global markets. With *Bride and Prejudice*, we still have a film that trades on national images and identities – and in both films the national is played out in its most banal, familiar form, something that is readily, instantly familiar around the world, even if the stereotypes are generally handled in a very subtle manner. Can less familiar assertions of the local survive in such a market? Possibly, in the small-budget film that finds a place in the international art-house market, and even the multiplex. Both *Billy Elliot* and *East Is East*, for instance, are principled attempts to depict a local community, yet both succeeded in a variety of markets and with a variety of audiences. The same might be said of critically acclaimed films such as *Last Orders*, *My Summer of Love* (2004) and *Kinky Boots* (2005), three more small-scale depictions of the local.

The Constant Gardener

The Constant Gardener engages in different ways with the local, the national, the transnational and the global. It is an English love story interwoven with a political thriller – a *global* thriller, as the publicity described it. Like *Notting Hill*, at the heart of *The Constant Gardener* is another eminently believable upper-middle-class, white Englishman, Justin Quayle, created through a thoroughly charismatic performance by Ralph Fiennes. Focusing on this figure and his associates, the film plays on an image of refined, upper-middle-class Englishness, which is shown to be bound up with the Establishment institutions of the Foreign Office, the Diplomatic Service, exclusive, old-fashioned London clubs and ancient buildings. As Justin drives through London midway through the film, there are occasional glimpses of the Union Jack flag flying from yet more solid institutional buildings. The unremarked flag may for Michael Billig be the pre-eminent symbol of banal nationalism, but there is also a sense of the exotic, the other, the foreign, in this view of what we might call official England.[15]

In the course of the narrative, the film dramatically challenges the perception of the English upper classes and their traditional institutions as bastions of uprightness and probity and shows the British government as caught up with corrupt and exploitative international businesses. Traditional and modern values thus come into conflict, and this is matched at the level of the imagery. Thus we have brief glimpses of traditional landmark London, sufficient to establish place and to invoke a set of values. But in the opening scene of the film, St Paul's Cathedral is seen from the Tate Modern, across the Millennium Bridge: London is caught between the tradition of St Paul's and the modernity of the Tate Modern. In a later sequence in the film, traditional London has been erased from the image altogether, to be replaced by a newly exotic vision of a postmodern metropolis in Canary Wharf.

The film also travels abroad, initially to Kenya – where ironically patriotism, or overt nationalism, is played out even more intensely, as the expatriate Brits rally round the corrupt businessman Curtis – as one of the diplomats puts it, he's 'one of us ... he's British'. It seems fitting that, at home, the central character can be defined without awkwardness as English, but as he moves abroad and is forced to negotiate with a wider public, he and his associates become British. Either way, the narrative clearly makes room for the heightened sense of national allegiance, or national belonging, felt by the expatriates, yet it also endeavours to critique this blind patriotism. When the expatriate Brits get together for a meal, there is a momentary image of another metaphorical national community, a Little England or Little Britain in the heart of Kenya, but it is a very troubled image, capturing perfectly the corrupt, incestuous and conflicted nature of the community. Although the community brings together people from different class and ethnic backgrounds, there is little sense of this as a culturally diverse, tolerant and open community; on the contrary, it is racked by infighting.

If the members of that community intersect with wider communities in the homeland, they are also part of much larger transnational communities, symbolised by the connectivities of the internet, international travel, and the Anglo-Italian family of Justin Quayle's wife, Tessa. This is the community of the new postmodern global village, where diasporic ethnic groups, extended families and professional relationships again stretch across continents. On the one hand, then, this is a film about Englishness. On the other hand, it is a film that is constantly on the move, crossing borders, exploring new and unfamiliar places, travelling between London, Kenya, Germany and Sudan. This transnational journeying is matched by an equally fluid camera style, a narrative structure and a collage of different *mises-en-scène* that suggest hybridity and edginess.

Where is the homeland, in this USA/UK/Canada/Germany co-production? After Tessa's death, Justin, by now an Englishman adrift in Africa, is told to go home. He responds: 'But I don't have a home – Tessa was my home.' On the one hand, then, home is no longer a physical place, but an emotional place, a state of mind, a state of being. On the other hand, England and Englishness are still there, at the charismatic heart of the film, in the very character of Justin. But it is also very clear that Africa is *not* home, featuring instead as an exotic other place, which is both ravaged by white people, and capable of being saved by whites. There is thus an inadvertent tension within the film, between a white liberal con-science and a lingering colonial sensibility. This inevitably cuts across and complicates the more overt concern of the film, with a narrative that con-fronts head-on the operations of the global economy, and in particular the impact of a corrupt global pharmaceutical business on the national auton-omy of Kenya and other African countries, and various local communities within those countries. The film thus provides ample material with which to think through the relationships between colonialism, nationalism and globalisation. Globalisation is not simply the bad object of international capitalism, however, since the loose network of resistance to which Tessa belongs also brings together people from different countries and cultures, who stay in touch with each other through the World Wide Web and digital technology. At the same time, it is clear that local allegiance and a sense of national belonging are vital to the identities of all involved.

Between the local and the global

The nation may sometimes be thought of in terms of a homeland, but home for most people will be envisaged in local terms. The characters in both *The Constant Gardener* and *Bride and Prejudice* visit various localities, but they are framed within a globetrotting web that rarely allows us to settle in one place. *Notting Hill* may tell the story of an American visit-ing London, thereby taking on a globetrotting dimension, but it is reso-lutely set in a local space, Grant/Thacker's Notting Hill. Other English filmmakers have tapped into (necessarily limited) funds for localised production or films with local settings or themes. Shane Meadows, for instance, has made several films set in the English Midlands – and his 2006 film *This Is England* boldly claims national status for a film that is decidedly local in focus, and that deals with a group of ethnically diverse working-class youths in the early 1980s, as they confront overtly nationalist politics. Like some of his other films, the production was part-funded by EM Media, one of a network of English regional screen agencies, this one responsible for the East Midlands. Such low-budget, local films emerge in the interstices of the global media economy – but they are still sometimes able to gain global critical success. As the title of *This Is England* suggests, the national does not simply disappear in such practices; rather, it takes different forms, moving beyond more traditional or dominant representations of the nation. Thus even if films are in so many ways transnational commodities, and even if some of them are local in setting and theme, they may still be branded in national terms, as one of their selling points, at least in selected markets.

Place is clearly vital to narrative fiction, and films must establish a sense of place to enable their fictions to unfold. Place also plays an important role in defining national and local identities; at the same time, it becomes an attraction to outsiders: this is the place of tourism. The English characters spending time in various African countries in *The Constant Gardener* are in some sense tourists; so too are Julia Roberts' American in London in *Notting Hill*, and the Indian Bakshi family as they visit London and Los Angeles in *Bride and Prejudice*. Many of the audiences for these films also become virtual tourists, but the film and tourism businesses have increasingly collaborated in recent years to turn virtual film tourism into actual film tourism. A report about film-related tourism in the UK commissioned by the Film Council concluded that films are more likely to have an effect on tourism where they 'link in to a wider, established "brand" '; whereas each of these three films is a contemporary drama, the report makes it clear that one of the most potent tourist brands is *historical* Britain.[16] As the writers of the report explain,

> the UK has a rich and well known history, and a large number of houses, buildings and sites from different eras still standing as testament to past times. The UK's history not only serves as inspiration for film and television drama enjoyed the world over, but at the same time acts as a powerful 'hook' for tourists, both domestic and inbound, to visit specific sites across the UK. Overall, the UK's history is possibly the most potent and effective mechanism for promoting the country's brand and image, and one which is easy to use in the widest variety of contexts.... The key benefit of historical films/programmes, whether based on fictional or real events and people, is that they both tap into, and reinforce, an overall brand for the UK as a country steeped in history.[17]

This sense of historical Britain can also be invoked in films with contemporary settings. Indeed, in both *The Constant Gardener*, with its

This Is England: a disorienting view of the nation.

brief images of ancient institutional and religious buildings in London, and *Bride and Prejudice,* with its distant view of Windsor Castle, a sense of traditional England is established through precisely this sort of banal nationalist imagery. That the sanctity of this traditional England is eventually undermined in both films aligns them with the equally disorienting view of the nation offered by *This Is England.* A more reverential view of traditional England is constructed in period adaptations of canonical English literature, such as the 2005 version of *Pride and Prejudice* and the various other period adaptations of Jane Austen's novels in the 1990s and 2000s. This is a view of England that feeds more easily into established patterns of tourism: as the film-tourism report further notes, such films tap into a much more substantially established brand that weaves together the cultural heritages of both 'English Literature' and England as a place steeped in history, and which has a life of its own beyond any particular film.[18] Place is never neutral, but is always invested with meaning; how those meanings are constructed by audiences will depend on how and where they are situated in the complex web of local, national and global relations that characterise the contemporary world.

It is certainly not the case that the national or the local simply disappear when global corporations move in on the action; global Hollywood, for instance, tries to tap into the local in various ways, both as corporate tourist and in partnership with local businesses, or indeed as corporate insider, with its own local branch. There is no getting around the fact that the major Hollywood distributors now expect their box-office revenues from world markets to exceed revenues in the domestic US market: they are now absolutely global corporations, and their business is about selling films to audiences worldwide. In some cases, this is achieved through a simultaneous worldwide release for a film. The global market, then, is no longer a bonus to American distributors, it is part of their core business. But it is not just about where films are shown but also about how and where they are made, which themes and issues they address, and where they are set. Major Hollywood films are designed to include ingredients – especially stars and locations – that might appeal to different markets. And they are made where the best deals can be secured in terms of production facilities, labour costs, tax breaks and other financial incentives. This is why, for the UK Film Council, tax breaks to encourage inward investment in the UK film business are so important. As one report noted, 'competition to attract film producers to shoot their film in a particular country is fierce. This competition partly focuses on the physical attributes of a country; the costs for labour and the renting of locations and sets; and the relative skills of the film production workforce. But a key element is tax competition.'[19]

I began this book by rehearsing the argument that cinema is one of the means by which national communities are maintained, the people of a nation are reminded of their ties with one another and with the nation's history and traditions, and those people are invited to recognise themselves as national subjects, distinct from people of other nations. But films are often funded from a variety of different national or transnational sources, control of those films may be in the hands of non-national creative workers or corporations, and they circulate beyond national borders and speak to other communities besides those depicted. It is also in many ways much easier to represent a local space or community than a nation. The argument about the role of films in maintaining national traditions and identities is thus challenged in various ways by the production of 'local' or 'national' films for global consumption, and by the creation of transnational products addressed to audiences that are defined not by national allegiance but by taste and sensibility.

This raises a number of issues in relation to the debate about national cinema. First, there is the argument that the globalisation of the media and entertainment industries progressively squeezes out local and even national cultures, whose specificity is thought of as both inexportable and economically unsustainable even within its own domestic market. Second, there is the concern that if the local or the national is depicted on screen, it will be 'diluted' to enable it to play more effectively to global audiences. And third, there is the question of how audiences actually make sense of any locally or nationally specific representations they are presented with.

Is the local or the national actually squeezed out by the forces of globalisation? The growth of 'world music' and 'world cinema' as marketable cultural categories, albeit specialised, niche categories, suggests in fact that globalisation does leave room for the local. Such 'local', 'indigenous' representations do enjoy a certain form of global distribution, thereby challenging that view of globalisation that sees it as a culturally homogenising force that obliterates heterogeneity, cultural diversity, local identity and difference. Indeed, as we have seen, Hollywood itself is in the business of creating global products that have local appeal: in such cases, it is possible to see the global and the local not as polar opposites but as interdependent. Globalisation, from this perspective, as Roland Robertson argues, involves 'the creation and incorporation of locality'.[20] Hollywood has on various occasions, for instance, invested in English heritage films – as in the production of Austen adaptations such as *Sense and Sensibility*, produced by Sony/Columbia, or *Emma*, co-produced by Miramax. In such instances, it is adopting a practice increasingly typical of global capitalism, addressing itself to and through specific local identities, adapting a global business to local conditions. As Robertson puts it, this is 'the tailoring and advertising of goods and services on a global or near-global basis to increasingly differentiated local and particular markets'.[21]

What the Anglo-Hollywood film industry produces in films like the Austen adaptations is in this sense a local, or particular, cultural product that is yet capable of commercial exploitation on a global scale. Robertson argues that this version of global capitalism is not simply about adapting to local conditions and particular, distinctive consumers, however, but also about '*the construction* of increasingly differentiated consumers, [and] the "invention" of "consumer traditions" (of which tourism, arguably the biggest "industry" of the contemporary world, is undoubtedly the most clear-cut example). To put it very simply, diversity sells'.[22]

Disney, for instance, as an American leisure and entertainments company with a global reach, decided that one way of breaking into the emerging and potentially huge market of China was to fund and co-produce films made locally and specifically for that market. Its first such release was *The Magic Gourd* (*Bao hu lu de mi mi*, 2007), adapted from a classic Chinese children's novel. In other words, here was an example of a global company appealing to local sentiments, exploiting the possibilities of 'glocalisation', creating its own brand of indigenous product: as a Disney executive put it, 'we make our brands more relevant to the local market'. But he also made it clear that the strategy in this case was not about exploiting a global product in a local market, but about producing material specifically for that market, since locally produced commodities have a greater chance of wide distribution in a heavily regulated market like China.[23]

Global capitalism, from this perspective, depends upon the production and reproduction of difference: the global is 'the generative frame of unity within which diversity can take place'.[24] Global capitalism, from this perspective, must embrace variety, it must acknowledge and attend to the indigenous and the local, and it must address niche markets. But can it do so only by imagining the local through the lens of the global? Can it do so only by creating and reproducing a standardised version of the local, a global version of the local, recognised and appreciated by a range of consumers, regardless of their location and sense of belonging? As a local culture is commoditised for global consumption, we must consider the extent to which the local is modified, reconfigured and translated for its new global niche audiences. Cultural representations designed for a consumer market must never be allowed to become too unfamiliar, too exotic, for fear of what media economists and others call 'cultural discount' – that is, the diminished appeal that products rooted in a particular culture might have for foreign audiences who 'find it difficult to identify with the styles, values, beliefs, institutions and behaviour patterns being portrayed'.[25]

In the Hollywood-funded Austen adaptations, for instance, Englishness is arguably reduced to a familiar brand, a series of stock images and generic stereotypes. On the other hand, the Austen adaptations are culturally much richer than this suggests. One might read these films as assertions of tradition, celebrations of the family, home and the sense of a homeland, affirmations of cultural rootedness. One might also read them as simple manifestations of a well-established ideology of Englishness, and one that is not so much local as hegemonic. Yet each of the films is in some sense about dislocation as much as rootedness, each problematises the image of the family, and each challenges settled ideas of national identity from the perspectives of feminism, or of class politics or of (post-)colonialism. This hardly suggests a series of ready-made stock images with no critical purchase.

The same is true of films like *Notting Hill*, *Bride and Prejudice* and *The Constant Gardener*: national identity may be inflected in terms of the local, the hybrid, the diasporic or the expatriate, while the iconography of the nation may be given a contemporary spin in some way or other; even so, the national is still usually anchored to a sense of tradition. In particular, the reproduction of familiar character types in novel guises suggests that traditional national images may be strengthened and renewed rather than weakened by the developments of globalisation – even if to some audiences those images will appear banal, while to others they will appear exotic. Sometimes those images will be highly reductive – as in the particular versions of upper-middle-class, Southern, white English masculinity on display in *Notting Hill*, *Bride and Prejudice* and *The Constant Gardener*. But in other ways, a film like *Bride and Prejudice* also attempts to construct a sense of complex individual and community identities. This complexity and specificity is achieved even more effectively in other films such as *Bend It Like Beckham*, *My Summer of Love* and *Bullet Boy*, films that may have been modestly budgeted but that still circulated in specialist niche markets around the world – and in the case of *Bend It Like Beckham* actually became considerable international box-office successes.

The international film trade in representations of England and Englishness clearly to some extent shapes those representations – but 'English culture' is by no means a 'pure' formation, and has from the outset been shaped by competing forces from within and beyond the geographical borders of what we now call England. In any case, the trade in filmic representations of Englishness does include films that retain a lot of indigenous cultural references, some of which still manage to achieve a certain success in export markets. Of course, there is plenty of evidence that cultural products intended for global markets are shaped by expectations as to what will work in those markets. Is this an unacceptable loss of cultural integrity, a threat to the representation of local cultural identities and stories, a dilution of the indigenous in order to overcome the problem of cultural discount? Or is it a way of ensuring a certain cultural diversity, a way of ensuring that a range of different types of film, representing different tastes and sensibilities, can be effectively produced, circulated and consumed?

For the purposes of trade on the international stage, 'national' cultures are often reduced to brand images, which can then be exported as known quantities, as signifiers of cultural difference, or at least of an acceptable and marketable cultural variety. One of the selling points of these brand images in international niche markets is then precisely their exoticism, their foreignness – so long as the sense of cultural difference is not too great. The indigenous and the exotic, seemingly polar opposites, thus blur into one another. It is perhaps significant, in this context, that so many 'English films' have been directed by 'outsiders', and that so many English characters have been played by American or Australian actors – effectively, foreign commentators on or interpreters of the English scene. And of course such representations depend in no small measure upon American commercial involvement. Paradoxically it would seem that the globalisation of the film industry has actually made it possible to continue to produce a range of local cultural products. From the top down, this may be because the strategy is capable of generating income; from the bottom up, it is equally a means of ensuring a certain sort of cultural diversity.

The problem is not simply a question of what films are about, however, but also of how they are experienced. A film about English characters watched in the USA, France or Japan may well work very differently from the same film watched by English audiences in England. Foreign audiences are unlikely to 'recognise' themselves on the screen in national terms, or to feel they belong to the national community invoked by the film. In that sense, the characters on display are likely to figure as exotic rather than as the vehicles of nationalist identification. But even in England there is no such thing as a *national* audience, and there will be many English spectators who reject the speculative narratives of belonging that can be formally identified at the level of the text. For the black communities that come together for the annual Notting Hill Carnival, the Richard Curtis version of Notting Hill will seem alien; for a Northern working-class Englishwoman, Grant/Thacker will not easily be accepted as the embodiment of ordinary Englishness. For these diverse audiences, whether foreign or English, films like *Notting Hill* may generate a sense of familiarity and recognition, but not of belonging; these are different processes, and it is possible to recognise an identity from outside, as it were – not to share or even to want to share that identity, but to see it as exotic, as other – familiar, maybe, but not banal.

Films such as those discussed in this chapter need then to be understood both from the bottom up as resisting the drift towards global homogenisation, and as products of global commodification, designed from the top down. The version of the local and the indigenous in the Austen films, for instance, is neither entirely invented by the global forces of Hollywood, nor entirely authentic, whatever that might mean. Of course to some extent these films are exotic fantasies; of course to some extent they are Americanised versions of Austen and of the English national past; of course they have been adapted to the 'local' conditions of what is perceived to be the taste of American audiences. At the same time, they remain culturally distinctive films, they retain a sense of difference – and that difference is crucial to their perception at home and abroad and a key reason for their commercial viability.

To this extent, their very presence as films is indicative of a certain cultural diversity, a certain attention to the local within an increasingly globalised film culture. Paradoxically, the attention to the local and the indigenous in the Austen adaptations is only possible because of international funding – and crucially American funding. In other words, it was the support of the Hollywood majors, as much as anything else, that enabled such films to be made. Hollywood's interest in relatively small-scale, specialist films thus suggests that the monolithic machine that some see in Hollywood may actually allow – even encourage – the production of difference. Hollywood in fact developed a business structure and a way of operating that allowed it to cater for different audiences, different tastes, different markets. This development needs to be seen as part of a wider trend, one that is a key feature in the evolution of the global media industry. As one commentator put it, 'international financing is sophisticated enough nowadays to support…fiercely localised work'.[26] Or as David Harvey has argued at length, the methods of global capitalism have shifted from mass production to flexible accumulation – wherein one of the flexibilities has been to exploit smaller markets with more specialised tastes.[27]

If the local and the national can now only ever be glimpsed through the imaginative lens of the global, this does not mean that the local or the national disappear altogether, or that they are transformed beyond recognition. Some representations may appear overly reductive, but others are more complex and subtle. In any case, different audiences will make sense of the same cultural product in a variety of distinctive ways. The global trade in an ostensibly national culture in this sense opens up possibilities, rather than closes them down. Cinema is not unique in this respect, and other contemporary cultural practices face a similar situation. In the international publishing business, for instance, there is still space for both mass-market fiction and self-consciously literary fiction with a much more limited appeal, for both texts that are designed to be widely accessible and texts that are much more challenging in terms of the themes they explore and/or the highly localised sense of place they establish. Indeed, the film business and the publishing business interact closely in all sorts of ways, to generate products, exploit markets and establish fan bases. It is this interaction that I explore in the next chapter.

4 English literature, the contemporary novel and the cinema

Literary adaptation: the English literary film and world cinema

The number of film adaptations of Jane Austen's novels in the 1990s and 2000s points to the ways in which the English literary heritage can be exploited as a source for contemporary cultural production. The Austen oeuvre is by no means unique in being on the one hand widely recognisable and therefore readily marketable, but on the other hand offering a highly distinctive and specific set of characters, themes, settings and values. A sense of openness, then, but also of of exclusivity; a sense of universality, where the appeal of a fictional world and its literary presentation transcends national boundaries, but equally a self-enclosed fictional world strongly defined in terms of a very specific sense of English tradition and identity. This duality is matched in the ways in which Austen novels have been reworked as films. Some are produced well away from England, their characters and settings transposed to altogether other cultures, as with the Hollywood-produced, modern-day version of *Emma*, *Clueless* (1995), set in and around an American high school, and addressed to a mainstream, youth-oriented audience. Others attempt to recreate the heart of old England, have a strong UK involvement at the point of production, and address what are generally understood to be specialist, niche audiences, as with *Persuasion* (1995) and *Mansfield Park* (1999). Somewhere in between are Hollywood-produced, star-driven films that at the same time make strenuous efforts to reproduce a traditional England, as in films like *Sense and Sensibility*.

What this diversity of Austen adaptations demonstrates is, first, that literary properties are a vital source of material for filmmakers, and second, that in a global film culture and film business, the national is a set of values and identities that can be exploited by a range of companies and enjoyed by a range of audiences, regardless of any

The Lord of the Rings: a major Brit-lit franchise of the 2000s.

national allegiances. To put it another way, English literature may be a highly fruitful resource with which the film business can work, but the rights to the English literary heritage are not owned by the UK state or by English-based companies. That such literature has proved of great interest to filmmakers around the world is demonstrated by UK Film Council statistics about the box-office success of films whose stories or characters were created by writers with strong British connections. As I noted in chapter 1, the Film Council has drawn attention to the fact that of the top 200 highest-grossing films worldwide between 2000 and 2007, some 30 fell into this category.[1] This figure includes both original screenplays by UK writers and adaptations of novels or short stories by UK writers. The list is of course dominated by the franchises organised around stories and characters created by J.K. Rowling (the Harry Potter films, 2001–10) and J.R.R. Tolkien (*The Lord of the Rings* trilogy, 2001–3).

If the scope is widened to cover the top-grossing films of the period from 1990 to 2009, but reduced to include only films adapted from novels or short stories by writers with strong British connections, the significance of these franchises is underlined even more strongly. Only 26 such literary adaptations appeared in the list of the top 400 highest-grossing films worldwide, and eight of them were based on the work of Rowling and Tolkien.[2] Other franchises also play a dominant role, with six adaptations of Ian Fleming's James Bond stories and character in the list, as well as two of C.S. Lewis's *Chronicles of Narnia* novels. The importance of children's stories and the family films adapted from them is also very clear, since the list includes adaptations of stories or characters created by Roald Dahl (*Charlie and the Chocolate Factory*, 2005), Philip Pullman (*The Golden Compass*, 2007), J.M. Barrie (*Hook*, 1991), Hugh Lofting (*Dr Doolittle*, 1998) and Dick King-Smith (*Babe*, 1995). Besides the Bond films, adult themes emerge in *The War of the Worlds* (2005), *Master and Commander* (2003), the two Bridget Jones films (2001, 2004) and *AI: Artificial Intelligence* (2001), adapted from stories by H.G. Wells, Patrick O'Brian, Helen Fielding and Brian Aldiss respectively.

These lists are revealing in a number of ways, not least about the pulling power and global cultural presence of English fiction, especially in the period since the publication of the first Harry Potter novel (1998) and its adaptation as a film (2001). Literary adaptation has long been an important strategy for those seeking to make successful films, and that has been particularly the case in the UK. If the statistics about worldwide box-office success are one way of drawing attention to this strategy, the literary adaptations that have attracted the most critical interest and debate have tended to be prestige or quality films adapted from canonical literary properties, especially the great tradition from Jane Austen at the turn of the nineteenth century to E.M. Forster at the start of the twentieth century. Indeed, there were more adaptations of Jane Austen novels between 1990 and 2009 than there were of J.K. Rowling novels, and there were twice as many adaptations of stories written by Charles Dickens.[3] There were also several adaptations of novels by the Brontës, George Eliot, Thomas Hardy and the foreign-born but Anglicised Joseph Conrad and Henry James, among many others. Novels by writers such as these have an unshakeable status as classics of English literature and that status has played an important part in establishing the Englishness of films adapted from those novels – although by no means all of them set out to faithfully recreate their characters and settings as English, and by no means all can be comfortably described as English productions. In this respect, the range of adaptations of Austen films can again be seen as typical.

The Austen franchise may be of a very different order to the Rowling, Tolkien or Fleming franchises, with none of the Austen adaptations securing box-office receipts anywhere near those of the top 200 highest-grossing films, but it has still contributed in important ways to the body of English literary properties exploited by the international film business. Looking at that process of exploitation in wider terms, it is worth noting that between 1990 and 2009 there were more than 200 films adapted from English novels and short stories. By no means all of them had any sort of UK production involvement; indeed, perhaps as many as 20 were adaptations in languages other than English, and some were marketed in ways that did not seek to draw attention to their English origins. Even so, English literature provided a starting point for a great many films, most of which featured English characters and/or settings. Around a quarter of these adaptations were of stories written in the nineteenth century; nearly a third were of stories first published between 1900 and 1985; and a slightly larger figure were of stories first published since 1985 – what we might call contemporary literature.

Around a third of the 200-plus films had no UK production involvement. Leaving those aside, adaptations constitute around 7 per cent of the total number of British films produced in that period – and the percentage remains fairly consistent regardless of how many British films are produced each year.[4] To put it another way, one in every 13 UK productions was an adaptation of English literary source material. Such statistics depend of course on how one defines English literature and British cinema; I have deliberately not been too finicky in this respect, aiming instead for a general picture of the relationship between the English novel and the cinema.

Most of the adaptations that had no UK financial involvement were American, but there were also several French adaptations, and others from India, the Philippines and elsewhere. These non-British productions included big-budget Hollywood versions of best-selling novels by such prominent mass-market authors as John le Carré and Patrick O'Brian, as well as children's writers such as Anne Fine, Dick King-Smith and Roald Dahl. There were also a few American adaptations of more self-consciously literary authors such as Pat Barker, William Boyd and Alex Garland, and modern-dress adaptations of canonical nineteenth-century writers such as Austen and Dickens. For some reason, most of the adaptations of English stories that had neither British nor American financial involvement were from source material written by women, including several French adaptations of novels by Agatha Christie, George Eliot, Doris Lessing and Ruth Rendell.

Clearly, then, English producers are not alone in adapting novels into films. On the contrary, this has long been one of the ways in which the film industry internationally has obtained its stories. Some of Hollywood's most successful films of the 1990s and 2000s were adaptations, with the work of John Grisham, Thomas Harris, Michael Crichton, Robert Ludlum, Lauren Weisberger and Dan Brown particularly prominent; Hollywood's involvement in several of the big 'English literature' franchises simply underlines how important literary adaptation has been to contemporary Hollywood. Nor would it be fair to conclude from the statistics above that English cinema is overwhelmingly a literary cinema, or that it has depended overly on literary adaptations. Even so, there remains a close and dynamic relationship between the English novel and the cinema, in both the highbrow and the middlebrow sections of the market, and for both established classics and contemporary novels. Given the established cultural resonance of 'serious literature', quality and prestige in the film business are frequently associated with literariness in one guise or another. Given the proven mass-market appeal of other novels, most notably the Harry Potter series, it is not surprising that the film business has also latched onto literature as a way of guaranteeing audiences.

The vibrancy and diversity of English literary culture has thus contributed in important ways to English film culture in the 1990s and 2000s and helped to consolidate what we might call English literary cinema. That cinema has certainly included some commercially and critically successful adaptations, but it is still only a small section of English cinema as a whole, and there are plenty of equally successful films that have no literary connections. But if a concept like English literary cinema is to have any real purchase, it must also be recognised as a global phenomenon, rather than a specifically national cultural practice, given the range of film industries, film companies and filmmakers from different parts of the world involved in the adaptation of English literary properties, and the range of audiences engaging with those adaptations.

Literate cinema and cinema about literature

The involvement of the English film business with literary adaptations has given it a mixed reputation. When it tackles canonical literature, English cinema is sometimes berated for the reverence with which it treats the source novel and a reliance on the verbal, the assumption being that cinema is primarily a visual medium. For some, this is a

betrayal of cinema and all that it is capable of as an aesthetic medium –
as one reviewer put it, describing Kenneth Branagh's adaptation of
Henry V (1989), it is about making 'movie[s] for those who don't like
movies'.[5] For others, it is simply an acknowledgement of the pervasive
interpenetration of cultural practices, the extent to which they are constantly feeding off each other, as they always have done. In any case,
the richness and diversity of literary adaptations, their visual qualities,
and the qualities of their performances hardly suggest that reverence is a
good description of the process of adaptation.

There is also the problem of fidelity, a term that has been absolutely
central to the debate about adaptation. Both professional literary critics
and ordinary readers, when confronted with an adaptation, will worry
about how faithful it is to the source novel. Novelists inevitably lose
control over their work once it is taken on by a filmmaker; so too do the
fans of that work, whether they are Janeites, the self-appointed guardians of Jane Austen's legacy, or the legions of young people who have
participated in the Harry Potter phenomenon. While some filmmakers
are certainly anxious to keep literary fans onside, many filmmakers
would also argue that it is vital that they shape their films according
to the needs of the film audience rather than the novelist or his or her
readers.

Cinema is thus conceived as both distinct from and yet at the same
time dependent upon literary culture. Some professional critics will
invoke the literary as a means of praising what they perceive as 'good'
cinema and recommending a film to 'sophisticated' audiences. Several
reviewers described James Ivory's adaptation of Forster's *Howards End*
(1992), for instance, as a 'literate' film – where literate meant intelligent,
subtle, civilised entertainment, as opposed to the 'mindless' attractions of mainstream Hollywood cinema; the adaptation thus 'achieved
just the right balance between the literate and the cinematic'.[6] *Ladies in
Lavender* (2004), an adaptation of a short story by William J. Locke, was
described in similar terms as 'a warm and literate film ... A film with
this kind of charm and sweetness and class may not be the usual fare
in a cinematic marathon dedicated to numbing the brain and deaden-
ing the senses, but every film festival should have one.'[7] It is not just
literary adaptations that are described in these terms. Thus the Oscar
Wilde biopic *Wilde* (1997) benefited from an 'intelligent, literate script';[8]
another biopic, *Shakespeare in Love* (1998), was 'one of the most satisfying – and literate – romantic comedies in years',[9] and 'that rare thing, a

literate crowd pleaser'.[10] *Gosford Park* (2001) and *To Kill a King* (2003), two more costume dramas, but this time with no literary connections, could also each boast a 'literate' script.[11] *Stage Beauty* (2004) too was 'refreshingly literate',[12] 'the sort of thoughtful, well-crafted movie intelligent film-goers yearn for'.[13]

The literate movie, made by literate people for literate audiences, was an important category for the specialised end of the film business too. The UK distributors of *Elizabeth* (1998), for instance, saw the film as a 'prestige' production, ideal for an 'upscale, literate dinner-party crowd'.[14] Elsewhere, in an interview in *Hollywood Reporter*, the president of Sony Pictures Entertainment sung the praises of his colleagues in Sony's boutique Classics division for small-scale films: 'They have a wonderful creative sensibility, and their emphasis on quality, taste and a truly global view of filmmaking is a model for our entire motion picture business.' He added that it was their 'sophisticated, highly literate and eclectic perspective that enables them to attract prestigious and innovative filmmakers from around the world'.[15] Associations with literary culture, however implicit, could thus be used to establish an aura of quality and intelligence around a cultural practice too often addressed to and understood in terms of the mass market. In the end, though, for the business, the literate film was still a marketable commodity, albeit one addressed to a highly specific niche audience.

Another important way in which cinema engages with literature, literary culture and literary readerships as audiences is through the literary biopic. There has been a surprising number of British and American films depicting the lives of prominent writers associated with England, and focusing in some way on the process of writing, including films about writers as diverse as Shakespeare and Wilde, as noted above, Jane Austen (*Becoming Jane*, 2007) and Beatrix Potter (*Miss Potter*, 2007), and J.M. Barrie (*Finding Neverland*, 2004) and C.S. Lewis (*Shadowlands*, 1993). There was also *The Hours* (2002), which, although hardly a biopic, nevertheless offers scenes from the life of Virginia Woolf. But only one such film in the 1990s and 2000s dealt with a contemporary English author, *Iris* (Richard Eyre, 2001), about Iris Murdoch. Such films appeal primarily to middlebrow audiences, to whom they offer an engagement with respectable literary culture that goes beyond the adaptation itself. They also tend to be dramas with a strong focus on human interest, a romantic vision of key moments in the life of a writer, a vision that often purports to throw light on the creative process or the source of the writer's fiction. They are also invariably costume dramas, period explorations of remarkable English characters.

Authors! Authors!

It is adaptations, however, that dominate the literature/film relationship. Looking at the full range of English novels adapted into films in the 1990s and 2000s, a surprisingly diverse range of authors have found their work appearing on the big screen. As noted above, many of the best-known authors of the nineteenth and early twentieth centuries have had films made from their work during this period, as have some of the most prominent authors of the mid-twentieth century, from D.H. Lawrence, Virginia Woolf and W. Somerset Maugham to Evelyn Waugh, George Orwell and Graham Greene. In the next chapter, I will explore the Jane Austen film franchise, with Austen standing in as a representative of the nineteenth- and twentieth-century English literary canon who happens also to be one of the most adapted authors of the 1990s and 2000s. In the remainder of this chapter, I concentrate on adaptations of contemporary fiction.

It is surprising to find that some of the biggest mass-market British authors of the contemporary period have not seen their work transposed to the big screen, including Joanna Trollope, the best-selling English female writer of the 1990s.[16] Nor did some of the biggest names in literary fiction find favour with the film industry, including Iris Murdoch and Salman Rushdie – although of course there is the biopic of Murdoch, while Rushdie appears briefly as himself in *Bridget Jones's Diary* (2001). Some authors seem to be preferred by television but overlooked by cinema, including best-sellers such as Jilly Cooper, Ken Follett and Terry Pratchett, and more self-consciously literary figures such as Alan Hollinghurst and Fay Weldon. But many of the most commercially and critically successful contemporary English novelists and others with a strong connection to the UK have seen at least one of their novels adapted as films.

Thus several of the novels that won the Booker Prize between 1985 and 2009 were adapted as films, including Kazuo Ishiguro's *The Remains of the Day* (1989/1993), A.S. Byatt's *Possession* (1990/2002) and Graham Swift's *Last Orders* (1996/2001); there were also several adaptations of other novels on the Booker shortlists, and a dozen or more winners of other prestigious literary prizes. A good selection of the authors listed by the high-profile English literary magazine

Granta in its influential surveys in 1983, 1993 and 2003 have been adapted, as too have been several authors honoured with a CBE or an OBE. At the mass-market end of the spectrum, most of the genres and authors that dominate the best-selling fiction lists found their way into the cinema too. Thus there were films adapted from thrillers by the likes of Nicci French and Jack Higgins; from crime novels by P.D. James and Ruth Rendell; from spy stories by John le Carré; from historical fiction by Patrick O'Brian; from 'chick lit' by Helen Fielding and Kathy Lette; from 'lad lit' by Nick Hornby; from teen fiction by Louise Rennison; from comic fiction by Ben Elton; and from horror by Clive Barker. Then of course there is the cult youth market, served by Danny Boyle's adaptations of Irvine Welsh's *Trainspotting* (1993/1996) and Alex Garland's *The Beach* (1996/2000), and another Welsh adaptation, *The Acid House* (1994/1998).

It was rare for contemporary writers to have more than two novels adapted into films in the period between 1990 and 2009, and most of the handful who did were associated with particular genres with their own quite specific markets, including Rendell's crime fiction, le Carré's political thrillers, Hornby's 'lad lit' novels, Patrick McGrath's Gothic fiction, Barker's horror writing and Rowling's children's books. The small number of contemporary authors such as these who have had several of their works adapted, and the characteristics of the fiction that has been so adapted, suggest that the film business is less interested in particular authors than in particular types of fiction and the fan bases associated with them, even if those fan bases are at times highly concentrated niche markets.

Another contemporary author who had several of his works adapted as films is Ian McEwan. It is perhaps surprising to find his name appearing here, since his writing is self-consciously literary and often cerebral; however, he also works with popular genre conventions, and this has ensured a strong crossover readership with healthy sales, especially as his career has developed. Adaptations of his stories have emphasised their eroticism and their thriller elements, and include *The Comfort of Strangers* (1981/1990), *The Cement Garden* (1978/1993), *The Innocent* (1989/1993), *Enduring Love* (1997/2004), *Atonement* (2001/2007) and *First Love, Last Rites* (1975/1997). Surprisingly, despite the provenance of the stories and the reputations of the directors, the scriptwriters and the casts, until *Atonement* none of these films was particularly successful, with none of them becoming the sort of crossover

Atonement: the most successful of the Ian McEwan adaptations.

hit at the box office that was surely expected. It was certainly the case that the production costs were in most cases too high to justify a release schedule that depended solely on art-house exhibition. *Atonement* was however a major critical and commercial success, as both novel and film, with the film version featuring two of the leading stars of the moment and tapping effortlessly into heritage drama territory, with its colourful evocation of upper-class English life in the 1930s.

McEwan's involvement with the cinema is in fact more extensive than the above list suggests, and is indicative of other ways in which writers engage with the film world. He adapted his own novel and wrote the screenplay for *The Innocent*, and wrote the stories on which two European films were based, *Schmetterlinge* (Germany, 1988) and *Rozmowa z czlowiekiem z szafy* (Poland, 1993). Perhaps more significantly, he also adapted Timothy Mo's Booker-shortlisted *Soursweet* (1982/1988), and wrote original screenplays for *The Ploughman's Lunch* (1983) and *The Good Son* (1993). McEwan's involvement in these films epitomises some of the ways in which writers seek to make a living from their work, selling the rights to their fictions and working on film and television scripts. Thus William Boyd adapted two of his own novels, *Stars and Bars* (1984/1988) and *A Good Man in Africa* (1981/1994), both American productions, wrote screenplays for several films and television programmes, and even directed his own script for *The Trench* (1999).

Hanif Kureishi wrote original screenplays for Stephen Frears in the 1980s (*My Beautiful Laundrette*, 1985, and *Sammy and Rosie Get Laid*, 1987) before publishing his first novel, *The Buddha of Suburbia* (1990), which he later adapted as a television series. He then wrote and directed *London Kills Me* (1991) for the cinema, adapted his own short story for *My Son the Fanatic* (1997/1997), and wrote the original screenplays for two films directed by Roger Michell, *The Mother* (2003) and *Venus* (2007).

Another writer whose involvement with the cinema makes for an interesting case study is Clive Barker, best-selling author of horror and fantasy stories, several of which have found their way to the screen. After two short stories were handled poorly as films, Barker took on the director's role for *Hellraiser* (1987), adapted from one of his novels (*The Hellbound Heart*, 1987). He subsequently directed two further films adapted from his own writing, produced several more, and either wrote or lent his name to screenplays featuring his stories and characters. Both *Hellraiser* and *Candyman* (1986, 1992) saw several sequels, some of them going straight to video with no theatrical exhibition. Such was his reputation among horror and fantasy fans that many of his films included his name in the title: *Clive Barker's Candyman, Clive Barker's Nightbreed* (1988, 1990), and so on.

Themes and variations

In many ways, cinema and literature run alongside each other – and not surprisingly, some of the same themes and trends can be identified in the two media. More specifically, filmmakers worked with various literary properties in order to tap into particular themes and trends. One of the themes often identified in recent English literature and which equally finds a place in contemporary English cinema is the exploration of the changing geopolitical landscape of the UK, the forces of devolution, regionalism and post-colonialism, and the emergence of multicultural and hybrid British identities. Adaptations of key novels and other material have thus enabled filmmakers to explore aspects of the British-Asian experience, for instance, via the work of Hanif Kureishi, in both his original screenplays and his adaptations, Meera Syal, in her adaptation of her own novel *Anita and Me* (1996/2002), and Monica Ali, whose novel *Brick Lane* was adapted in 2007. Adaptations of novels by Graham Swift (*Waterland*, 1983/1992, and *Last Orders*) and Helen Cross (*My Summer of Love*, 2001/2004), among others, enabled filmmakers to focus on very specific local or regional identities. Moving beyond the space of Englishness, other filmmakers used Irvine Welsh's novels *Trainspotting* and *The Acid House*, and a short story by A.L. Kennedy, which became *Stella Does Tricks* (1994/1996), to address the question of what it means to be Scottish.

Another trend saw filmmakers adapting novels by women writers that enabled them to explore the diversity of female experience. *Dirty Weekend* (1991/1993), for instance, was an adaptation of what is regarded by some as a feminist vigilante novel by Helen Zirhavi, who co-scripted the film version with Michael Winner, while later adaptations included Tracy Chevalier's period novel about a servant girl in the seventeenth-century Netherlands, *The Girl with a Pearl Earring* (2000/2003), Esther Freud's semi-autobiographical *Hideous Kinky* (1992/1998) and Zoë Heller's contemporary drama *Notes on a Scandal* (2006), all of them featuring female protagonists. Some of the most critically acclaimed British female writers of the late twentieth century saw their work adapted as films, including A.S. Byatt (*Angels and Insects*, 1992/1995, and *Possession*), Rose Tremain (*Restoration*, 1989/1995) and Pat Barker (*Regeneration*, 1991/1997). But if some of this material explores female experience from a self-consciously feminist perspective, there is also the post-feminist chick lit of Kathy Lette's *Mad Cows* (1996/1999), and the immensely successful adaptations of Helen Fielding's *Bridget Jones's Diary* and its sequel, *The Edge of Reason* (1999/2004). Such films appeal to the film industry because they have the potential to attract a range of different audiences, including both the niche literary audience and the female audience, with the Bridget Jones films in particular attracting substantial numbers of women cinema-goers of all ages; some of the films work too as romantic drama or comedy, with the potential to succeed as date movies.

The engagement with the past, a key feature of English cinema in the 1990s and 2000s, and explored in depth in later chapters, also owes a great deal to trends in English literature and literary culture. Of course, some of the films set in the past are based on original screenplays about real or imagined historical characters or events, but a good many are adaptations of novels. On the one hand, there are adaptations of nineteenth- and early twentieth-century novels, contemporary dramas in their day, but generally reworked as period pieces by the film business. On the other hand, a good many films set in the past are adaptations of more recent novels that engage with the past, and with ideas of heritage and tradition. This is hardly surprising since various surveys of the contemporary English novel have commented on the turn towards historical fiction, to memory and the past. Adaptations of such films tend to work as tasteful period pieces for the niche art-house market, and where possible for the crossover market, although others were made with much more of an eye on the mainstream.

At the populist end of the market was the star-driven 2008 adaptation of Philippa Gregory's historical romance *The Other Boleyn Girl*, set in the sixteenth century and dealing with a key moment in the history of the monarchy and the nation. The 1995 adaptation of Rose Tremain's *Restoration* dealt with a similarly momentous period in the seventeenth century. Several more adaptations were set in nineteenth-century England, including *Angels and Insects*, from Byatt's story, and *Mary Reilly* (1990/1996), a Hollywood adaptation of Valerie Martin's novel. Rather more were set in the early twentieth century, including the low-budget art-house adaptation of Barker's *Regeneration*. Moving into the middle decades of the twentieth century, Ishiguro's Booker Prize-winning *The Remains of the Day* was reworked by the Merchant Ivory team, specialists in highly tasteful, quality adaptations of prestigious novels with period English settings; also set in this period were adaptations of McEwan's *Atonement*, Angela Huth's *The Land Girls* (1995/1998) and Sebastian Faulks's *Charlotte Gray* (1998/2001). Some of the 'historical' novels and their adaptations move between past and present in postmodernist fashion, including Byatt's *Possession*. There are also adaptations of 'post-colonial' novels that deal with English characters abroad but are written by non-English writers, such as Peter Carey, in *Oscar and Lucinda* (1988/1997), and Michael Ondaatje, in *The English Patient* (1992/1996), both Booker Prize winners successfully remade as films. In a similar vein are projects like *The Last King of Scotland* (1998/2006), from the novel by Giles Foden, about the Ugandan dictator Idi Amin.

In appropriating literary source texts, the film business makes few distinctions between living and dead writers, or between contemporary and classic literature – or indeed between writers of different nations. The Merchant Ivory team provides an interesting example here. Both *Howards End* (1910/1992) and *The Remains of the Day*, for instance, are tasteful heritage films set at least in part in the first half of the twentieth century, in southern England, amongst fine heritage properties; both were produced by the Merchant Ivory team; and both star Anthony Hopkins and Emma Thompson – but one was adapted from a novel by the long-dead English writer E.M. Forster and the other from a novel by the living Anglo-Japanese writer Kazuo Ishiguro. For the film industry, both were marketable products, at the prestige end of the market – and perhaps more to the point, both were pre-sold properties, with a guaranteed core consumer base in the literary audience.

It is perhaps here, in the turn to the past, that the English literary cinema has most taken hold, but if many of the films about the past are adaptations, the heritage film set in the nineteenth or early twentieth century has at the same time developed its own filmic conventions, its own ways of embracing heritage. The frequently rich and spectacular visual qualities of these films, their pictorialist use of the image, their character-led rather than event-led narratives, their strong performances and their preference for the long take and the medium shot, rather than fast cutting and close-ups, for instance, are all features that owe little to the novel. The literary connections are important, but all of these adaptations work effectively as films in their own right, their artfulness and their cinematic cross-references enabling them to inhabit a world of their own while at the same time benefiting from their literary intertexts.

There are other ways in which film style and literary style part company. *The Remains of the Day* happens to be one of several contemporary English novels reworked as films that involve some form of first-person narration. Nick Hornby's male confessional style, Bridget Jones's diaristic form, the perverse narrators of *Remains ...* and *Enduring Love*, the more straightforward narrator of *The Girl with a Pearl Earring*, the twin narrators of *Chocolat* (Joanne Harris, 1999), and the multiple narrators of *Last Orders*: all are variants of first-person storytelling. Feature films however have rarely been able to sustain explicitly subjective narration, and the adaptations of these films use various devices to overcome this difficulty without losing the spirit of the novel. In *Girl with a Pearl Earring*, for instance, the camera stays with the eponymous heroine most of the time – but no effort is made to actually render her point of view as the point of view of the film or the spectator. Much the same is true of *Chocolat*, where the film again adopts a third-person narrational style that irons out the multiple perspectives of the novel. *Enduring Love* too eschews the novel's highly self-conscious first-person storytelling, although several scenes in the film attempt to create a sense of interiority, of inhabiting a consciousness. In the Bridget Jones films, fragments from the titular diary are occasionally written on the screen – but more as a reminder of the way the novel works than as a consistent style; likewise, scenes featuring the diary are there more to justify the title than to carry any narrational responsibility. Once again, established filmic conventions overwhelm the specific stylistic characteristics of particular novels.

Looking at these same films adapted from first-person novels, it also becomes clear once again that national identity is a slippery concept, not one that can easily be attributed to the films, even if they have all been adapted from English novels. The author of *The Remains of the Day* is Anglo-Japanese, the director of *Last Orders* is Australian, *Chocolat* is set in France and directed by a Swede, *The Girl with a Pearl Earring* is set in the Netherlands, the English protagonist of the Bridget Jones films is played by an American... Several of the films mentioned deal with quite specific London locations and characters, including the Bridget Jones films, *Enduring Love* and *Last Orders*; as such, they deal variously with the local and the metropolitan; national identity may be established at a banal level in each of these films, but it would be difficult to argue that it becomes the thematic focus of any of the films. As noted in chapter 3, in one of the adaptations of a Nick Hornby novel, *High Fidelity* (1995/2000), another local London location is transposed to Chicago. English literary source material cannot therefore in any sense guarantee the ways in which national identity is established, let alone addressed in film adaptations.

Adaptation and the marketplace

In market terms, the relationship between a book and its adaptation can be extremely valuable. Adapting a best-seller means working with a product that already has massive visibility to a range of consumers – but the process works the other way round as well. Most adaptations are accompanied by a tie-in edition of the source novel, released by the publishers to capitalise on the new visibility of the title. 'Now a major motion picture', it will say on the cover of most of those tie-in publications, over an image from the film version featuring the stars. Film tie-in editions can send books right to the top of the best-seller charts, even if the film itself is not particularly successful. For instance, 'the two Picador paperback editions of *Bridget Jones's Diary* sold an extra 1,730,535 copies', while the tie-in edition of *Chocolat* 'put Joanne Harris up alongside her namesakes Thomas and Robert. Her Black Swan paperback, 357,287 last year, is now close on 1,200,000.' Even the expensive but critically and commercially disappointing film version of *Captain Corelli's Mandolin* (1994/2001) 'contributed another 548,148 to Louis de Bernières's sales to make up a total of 2,358,446'.[17]

All of these titles are examples of the publishing and film businesses exploiting new markets in the 1990s and early 2000s: on the one hand the crossover product, which has the capacity to shift out of a niche market into the mainstream; and on the other hand chick lit, or the 'city girl' novel, as represented by the Bridget Jones franchise. Like chick lit's masculine variant, lad lit, these were generic categories that emerged in the 1990s and were carefully nurtured by the publishing business and subsequently by film distributors. Behind these relatively new developments is a more established context in which fictional experiences are sold to consumers. Traditionally, there are two relatively distinct markets for both novels and films – and the distinctions between them are routinely upheld by critics.

On the one hand, there is what is often dismissed as mass-market genre fiction, the best-seller, the novel as popular culture – or what in film terms can be described as the multiplex market. This in turn can be further subdivided by genre and consumer base. Thus there are the primarily action-based genres, which tend to be popular with male readers, and in due course cinema-goers. And there is women's romance fiction, which has not in recent years been much taken up by the film industry. Hence the significance of both the chick lit phenomenon and the crossover success of titles by the likes of Joanne Harris, which can work both as serious literature and as romance fiction. Mass-market genre fiction tends to be judged primarily in terms of sales and fan bases, or readerships. It is often assumed to be less reflective about its own form, its subject matter, and the world in which it is set. But often so-called genre fiction can be self-conscious about both form and content – and critics will claim that writers such as Ruth Rendell, John le Carré and P.D. James rise above the constraints of their genres. Such debates mirror closely the debates about popular cinema.

At the other end of the market is the so-called serious novel, self-consciously literary fiction for 'middle to highbrow', 'discriminating readers'.[18] This is the arena of prize-winning fiction and the so-called 'literary novelist', who specialises in slow-moving character studies rather than narratives of action, and in the novel of ideas. This is the literary equivalent of art-house cinema and the festival circuit, with its own system of prizes and awards that validate the film business's sense of quality and specialised niche markets. As with literary culture, it is a market traditionally defined less in terms of commercial success and more in terms of critical impact and reputation, with the reviewing practices of the quality press playing a vital role in this respect. And as with literary culture, the core consumer group is educated and middle-class, and expects certain sorts of production values, moral dilemmas, intellectual enigmas and aesthetic experiences. As a market, though, it is not nationally specific, even if some of the representations on screen might be read in that way.

If mass-market genre fiction and serious literature are traditionally considered two quite distinct markets and cultures, those markets and cultures have increasingly overlapped in recent decades, and the film industry has been quick to exploit this overlap. Booker Prize winners have frequently found their way into the top echelon of the best-seller lists, as in recent years have novels without that accolade, by the likes of Ian McEwan and Zadie Smith. It is no coincidence that there have been adaptations of *Possession*, Byatt's commercially successful Booker winner, and *Enduring Love* and *Atonement*, two of McEwan's most successful novels. As the publisher Dan Franklin notes, people in his business are always on the lookout for the 'novel that is at once literary and commercial, a book with big ambitions that will appeal to a very wide audience'.[19] Franklin also makes it clear that the possibility of securing an advance from a film producer is an important factor at a certain level in the fiction publishing business.

High Fidelity: adapting lad lit for the screen, re-working London as Chicago.

Other fiction is much more self-consciously middlebrow and mid-market from the outset, and this is where the emergent genres of chick lit and lad lit fit in. *Bridget Jones's Diary*, with its Jane Austen subtext indicating its pretensions towards the highbrow, was not initially an obvious best-seller, yet with its sequel and its adaptations, it became a major literary and filmic phenomenon, and attracted readers and audiences well beyond its target female twenty- to thirtysomethings. The key lad lit author was Nick Hornby, whose novels were again both critically applauded and immensely successful (including in the USA) – with *Fever Pitch* (1992/1997), *High Fidelity* and *About a Boy* (1998/2002) all being made into films. The cycle of films about football hooliganism was another way in which lad culture and young male audiences were addressed, and this too benefitedfrom an adaptation, of John King's *The Football Factory*, made into a film in 2004.

The Harry Potter series can also be seen as crossover fiction, with its adult editions, the prizes it has attracted and its success in the American market. The film business clearly likes this sort of best-selling but upmarket genre fiction aimed at the core family and youth markets – especially when it takes on franchise proportions, as it did with the Harry Potter series. But it also likes the crossover fiction that has its feet planted firmly at the 'serious literature' end of the market even if it still plays vibrantly with the conventions of more accessible genre fiction. It is worth noting some overlapping cycles here. In the space of four years, between 2000 and 2004, the English production company Working Title made adaptations of both of the Bridget Jones novels, *High Fidelity* and *Captain Corelli's Mandolin*, one of the most commercially successful 'serious' books of recent years. The company continued to produce the occasional well-crafted literary adaptation over the next few years, again tapping into the crossover market with *Pride and Prejudice* and *Atonement*, both directed by Joe Wright and starring Keira Knightley – but with the former film it endeavoured to do for Austen what it had earlier done with contemporary crossover fiction.

The American company Miramax, which had made its reputation turning apparently niche-market films into major crossover hits, was also involved with *Captain Corelli* and *Bridget Jones: The Edge of Reason*, which were part of its own cycle of mid-market, middlebrow literary adaptations. These included *Mansfield Park* (1814/1999), *Chocolat*, *The Hours* (1998/2002) and *Cold Mountain* (1997/2003) – respectively a racy adaptation of an English literary classic, a reworking of a contemporary English novel set in France, a version of an American novel in part about an English author, Virginia Woolf, and an adaptation of an American novel directed by an Englishman. Precise cultural provenance is an irrelevance in the film business, so long as a market can be identified.

A film adapted from a novel takes the shape it does partly from the source novel, and partly from a whole range of other circumstances. *Captain Corelli* must have seemed an ideal text to work with since it already had a huge market presence, and could be presented as solidly middlebrow fare. On the one hand, it drew on the kudos of serious literature, on the other it had all the attractions of a romantic Mediterranean holiday setting, a gender-inclusive blend of the war film and the romance and an apparent nostalgia for simpler times. It needs then to be seen alongside other middlebrow literary adaptations of the period, especially those produced by Working Title and Miramax, but also middlebrow material without a strong literary connection, whether produced by those same companies (for instance, *Notting Hill*, 1999) or with similar ingredients (such as *Mamma Mia!*, 2008, with its Greek holiday romance). In that context, it is hardly surprising that the trenchant political discourse of Louis de Bernières's source novel all but disappeared from the film. Cinema is a fickle business, however, and the film was in the end both a commercial and a critical disappointment.

The process of adaptation: *Possession*

There are perhaps two defining motivations that inspire filmmakers to adapt a novel. On the one hand, the novel provides a well-crafted story, carefully drawn characters, narratively meaningful settings, and a world view, a moral and ideological framework – that is, the raw ingredients for fiction whether on the printed page or on film. On the other hand, to adapt a novel may mean taking on a product that already has a market presence, and that can be further marketed on the basis of that reputation. Working with a pre-sold property in this way may reduce the risk involved in financing the production. Most adaptations combine the two motivations, though some will involve a source novel that has virtually no market presence. To take on a well-known novel, or a novel by a well-known author, may require a third motivation to come into play: the desire to reproduce the novel as faithfully as possible. But that aspiration will always be counterbalanced by the need to create something that will work well as a film, and that will engage both those audiences familiar with the novel and those that are not. The film must be able to play off the reputation of the novel, and summon up sufficient memories of it for audiences who have read the novel, but it must also work in its own right as a film.[20]

The process of adaptation is necessarily a process of reshaping and repackaging. A written text must become an audio-visual text, and it must have some of the ingredients that will encourage financiers to invest in the project and audiences to watch it. There is almost invariably a process of narrative condensation in adapting novels as films: screenwriters will often pare down the range of events and the number of characters. But at the same time there is a process of opening up, of creating a fuller diegetic effect, filling out the world of the fiction – whether in the settings or in the physical presence and performances of the actors. The film must reshape the source material according to its own conventions, while not losing sight of the novel, if it is well-known enough for the film to be marketed on that basis. Events may be reordered, narrational material transposed into dialogue. Novels as long as *Possession* and as short as *Orlando* (1928/1992) must come out at roughly the same length. And the readily recognisable genre features of novels such as *Possession* and *Enduring Love* will often win out over the more philosophical aspects of such self-consciously literary works, rendering them as much more straightforward narratives. A perversely multi-stranded epic like *Captain Corelli* will be turned into a more straightforward linear narrative with a central romantic couple and not too many distracting characters and stories around them. Even a spy thriller like le Carré's *The Tailor of Panama* (1996/2001) may find a new, less nuanced, more conventional happy ending imposed on the film version.

The conventional mythology of literary authorship is that the process of creating a book is entirely the responsibility of the individual author. But of course the publishing business also plays its part, in the guise of editors, marketing people, book designers, and so on, as does the business of criticism, literary reviews and the like. In the case of cinema, the business end of things is much more elaborate and multi-layered, whether it is the business of creation or the business of the moving image industry as a whole.

Take the film *Possession*, for instance, directed by an American, Neil LaBute, and adapted from Byatt's Booker Prize-winning novel of the same name. The screen rights to the novel were evidently purchased by

Warner Bros., one of the major American studio-distributors, shortly after the book was published. But it was not until some ten years later that LaBute and his scriptwriting collaborators produced a screenplay that Warners were happy with.[21] The credits for the finished film in fact list *three* writers, LaBute, David Henry Hwang and Laura Jones; the next credit states that the screenplay was 'based on the novel by A.S. Byatt'. Note 'based on', not 'adapted from'; and note too that this credit appears at the end of the film, not the beginning. The cinema trailer, on the other hand, made no bones about the fact that this was an adaptation, of the '*best-selling*' novel by Byatt. In the film itself, however, the connection to Byatt's novel is signalled more subtly, with the title credit for instance adopting the calligraphic design of the cover of the novel.

So, three writers rather than one produce the screenplay, which clearly plays intertextually with the source novel, but neither flaunts that relationship too openly, nor makes too bold claims about the fidelity of the adaptation. Other film adaptations will do this differently, especially where the adaptation can be sold widely on the name of the author of the source novel. But almost all adaptations of novels are faced with the problem of narrative scope. In this case, a massive 500-page novel becomes a mere 98-minute film, with events and characters refigured, or omitted altogether.

Byatt's *Possession* is subtitled *A Romance*. And indeed it is, but it is also a novel of ideas, an imaginative but also erudite exploration of literary history, and an intelligent and witty satire about the modern academic enterprise. The film retains some of this narrational richness. It is still decidedly a romance, but the details of academic research become something closer to a detective thriller, albeit one that retains an academic veneer. The film also lacks the novel's intellectual pretensions. The basic outline of the story and some of the key characters and events remain the same. But other material that is vital to the novel must make do in the film with a passing visual reference or a suggestive moment of dialogue.

The narrative is about a group of academics piecing together the story of a love affair between two Victorian poets. Perhaps one of the main changes is that in the novel we only know the Victorians through their letters, poems, diaries and journals, and through academics reconstructing their lives. In the film, however, the past is brought to life, given an aural and a visual substance, with the characters taking on a flesh-and-blood existence that is as real on the screen as the academics in the present. These are then two quite distinct modes of narration, the

one reworking in postmodernist fashion the conventions of the epistolary novel; the other adopting throughout the familiar present historic
tense and third-person narration of the classic story film.

Of course, it is not as simple as this. The film, for instance, moves
enigmatically between present and past, often in the same shot,
interweaving its two sets of characters in a richly suggestive manner. It
also in various ways absorbs extracts from the letters, poems and diaries
by various aural and visual means. Much of the novel, on the other hand,
adopts a familiar third-person narration for the present-day events –
but also for three brief passages set in the past, which are, in a quite
surprising way, given the same treatment as the present-day scenes.
But where Byatt views all her characters through a strongly ironic lens,
LaBute and his collaborators present them straight.

Adaptations of self-consciously literary novels will often include scenes
of people reading or writing, in an effort to regain something of the literate quality of the word. This wordiness will sometimes attract criticism,
since it is felt not to do justice to the 'essentially visual' quality of cinema. Such criticism seems misplaced if the point is precisely to establish
overtly literary reference points. In the case of *Possession*, it seems entirely
appropriate to adapt a sometimes epistolary novel about two poets, and
the effort to know them through contemporary written archival material,
by including scenes of people reading or reciting poetry, or extracts from
journals and diaries. Sometimes the recitation is in voice-over, sometimes
it is delivered on screen, sometimes we see the author writing something,
which we also hear spoken both in their own voice and in the voice of one
of the present-day detective-academics. These are highly conventional
strategies of the self-consciously literary adaptation at the quality end
of the market. Another familiar strategy is to take material that is given
as authorial commentary in the novel and refigure it as character dialogue in the film. An interesting instance of this comes in the final scene
of *Possession*, interesting partly because it is one of the very few passages
in the novel where historical characters come to life rather than exist only
through the writing they have left behind. But it is also notable for the
self-consciousness of the narration in both novel and film.

In the opening paragraph of the postscript, Byatt writes:

> There are things which happen and leave no discernible trace, are not spo-
> ken or written of, though it would be very wrong to say subsequent events
> go on indifferently, all the same, as though such things had never been.

Two people met, on a hot May day, and never later mentioned their meeting. This is how it was.[22]

Byatt goes on to describe a meeting between one of the Victorian poets, Ash, and the little daughter he never knew he had. The scene is reproduced in all its essentials in the film. It opens with Ash, played by Jeremy Northam, walking through a summer field. In voice-over, Northam delivers an abbreviated and slightly reworded version of Byatt's opening paragraph, finishing, like Byatt, with the self-consciously narrational phrase 'This is how it was'. Northam and a young girl then play out the scene almost as Byatt has described it, reusing some of her dialogue. The incongruity of Northam commenting on his own character's destiny may be unusual, but the details of how a passage from a novel is refigured for the screen are in many ways typical: narrative condensation, the audio-visual rendering of characters, events and settings, the transposition of the written word as the spoken word, and so on.

There are other changes at the level of the script, three of which LaBute himself has commented on, noting that the changes were designed to improve the dramatic structure of the film as a film, rather than as an obsessively faithful adaptation.[23] First, the number of present-day academics centrally involved in the story is reduced to two, with some being cut altogether and others playing bit parts that are quite different from the much fuller development they receive in the novel. Second, one of those two characters, Roland, is transformed from an English research assistant to an American, ostensibly to create a greater dramatic tension with his (English) counterpart, Maud, as they work out their own romantic relationship. (Ironically, Maud is played by the American actress Gwyneth Paltrow.) LaBute claims that the refiguring of an Englishman as an American was 'not [done] as a way to reach a wider American audience', but it will certainly have helped in that respect, and will no doubt have helped win Warner Bros. over to the script. Third, another of the academics, Cropper, who plays a large part in the novel but is reduced to a much smaller character in the film, is at the same time required to take on the role of evil antagonist, in effect a mere cipher of a felt dramatic requirement, to act as a foil to the two protagonists.

All these changes were made at the scripting stage. The screenplay, however, is by no means the end of the process of adaptation. As LaBute puts it, 'You make [the film] one time when you write it and you make it again when you shoot it and you make it a third time when you edit it'.[24] Each time, a different set of creative workers, a different set of collaborators, is involved. Actors, and especially stars, must be cast to play the characters; they must be dressed by the costume designer, and must inhabit buildings and landscapes created or chosen by the production designer; and all of this must be filmed by the director of photography and his or her team. The director will interact with each of these co-workers to produce the look or feel they are aiming for.

One of the effects of envisaging the past in the film, filling out the diegesis of the Victorian period, is to give the film a generic texture that is not there in the novel. For part of its screen time, the film thus adopts the conventions of the period costume drama, the English heritage film. With actors such as Jeremy Northam and Jennifer Ehle, rich mid-Victorian costumes, interior designs and modes of transport, ancient buildings and stately homes set in rolling green parkland, all familiar from a host of other costume dramas about the modern English past, a whole new dimension of intertextuality is thereby brought into play. Even the shooting style, with its frequent long takes and ornate tableau shots, is reminiscent of other heritage films. The problem of adaptation is in one sense about the degree and type of intertextuality that is allowed or encouraged – and in some cases unexpectedly made possible by historical circumstances beyond the control of the filmmakers. For the literary faithful, the intertextual references should be limited to a strong sense of resemblance between the source novel and the film adaptation. But for others, it is recognised that the film must have a life of its own, that its dramatic structure, its audio-visual design and the interplay of its characters must work in their own right, without spectators feeling they have to read the novel to make sense of the film.

This is not to suggest for a moment that the film operates in a vacuum; it is to demonstrate that the source novel is far from its only intertext. In fact, each new ingredient introduced to the film will make its own aesthetic and cultural demands on the shape and feel of that film. Casting any star brings with it memories of the star's previous roles and their public image above and beyond any particular roles. Casting Paltrow as Maud for instance enabled the film to benefit from several other films of the period in which Paltrow played refined English characters (*Emma*, 1996; *Shakespeare in Love*, 1998; *Sliding Doors*, 1998). On the other hand, it also brought her presence as an American star of a particular type, and LaBute notes that he consciously modelled her first entrance in the film on that of Grace Kelly in *Rear Window* (Alfred Hitchcock, 1954).[25]

American star Gwyneth Paltrow plays an English woman in *Possession*.

Finally, there is the post-production stage, where the material that has been shot must be edited into shape, and often a music track added. There is no music in Byatt's *Possession*, of course, but the events in the film are insistently overlaid with a romantic music track that plays a large part in colouring the way that audiences respond to particular scenes and characters. At the editing stage, story material may well be reorganised, or scenes and even whole characters cut out. Occasionally, this final shaping of material may suggest that a new scene needs to be added, as happened with *Possession*, when the two stars were recalled to shoot some extra footage which it was felt was needed to give the film required dramatic shape and density.[26]

Possession the film is then very different from *Possession* the novel. The latter was a tour de force, both critically and commercially. The adaptation endeavoured to exploit that cultural presence and to find a means of reproducing the novel in a way that would work for cinema audiences. As such, it can be seen as an example of English literary cinema, a distinct niche within the transnational arrangements that I'm calling English cinema – this film was, after all, made very much under the sway of Hollywood. Those involved with the production clearly hoped that its middlebrow qualities as a film would enable it to bridge the gulf between the mass market and the art house, in the same way that Byatt's novel had evidently crossed over from the serious literature market to become a best-seller.

As ever, the question of national identity in the film is complex. There is no escaping the Englishness of the source material, in the sense that this is both an adaptation of a novel by an English writer and a story about English characters. That Englishness is played up in generic terms in the film, with the Victorian past created according to the conventions of so many other English heritage films, and especially costume dramas set in the nineteenth century. Arguably, this lends the film an English exoticism that can be exploited in the international marketplace, including the English market. On the other hand, the Englishness is played down, by reworking one of the English characters in the novel as an American in the film, while the danger of cultural discount for audiences accustomed to American cinema is further assuaged by casting the American star Paltrow in the role of the lead English character in the present-day sections of the film.

Adaptations of stories by English writers and others with a close connection to the UK featured prominently in cinemas worldwide in the 1990s and 2000s. Versions of novels by the likes of Ian Fleming, Rudyard Kipling, C.S. Lewis, Patrick O'Brian, J.K. Rowling, Dodie Smith, J.R.R. Tolkien and H.G. Wells ensured that what we might call an English sensibility maintained a presence in mainstream cinemas. But there were also plenty of critically acclaimed adaptations of English stories at the middlebrow or specialist end of the market, from *Howards End*, *The Wings of the Dove* and *Pride and Prejudice*, to *Possession*, *Last Orders* and *Atonement*. If these collectively constitute an English literary cinema, it is worth noting the diversity of that cinema. The film business has consistently expressed an interest in four different types of published fiction. First, there are the best-sellers, contemporary fiction that proves its commercial clout through sales figures; second, there are the critically acclaimed, self-consciously literary novels by contemporary writers; third, there are adaptations of classic literature from the historical canon; and fourth, there are one-offs, adaptations of stories that have no real reputation or commercial track record, but that have appealed to filmmakers – as in the case of *Ladies in Lavender*, an adaptation of a little-known short story by a long-forgotten writer.

The diversity of English literary filmmaking is also evident in the types of films that have been adapted from English stories, ranging from big-budget, Hollywood-led franchises, via European and other foreign-language adaptations, to low-budget English productions. Through such films, a great many versions of Englishness feature on the screen – although in some cases, Englishness simply doesn't feature, either because of the type of story or the way it is presented (in dubbed versions for foreign-language markets, for instance, or in adaptations that rework the characters and settings of the source novel in quite radical ways). If the English literary cinema embraces the Bond films and the Harry Potter films, as well as adaptations of Booker Prize-winning novels, it cannot be said that all such films are likely to be described as *literate* films by reviewers: in the field of literary adaptations, such a description will be reserved for prestige or art-house films adapted from so-called quality literature. At the same time, of course, prestige films or art-house films with no literary source text are just as likely to be described as literate. What is at stake here is a particular conception of both literature and cinema, a particular sense of cultural value.

As the case of *Possession* illustrates, literature and cinema remain distinct media, yet feed off and are coloured by each other in a variety of often quite intricate ways. As businesses, publishing and the film industry frequently engage with each other, to their mutual benefit. The English literary cinema and the wider field of literary adaptations have undoubtedly made their mark on English film culture – but not as indelibly as some have claimed. The cultural status of 'serious literature' has certainly helped shape a particular strand of English cinema, its audiences and its apologists – but there are many other strands to English cinema, both as a historical phenomenon and in its contemporary guise, and mainstream filmmakers have found it as productive as those at the more specialised, niche end of the market to work with literary sources. The ways in which the process of literary adaptation has shaped cinema are by no means necessarily to the detriment of cinema as a cultural practice; nor are they by any means clear-cut, as the diversity of films adapted from novels should make clear. That diversity can be seen in the various ways in which Jane Austen's life, work, characters and cultural reputation have been taken up in contemporary cinema and television, which is the subject of the next two chapters.

5 Jane Austen: 'the hottest scriptwriter in Hollywood'

Austen on screen

Across the history of cinema, the two English authors that have perhaps held the most fascination for filmmakers have been William Shakespeare and Charles Dickens. Since the early days of silent cinema, there have been versions of their plays and novels produced for the screen, as well as films depicting the lives of the authors. But the 1990s and the 2000s were surely the moment of Jane Austen: for an author who had been dead for nearly 200 years, Jane Austen was remarkably prolific in generating material for the screen in this period. The Anglo-American film and television industries went out of their way in these years to sell Jane Austen to audiences in cinemas and in the living room. And there is no doubt they did a good job too, if we measure their success in terms of ticket sales and television ratings, critical adulation and audience interest.

When *Sense and Sensibility* appeared in cinemas in 1995, it was the first English-language Austen adaptation with a period setting to do so for more than half a century. Since then, Austen has inspired films that engage with the literary process from authorship to readership – from the biopic *Becoming Jane* (2007) to the contemporary drama about a reading group *The Jane Austen Book Club* (2007). Five adaptations of her novels adopted period settings and found their way into cinemas, from *Persuasion* in 1995 to *Pride and Prejudice* in 2005. Alongside those adaptations that played as period dramas that attempted to reproduce the historical period in which Austen was writing were other reinterpretations of her work that adopted a modern-day setting, from the American high-school romantic comedy *Clueless* (1995) to the Anglo-Bollywood musical *Bride and Prejudice* (2004).

In 1995–6, when a spate of Austen adaptations appeared on cinema and television screens, commentators coined the term Austenmania – a

Clueless: re-working Jane Austen's *Emma* as an American high school romantic comedy.

mania in which Colin Firth as Darcy in the BBC adaptation of *Pride and Prejudice* (1995) played a central part. Subsequent productions explored the possibilities of a fanatical obsession with Austen's novels, themes and characters – in *Bridget Jones's Diary* (2001), for instance, where Colin Firth reappeared as a modern-day Darcy, and in *Lost in Austen* (2008), a television series that saw a young twenty-first-century fan of Austen play out the ultimate literary fantasy as she was transported back in time to the fictional-historical world of *Pride and Prejudice*. At the time of writing, *Pride and Predator* was reported to be in development, combining the pleasures of an Austen period adaptation with the alien/horror genre: 'it felt like a fresh and funny way to blow apart the done-to-death Jane Austen genre by literally dropping this alien into the middle of a costume drama, where he stalks and slashes to horrific effect'.[1] Whether this will see the light of day probably depends upon another production in development at the time of writing, an adaptation of a mash-up novel, *Pride and Prejudice and Zombies*, in which a deadly virus has an equally horrific effect on Austen's characters.[2]

Jane Austen's status is as a canonical *English* author, whose work chronicling a particular moment in English history is at the same time one of the high points of English literature. Part of the appeal of the period adaptations is their reproduction of a self-consciously English historical milieu, even if that milieu is shown to be problematic in all sorts of ways. In some of the looser modern-day adaptations, however, Englishness is no longer on the agenda, as in the two adaptations set in contemporary USA, *Clueless* and *Pride and Prejudice – A Latter-Day Comedy* (2003), a low-budget film made primarily with the Mormon community in mind. *Kandukondain Kandukondain* (2000), meanwhile, is a modern-day Indian version of *Sense and Sensibility*, done in Bollywood musical style with the characters speaking in Tamil. *Bride and Prejudice* does something similar, but this time the drama involves relations between the Indian characters and various English but also American characters, and moves between India, England and the USA.

It doesn't really work to define these various Austen films as a genre, but in a film business increasingly driven by franchises, there is some logic to seeing the fascination with Austen in terms of a franchise or a brand, a sort of respectable middlebrow niche version of the Harry Potter or the James Bond movies – except that the brand is spread across a variety of producers and distributors, and across film and television screens, rather than being jealously guarded by one particular company. The brand extends beyond the film/television/publishing tie-ins too. Outlets like the gift shop at the Jane Austen Centre in Bath do a good business in Austen-branded fridge magnets, mugs, figurines, prints, tea towels, cross-stitch kits, needlepoint gifts, stationery sets, board games and foodstuffs, as well as books, audio CDs, DVDs and magazines like *Jane Austen's Regency World*, 'the only colour magazine about Jane Austen'. Some 42,000 people visit the Centre each year, 90 per cent of them women, while its website is even more popular. At the height of the mid-1990s Austenmania, one year 57,000 people visited Austen's family home at Chawton in Hampshire, and by the mid-2000s admissions were still at a steady 25–30,000 yearly. There is also a host of dedicated Austen websites, most notably the Republic of Pemberley website, 'Your haven in a world programmed to misunderstand obsession with things Austen'.[3] And there are numerous sequels to Austen's novels, rewrites and other literary extensions of Austen's writing, including Arielle Eckstut's *Pride and Promiscuity: The Lost Sex Scenes of Jane Austen*.[4]

For the self-appointed guardians of Austen's legacy, such as David Baldock, director of the Jane Austen Centre, 'there is always a worry [that the Austen industry] will become too commercial', but it could always be justified because 'it is bringing new people to her work'. Maggie Lane, honorary secretary of the UK's Jane Austen Society, also argued that 'the more people that know about her the better'.[5] Janeites, as the dedicated fans of Austen are referred to, are among the most vigorous and vociferous of cultural guardians, and have an ambivalent relationship with screen versions of the literary Austen. Some of the adaptations, reworkings and spin-offs done for film and television have certainly proved controversial – and there is clearly a wealth of difference between those adaptations that are sold as 'authentic' and faithful period reproductions and those that much more self-consciously play with Austen's themes and characters. The much looser, modern-day adaptations are obviously much less concerned with questions of historical realism or with what is traditionally regarded as faithful adaptation, and approach Austen, her novels and her characters in very different ways.

In one way or another, though, all these screen dramas engage with the literary Austen, and all of them have been discussed in relation to the author, her novels and her life and times. Indeed, there is an extensive academic debate about Austen screen dramas as literary adaptations, a debate which itself, even when it is least complimentary about the dramas, reinforces the relationship between them and their literary forebears.[6] It is therefore important to engage with the adaptation debate and to consider its terms of reference. But it is also important to move beyond that debate and to look at the films and television programmes as cultural products in their own right, cultural products that engage with other concerns besides Austen's, and whose intertextual references are by no means limited to her novels. Indeed, for some audiences, the novels are simply not part of the world in which the films and television programmes operate.

It is difficult, though, when looking at the films and television programmes, and at the debate surrounding them, to escape the traces of the literary Austen or of the broader literary process. The credits at the start of the 1995 *Sense and Sensibility* tell us that the film has been 'adapted from the novel by Jane Austen', or, as the theatrical trailer puts it, 'from Jane Austen's timeless classic'. Patricia Rozema's 1999 adaptation of *Mansfield Park*, meanwhile, is credited on screen as 'based on

Jane Austen's novel *Mansfield Park*, her letters and early journals'. Such on-screen homages are both frequent and important to the cultural status of the films – although by the time of the 2005 *Pride and Prejudice*, all but the main company credits have been moved to the end of the film, so the acknowledgment of Austen's authorship is much more reticent. Her name also rarely appears on the front covers of DVD versions of the films, to make way for other invitations to consumers. The front cover of the British *Pride and Prejudice* DVD, for instance, quotes the *Daily Mail*'s judgement that this is 'beyond any doubt the romantic comedy-drama of 2005'.

If Austen's authorship is sometimes kept in the background, writing and reading as activities are frequently part of the diegetic worlds of these dramas. Thus the central characters of *Mansfield Park*, a period adaptation, *Pride and Prejudice – A Latter-Day Comedy* – which, as its title suggests, is an updated version of the story – and, of course, the Austen biopic *Becoming Jane* write fiction, while Bridget Jones writes her diary. In the period versions of the novels, there are scenes set in the grand libraries of country houses, and characters read aloud to each other or quietly to themselves. Thus Marianne and Willoughby read poetry in *Sense and Sensibility*, Lizzie reads a novel as she strides into view at the start of the 2005 version of *Pride and Prejudice* – while the premise of *The Jane Austen Book Club* is that the protagonists get together in modern-day California to read and discuss Austen's novels. *Mansfield Park*, *Becoming Jane* and *The Jane Austen Book Club* all engage in their different ways with literary authorship and specifically the production of Austen's oeuvre.

Another of the key ways in which the literature/film relationship is mobilised is through publishing tie-ins – and most of these films were tied in with novels appearing in new editions, featuring publicity material that linked them directly to the films: 'now a major film', reads the banner on the front of such books. Bloomsbury, for instance, brought out a British paperback edition of *Sense and Sensibility* to tie in with the film release in 1996, using the main publicity images, title design and stars' names on the front cover. Meanwhile, in the USA, Signet Publishing printed 250,000 copies of the book rather than the usual 10,000 a year of their mass-market tie-in, Everyman's Library/Knopf Publishing printed 50,000 hardcover copies, and Penguin Audiobooks brought out a version of the novel read by Julie Christie.[7] There were other kinds of literary tie-in too. For instance, Emma Thompson's script for *Sense and Sensibility* was published, along with extracts from a diary she kept during the making of the film, in both a hard-bound coffee-table version with copious colour photographs, and a paperback version, minus the script and the photographs – and even the hard-bound version sold 28,500 copies in its first printing in the USA.[8] Another important way in which the literature/film relationship is mobilised is through the appearance of weighty pieces on the various Austen adaptations in upmarket journalistic outlets such as the *New York Review of Books* and the *Times Literary Supplement.*[9]

There is now a good deal of academic writing about the various Austen adaptations of the 1990s and 2000s.[10] When this work deals with the films, it deals with them precisely as Austen adaptations, and is therefore interested in their relationships with the novels and with the historical period in which they were written. Much of it is written by literary historians and critics who have an intimate knowledge of Austen's novels and their historical context. And of course much of this writing focuses on the way that the novels have been adapted to the circumstances of the moving image business and its audiences in the 1990s, the changes that have been made in order to sell Austen's work to late twentieth-century and early twenty-first-century consumers.

Much of this work on the Austen films is fascinating, but there is much more to the films than the ways in which they compare to the novels. I certainly don't ignore the literary connection and the question of adaptation in what follows, but my purpose is to focus on some of the other circumstances of the films. Thus I want to take account of the fact that the Austen films are cultural products that were produced and then circulated in a particular industrial context. From this point of view, it's important to acknowledge the fact that the film business was more concerned to provide experiences that might meet the expectations of contemporary movie audiences than it was to create texts that reproduced exactly what Austen intended, or that represented the early nineteenth-century world in precise historical detail. I also want to consider some of the intertextual frames within which audiences enjoyed and interpreted these films besides the adaptation frame or the Austen frame. To put it crudely, I want to examine how Jane Austen was sold to non-Janeites, how a particular type of period chick lit, albeit an upscale version of chick lit much appreciated by male intellectuals, was transformed into the multiplex-friendly frock flick or the contemporary romantic comedy-drama.

The problem with the adaptation debate is precisely that it situates the films first and foremost as adaptations, affording far too much primacy to the novels and to Austen's authorship. It assumes too often that film audiences only relate to the films through the novels – and that if they don't, they should. It overlooks the fact that the 1996 film version of *Emma* could for some audiences be marketed as 'based on the story that inspired the hit movie CLUELESS!'[11] Or that reviewers could describe *Sense and Sensibility* as 'a beautifully crafted, witty, moving film likely to overcome even the stiffest Austen prejudice'.[12] Adaptations are clearly readings of the source text – and very public readings at that. But because the adaptation debate generally starts from the point of view of the novels and their canonical status, it too often sees the films as a form of cultural debasement, what American Austen scholars have referred to as '"E-Z" Austen',[13] or 'the harlequinization of Austen'.[14] Too often, then, the adaptation debate will suggest that films offer inadequate, or inappropriate, or unfaithful readings. From this point of view, film adaptations are seen as dreadful travesties of the source text, violations of its cultural integrity, mass-market commodities that fail to do justice to the cultural complexities of the source.

As John Wiltshire points out, the debate very often seems to be about trying to rescue Austen from the adaptations, and from popular culture in general, rather than about responding to the adaptations as films in their own right.[15] The adaptation debate will thus often focus on what seems to have been lost in adapting a culturally prestigious source text as a film, or about how the author of the source text has been misrepresented. Of course it would be foolish to deny that the films give Austen's characters, plots and themes a late twentieth-century or early twenty-first-century slant, rendering them closer to Hollywood, recreating them for contemporary consumers. But then much of the literary-historical scholarship around Austen is about situating her in the culture, society and political economy of her period, explaining why her novels take the shape that they do, so it seems rash to admonish the film adaptations of the 1990s or the 2000s for being similarly steeped in the culture, society and political economy of the period in which they were produced.

In any case, it's important to recognise that if by some standards the films are closer to Hollywood, some of the filmmakers at the same time endeavour to keep their distance from Hollywood, by insisting on the literariness of their films, by insisting on their fidelity to Austen, their historical authenticity, their English cultural refinement, their sense of good taste. It's also important to think about what has been *gained* in the process of adaptation, rather than lost from the 'original'. The most productive accounts of adaptation from this point of view are those that try to understand an adaptation in its own terms, as a product of the moment in which it was produced, and addressed to audiences with their own contemporary preoccupations and interests.

Accounts of adaptation from this point of view will focus on the process of authorship involved in the production of the adaptation, rather than fetishising the author of the source text and focusing on the fidelity or otherwise of the adaptation. They will also take on board how the adaptation works for *all* of its audiences, and not just the dedicated readers of the source text. Literature is thus treated rather differently from this perspective. The novel tends to be regarded as a cultural commodity that is bartered in the marketplace, rather than as a text that needs to be examined subtly and in detail. What the film industry buys into, as much as anything else, is the cultural status of the novel and its author. From this point of view, it is less a question of how faithful an adaptation is to its source text, and more about how the discourse of fidelity is mobilised in the promotion and reception of the film.

The ability to appeal to different audiences was important to the design of the Austen films of the 1990s and 2000s. Thus several of them were designed to work both for those who want to see a Hollywood love story or a romantic comedy and for those who want to see an 'authentic' Austen adaptation. Talking about his 1995 film version of *Sense and Sensibility*, for instance, the director Ang Lee explained: 'we wanted to do something that breaks away from the stereotype of the period drama. … We want people to laugh and to cry and to think about the movie. The same thing, we believe, Jane Austen was doing to her readers, except that we have to do it with the modern movie goer, a broader audience.'[16] It was the same; but it was different. The extensive debate about the films among reviewers, cultural commentators and academics is testament to their success in reaching different audiences. And the contrariness of that debate, the fact that there are so many divergent readings of the films, some seeing them as feminist, some as having edited out Austen's feminism, and so on, is, I would argue, testament to both the richness of the films and the fecundity of the reception process.

'Austenmania' in the mid-1990s

There have of course been numerous *television* adaptations of Austen's novels over the years – classic serials, one-off dramas, and mini-series.

But until the mid-1990s, *film* adaptations intended for theatrical release were very rare indeed. MGM had made a version of *Pride and Prejudice* in 1940, starring Laurence Olivier and Greer Garson – and it's worth noting that this was sold both as an Austen adaptation and as a romantic comedy with no apparent literary reference points, a dual address that would become increasingly familiar with Austen films in the 1990s and 2000s.[17] But after that production, Janeites had to wait more than half a century for another immediately recognisable English-language Austen adaptation to appear in cinemas. And having waited all that time, what should happen but that several such adaptations came along all at once?

In 1995, *Persuasion* was made as a one-off television drama by the BBC, although it later enjoyed an art-house cinema release in the USA. It was followed onto British television screens later in the year by a six-part serialisation of *Pride and Prejudice*, again on the BBC. The enormous success of this adaptation, and the adulation that audiences showed for Colin Firth's Darcy, prompted the press to coin the phrase 'Austenmania'. Nor did the phenomenon stop there. Midway through *Pride and Prejudice*'s run, the modern-day reworking of *Emma*, *Clueless*, appeared in the UK's cinemas, to be followed early the following year by a film version of *Sense and Sensibility*. Later in 1996, two adaptations of *Emma* reached British audiences, with the film version being released in cinemas just two months before ITV showed a new television version, this time as a single drama – and like the BBC *Pride and Prejudice*, it was scripted by Andrew Davies. With new adaptations of four of Austen's six finished novels reaching British screens, Austenmania had really taken hold in the UK.

In the USA, too, Austen adaptations were experienced in a rush. Numerous heavyweight reviews in the press took advantage of the appearance between August 1995 and January 1996 of *Clueless*, *Persuasion* and *Sense and Sensibility* in the cinemas, and *Pride and Prejudice* on the Arts and Entertainment cable network. The press frequently referred to Austen as 'the hottest writer in showbusiness',[18] or 'the hottest script property in Hollywood these days',[19] while *Newsweek* ran a headline 'Jane Austen Does Lunch', and quoted Charles Denton, head of BBC drama, proposing that 'Jane Austen is obviously the Quentin Tarantino of the middle classes'.[20] This rush of adaptations was clear evidence that the cult of Jane Austen had reached a new level, with film, television and the publishing business all getting involved. The mix

Persuasion: deliberately low-key and de-glamorised.

of 'authentic' period adaptations and looser reworkings like *Clueless* was also indicative of the effort to spread the appeal of Austen across a range of markets. The fact that *Persuasion* was shown in the UK as a television drama and in the USA as an art-house film simply underlined the various ways in which such products could work – although its difference from the other two period film adaptations, *Sense and Sensibility* and *Emma*, was also revealing. Where *Persuasion* was deliberately low-key and de-glamorised, the other two films both had up-and-coming or established stars and production values to match.

Did this sudden onslaught of six separate Austen adaptations also say something about the period in which they all appeared in the mid-1990s? Was there a good reason for so many Austen adaptations seeing the light of day at the same time? Several commentators argued that there was. It was a response to the loss of genuine social values, argued some, a response to the collapse of a caring, ordered society, a search for a more ethical stance in an increasingly unethical world. The screen dramas thus represented 'nostalgia for a more decorous and polite age'.[21] Yet others argued that Austen's work had a timeless, universal quality which ensured that the films possessed a different sort of contemporary relevance – although this could hardly explain why so many Austen adaptations appeared in the mid-1990s. Austen films were also an antidote to 'so much of what Hollywood has offered lately'; *Sense and Sensibility*, for instance, was a film in which, precisely, 'sense and intelligence ... prevail'.[22] This was another version of literate cinema.

There is little evidence that film and television producers went out of their way to produce an Austen cycle, however – although apparently Orion Pictures did at one point at the height of Austenmania option Austen's unfinished novel *Sanditon* for production.[23] The marketing people of course had a field day, tying each new adaptation into the audience base and public awareness that had been established for the previous one. But there is little evidence of producers carefully planning these films and television programmes as a coherent cycle at the production stage. In fact, like James Collins,[24] I think the appearance of four Austen adaptations in cinemas in the space of just over a year is probably much more coincidental, especially given the length of time some of the films were in gestation, and the fact that there wasn't enough time between the success of one film and the appearance of another for the latter film to be conceived and produced. They were all quite different productions, handled by separate companies, the only common ground being that *Persuasion* was handled by the specialty distribution division of Sony, while *Sense and Sensibility* was produced by the their mainstream arm, Columbia Pictures. There were much closer connections between the television adaptations of *Pride and Prejudice* and *Emma*: both were scripted by Andrew Davies, produced by Sue Birtwistle, and co-funded by the American company A&E Television Networks – but the first was made by the BBC and the second by Meridian/ITV.

To provide a more thorough explanation of why four Austen films appeared in cinemas in such a short space of time, it is necessary to look at the productions in a broader context, and especially to look beyond the Austen connection. I would argue that it is in fact much easier to see the emergence of these four Austen films in the mid-1990s as evidence of the intense exploitation of two broad industry production trends than it is to see them as evidence of a very specific cultural turn that required the rediscovery of Jane Austen. The audiences for Austen films were not simply, and in some cases not at all, looking back to Austen as a key woman writer of the early nineteenth century. Nor were they necessarily particularly interested in the historical details of the period.

Clearly, the fact of adaptation is important to how these films are conceived, how they're developed by the filmmakers, how they're discussed by critics and how they're received by audiences. Adaptation is thus an important framing device, and an important promotional strategy. But fidelity to the source text is by no means the only interpretive frame through which audiences make sense of the films. For many audiences of the Austen adaptations, they were perhaps above all engaging with particular types of films of the 1990s: on the one hand, the tasteful, middlebrow period drama with an English setting and characters, strong literary connections, and an intense appeal to female viewers; and on the other hand, the romantic comedy-drama, which embraces both the period version of *Emma* and the contemporary update, *Clueless*.

The three Austen films with period settings are very much symptoms of the middlebrow English period drama production trend. That is, they are the products of a particular business strategy, a particular way of operating within the global film economy. *Emma* and *Sense and Sensibility* – and later in different ways the 1999 film version of *Mansfield Park* and the 2005 version of *Pride and Prejudice* – were produced by a Hollywood fascinated by the potential of the co-production and the modestly budgeted crossover film that might work in both specialised, art-house cinemas and in the multiplexes, a type of film that might cross over from the niche market to the mainstream. *Emma*, *Sense and Sensibility* and later *Pride and Prejudice* simply ratcheted up the strategy a notch or two closer to the mainstream.

The Austen period films were thus variants of the English heritage film, attempts by the industry to prolong the Anglo-Hollywood costume drama production trend. Thus, while they share a great deal as Austen adaptations, they also share much with a great many other tasteful costume dramas, historical films and period literary adaptations of the 1990s and 2000s, from *Howards End* (1992) and *The Remains of the Day* (1993) to *The Wings of the Dove* (1997) and *Gosford Park* (2001), from *Mrs Brown* (1997) and *Elizabeth* (1998) to *Atonement* (2007) and *The Other Boleyn Girl* (2008). The particular commercial success in the early 1990s of the Merchant Ivory films, and especially *Howards End* and *The Remains of the Day*, and other films adapted from classic literature, like *Little Women* (1994), produced by Columbia, the same company that produced *Sense and Sensibility*, clearly paved the way for the appearance of several Austen films in the mid-1990s.

By situating the period film adaptations of Austen's novels in the context of this production trend, I want to divert attention away from the specifics of adaptation and the relationship with the source text. Audiences make sense of films in relation to representational traditions with which they're already familiar – and that won't always be by reference to Austen. Accordingly, in the pages that follow, I outline some of the features of the Anglo-Hollywood costume drama production trend that shaped the production and reception of the period Austen adaptations. Although much of what follows applies as much to the 2000s as the 1990s, I will concentrate here on the context of the mid-1990s.

The Anglo-Hollywood costume drama production trend in the 1990s

As I have demonstrated elsewhere, the costume drama produced or co-produced by English companies, and/or with some engagement with the English past and the English cultural inheritance, was a prominent feature of English filmmaking in the 1990s.[25] While Austen's novels are historically specific, for many people the adaptations are simply period films, and so belong with other period films, almost regardless of the period in which they are set, so long as it is far enough back in the past. Even if we ignore films set in or after the Second World War, there were some 80 English period dramas produced between 1990 and 2000 that fell into this category. This meant that something like one in every ten British or Anglo-Hollywood films of the period was a frock flick set before the Second World War – and the Austen adaptations clearly form only a very small proportion of those 80 films.[26]

The literary connection is of course vital to this production trend. Of the 80 pre-Second World War Anglo-Hollywood costume dramas produced between 1990 and 2000, some 55 were literary or dramatic adaptations of one sort or another, while several others had strong literary connections, including the various biopics about writers, such as *Tom and Viv* (1994), *Carrington* (1995), *Wilde* (1997) and *Shakespeare in Love* (1998). In other words, around 70 per cent of the English period films of the 1990s had strong literary connections. The Austen films are again just a small part of this English literary cinema, a cinema addressed in part to audiences who have a strong attachment to literary culture. From the point of view of the film industry, as noted above, adaptation is in part a marketing strategy, a way of producing a film that is in some significant way 'pre-sold'. For the industry, the adaptation of canonical literature is thus both a way of engaging with particular niche tastes and niche audiences, and a way of ensuring that the film has an audience on its release. In this context, as noted above, it is less important whether a film adaptation is faithful to its literary source text than how the discourse of fidelity and the cultural status of the source text and its author are mobilised in the production, promotion and reception of the film.

Female authorship is another significant feature of the English costume drama of the 1990s on the one hand and the Austen film franchise on the other. Thus, of those 80 pre-Second World War period films produced between 1990 and 2000, 11 were directed by women, including the 1999 version of *Mansfield Park*; 12 were written by women, including *Sense and Sensibility* and *Mansfield Park* (and later the 2005 version of *Pride and Prejudice*); 20 were adapted from novels by women, including of course all the Austen adaptations; 21 had female production designers, including *Sense and Sensibility*; 25 had female producers or executive producers, including *Persuasion*, *Sense and Sensibility*, *Emma* and *Mansfield Park*; and, perhaps least surprising of all, 70 had female costume designers, including all four Austen adaptations. All of these women – as well as the many female stars of these films – can lay some claim to having authored the films, shaping how they appeared to audiences. Female authorship, in a broad sense, thus plays an important role in the development of the English heritage film, including the period Austen adaptations. It is worth noting that several of the contemporary reworkings in the Austen franchise also draw on female authorship. *Clueless*, the two Bridget Jones films, *Bride and Prejudice* and *The Jane Austen Book Club* were all written (or co-written) and directed by women, while the novel of *The Jane Austen Book Club* was also written by a woman, as were the Bridget Jones novels.

Even so, there is no getting away from the fact that the period film versions of *Persuasion*, *Sense and Sensibility*, *Emma* and *Pride and Prejudice* were all directed by men, while Andrew Davies scripted the television adaptations of *Pride and Prejudice* and *Emma* and co-scripted both the Bridget Jones films – and came back to write two of the more recent television adaptations, *Northanger Abbey* (2007) and *Sense and Sensibility* (2008). Authorship could also take films in quite different directions as well: the 1995 version of *Sense and Sensibility*, for instance, was occasionally discussed on its release not as an Austen film, but as 'a film by Ang Lee', as the on-screen credits would have it, and in this context it was compared with his two previous films, both of them Taiwanese – *The Wedding Banquet* (*Xi yan*, 1993) and *Eat Drink Man Woman* (*Yin shi nan nu*, 1994).[27]

If female authorship is nevertheless a significant marker of both the Austen screen dramas and the broader Anglo-Hollywood costume drama production trend, so too are female audiences. The core audience for the costume dramas, Austen-based or otherwise, was identified by distributors as more upscale than the mainstream, and more female-oriented.[28] Choice of subject matter was thus to a great extent dictated by what it was felt this audience was interested in. In terms of the upscale female audience, Austen was obviously a real winner, especially when, as in the 1990s productions of *Sense and Sensibility* and *Mansfield Park*, the feminine tropes of romance, domesticity, strong female protagonists and elegant costumes could be given a modern feminist spin. But even the fact of presenting drama resolutely organised around female characters was seen as noteworthy: 'Watching Ang Lee's adaptation of *Sense and Sensibility*, one is reminded how fresh, even how daring, portraying the daily lives of intelligent women on film can be.'[29] There were more traditional attractions too: Emma Thompson, scriptwriter and star of *Sense and Sensibility*, comments in her diary on the highly romanticised scene in the film where Willoughby emerges from the mist on a white horse to rescue an injured Marianne. She records the (male) director, Ang Lee, laughing: 'This scene is ridiculous'. Thompson and Lindsay Doran, the female producer, reply, 'it's a girl thing'.[30]

Austen's novels may be regarded by many as among the high points of English literature, but they also read as romantic stories. More generally, romantic plots are central to the costume drama production trend. While some of the films are played as straight romantic dramas, another variant is the romantic comedy – and *Emma* and *Sense and Sensibility* are clearly played in part as Hollywood romantic comedies, albeit in period garb, and with scripts 'literate' enough not to frighten off those horrified by such downmarket generic signifiers. The American trade paper *Variety*, for instance, described *Sense and Sensibility* as 'classy', but also as an 'entirely enjoyable comic melodrama' bound to do well at the box office.[31] It was evidently this sense that the story had all the qualities of good romantic comedy that attracted Lindsay Doran, the film's producer, in the first place: 'wonderful characters, a strong love story (actually, *three* strong love stories), surprising plot twists, good jokes, relevant themes and a heart-stopping ending'.[32] The production notes circulated to the press meanwhile described the novel as 'Jane Austen's celebrated and best-loved romantic comedy' and the adaptation as 'a sparkling love story'.[33] Reviewers of *Sense and Sensibility* also enjoyed the way it worked with and sometimes reworked familiar genre conventions, and thought as a result it 'might just be the heritage movie that girls who like boys who hate heritage movies will get away with taking those boys to see'.[34] Or as *Glamour* magazine put it, 'it will even please the guy you may have had to drag there kicking and screaming'.[35]

Two other films with Austen links make the romantic comedy connection even stronger: *Clueless* and *Bridget Jones's Diary*. In this vein, one might also situate the Austen adaptations alongside the broader cycle of Anglo-Hollywood romantic comedies with contemporary settings. Not just *Bridget Jones*, then, but also *Four Weddings and a Funeral* (1994), *Notting Hill* (1999) and *Love Actually* (2003). When placed in this context, it is hardly surprising that the Austen films play up desire and eroticise the characters, and especially the male characters, in a very 1990s fashion.

Of the adaptations that made their way into cinemas in the mid-1990s, the one that most impressed the more upmarket critics was the downbeat, de-glamorised *Persuasion*. What was admired was what such critics saw as its restraint, subtlety and authenticity: as one critic put it, this was 'the most thoughtful' Austen adaptation; another called it a 'supremely intelligent' adaptation, of which 'Jane Austen would have approved'.[36] For the producer, Fiona Finlay, however, the appeal of *Persuasion* was that it was above all 'very romantic':[37] 'it's a story that everyone can relate to. There's something very touching about long-lost love: I think everyone can relate to that.'[38]

As a result, even this tasteful and reserved drama was promoted in part as a conventional romantic period piece. Thus the American poster for the film showed the central couple, Anne and Wentworth, kissing, accompanied by the tagline 'It's never too late for true love'. The kiss itself caused some consternation to Janeites, since it was included in the drama at the request of the American television co-production company, WGBH/Boston, in an attempt to give the film wider appeal.[39] That attempt to widen the appeal of the film was taken a step further when the film was released for video rental. Now the cover showed two entirely different actors involved in a much more passionate and revealing pose, suggesting a much racier drama. 'Hot Austen', commented the *Times*.[40]

In many ways, the kiss at the end of *Persuasion* set the tone for most of the Austen adaptations that followed – and the reception they attracted. Emma Thompson comments in her diary on shooting a scene for *Sense and Sensibility* with her co-star Hugh Grant: 'Kissing Hugh was very lovely.

Glad I invented it. Can't rely on Austen for a snog, that's for sure.'[41] In fact, the kiss failed to make it into the final cut of the film, which remains chastely snog-free. Darcy and Elizabeth are allowed a brief kiss in the final shot of the 1995 *Pride and Prejudice*. A decade later, Keira Knightley and Matthew Macfadyen, the new Lizzie and Darcy, enjoy a very romantic kiss in the final scene of the 2005 *Pride and Prejudice* – but only in the American release print, since the British release print has a different ending. Two years later, Jane Austen herself enjoys a very sensuous screen kiss in the biopic *Becoming Jane*, a kiss which again worried Austen purists. More radically, while Fanny and Edmund enjoy a kiss at the end of the 1999 version of *Mansfield Park*, there is also a full-on sex scene – which was this time cut from the American release print, to ensure a child-friendly censorship rating.

Even with *Persuasion*, what appealed to Roger Michell, the director, was 'the idea of the author, shortly before her death, writing a novel about lost opportunities. She dies a virgin in 1817 and here she is writing an erotic love story which is full of sexual yearning.'[42] Romance, rather than openly sexual yearning, was the key selling point for the Austen films, however. The tagline used in publicity for the film version of *Emma*, for instance, presented the film as a romantic comedy rather than a Jane Austen adaptation: 'this season, cupid is armed and dangerous'. (Although, strangely, in the publicity images used in the USA, Emma is armed with a bow and arrow, and a very cheeky expression, whereas in the images used in the UK, she's armed with a teacup!)

The centrality of romantic plotlines in English costume dramas takes the 1990s Austen period adaptations in one direction. The relationship of such films to the heritage and tourism industries takes them in another. For these are also films in which a particular version of heritage England is presented as spectacle, a spectacle which tourists are encouraged to visit. For instance, the American magazine *Town and Country* ran a lavishly illustrated six-page piece at the time of the release of *Sense and Sensibility*, under the title 'Jane Austen's England'.[43] The article opened with a double-page spread, a giant photograph of Elinor and Marianne walking across a green hill, with heritage sheep in the background. The text superimposed on this photograph informed readers that 'The film version of *Sense and Sensibility* takes us to the England that was – and, in some places, still is'.[44]

In a trope typical of such journalism, it was suggested that 'the English landscape itself plays a starring role', that England 'becomes a vivacious character in a roster already rich with personalities': 'With sweeping wide-angle shots of Devon and close-ups of the human heart, it brings to life an era and a place, with present-day England doing a thoroughly convincing imitation of the turn of the 18th century'.[45] The article then moved into tourist guide mode, listing the various locations, noting that many of them were owned by the National Trust and were therefore open to the public. This England, then, is a place that can be visited, and every opportunity was taken to establish this fact. Thus the press book produced to promote *Sense and Sensibility* also listed all the locations used in the film, as did Emma Thompson's *Diaries*.[46]

An article in the *Los Angeles Times* went out of its way to sell these English settings, and especially Plymouth, to Americans: 'This historic southwestern port city has a long proud tradition of making its influence felt on America', it noted, citing Drake's voyage round the world, via California, and the Pilgrim Fathers in the *Mayflower*, which had both set off from Plymouth. Locals are quoted remarking that here is 'some of the prettiest countryside in England', which is bound to appeal to American tourists.[47] And Austen film and television adaptations do have a demonstrable effect on heritage tourism. Thus Lyme Park at Disley, Cheshire, saw a 178 per cent increase in attendances after featuring in the BBC's *Pride and Prejudice*, while Saltram House, in Devon, used in *Sense and Sensibility*, recorded a 57 per cent rise.[48] *Pride and Prejudice* was even given an award by the British Tourist Authority, in honour of the series' 'outstanding contribution to English tourism'.[49]

More generally, the 'gorgeous countryside' and 'exquisite landscape' in films like *Sense and Sensibility* was frequently noted in an approving manner by reviewers, especially American reviewers.[50] 'Deftly setting the stage in late 18th-century rural England',[51] 'the screen teems with superlative actors, brilliant costumes, [and] gorgeous landscapes'.[52] The film is 'beautifully photographed by Michael Coulter, whose camera caresses the glorious and ever moody English landscapes and the warm candelit interiors of country homes'.[53] As a result, 'Lee's vision of Austen's England is pictorially opulent... Lee lets the colors of the Devon countryside dominate...',[54] and we are provided with a vision of 'the empty skies and wooded slopes of an eighteenth-century England'.[55] 'Oh, to be in the English countryside', mused one American reviewer.[56]

For others, though, this *mise-en-scène* of the English countryside in this 'charming adaptation of Jane Austen' was more than just a series of pretty pictures, for it also played an important function in the development of character in the film.[57] 'Ang Lee triumphs. He never permits his camera to be a tourist of the English countryside but uses the settings to support the emotions of any given scene.'[58] This was seen as rather different from the BBC's version of *Pride and Prejudice*, where the camera 'looked at the countryside as if it were a National Trust guide showing yuppie Yank tourists the Stately Homes of England'.[59]

It's worth noting the effect of the iconography of English heritage cinema on the Austen films. *Sense and Sensibility* and *Emma* may have been produced by American companies but, like the BBC-produced *Persuasion*, they were shot on location in England, and frequently provide sweeping landscape shots of an apparently pre-industrial countryside. In adopting this iconography, as Ros Ballaster and Julianne Pidduck have noted, the Austen films shift away from the domestic interiors of the novels to what Pidduck calls 'the picturesque outdoors'.[60] But there are gradations of picturesqueness. In *Sense and Sensibility* and *Emma*, the landscapes are glorious; in *Persuasion*, there are still some fine landscapes, and some impressive architectural properties, but the overall tone is of a gritty realism rather than swooning spectacle. As such, *Persuasion* was establishing a tone that would be reproduced later in the film versions of *Mansfield Park*, *Pride and Prejudice* and *Becoming Jane* – although on each occasion the production team seemed to think they were doing something new.

The 'realist' approach to landscape was matched by a similar approach to costume design. Roger Michell wanted the clothes in *Persuasion* to look rumpled, for instance, the hair to look windswept when appropriate and the make-up to be very low-key. If costumes got dirty, then that was fine: 'for me, it's thrilling to see a lot of Georgians in a ploughed field getting muddy'.[61]

Englishness is clearly a vital feature of the Anglo-American period films of the 1990s. One reading of the films, as in the article from *Town and Country*, is that they are nostalgic, conservative visions of Old England, a green and pleasant land, pre-industrial, safe and welcoming ('impressions of order are supplied by its deep, green, manicured farmlands...'[62]). Reviewers who see the films in this way will frequently describe them as 'quintessentially British' (for which read 'English'),[63] while the films themselves do seem to offer a very class-bound vision of a national identity steeped in the past, but still heavily traded in the global marketplace today. But it is also possible to see these same films as offering much more complicated and ambivalent versions of national identity. Thus, many of the films depend on the spectacle of class privilege – grand houses, landscaped grounds, lavish interiors, extravagant costumes, and so on – while at the same time weaving narratives in which those privileges are critiqued or at least presented ironically, and class tensions revealed. Arguably, too, some of the films, and especially the Austen films, offer a feminised vision of Englishness, telling stories of how women were disenfranchised, disinherited and disempowered in the past.

It's also worth noting that in the Austen films, as in so many other films of the costume drama production trend, but also in English films more generally, we are invited to look at England from afar, and often from the perspective of another culture. This sense of cultural distance is built into many of the films from the moment of inception. Thus *Emma* and *Sense and Sensibility* were made for an international rather than solely English market, enjoyed American financial backing and were directed respectively by an American and a Taiwanese, while the eponymous heroine of *Emma* was played by an American. In this sense, then, these films, like so many other culturally English films, cast an un-English eye on Englishness – although this didn't stop reviewers from continuing to treat them as 'quintessentially British'. What this draws attention to once again is the paradoxical interplay of the national and the international, the local and the global, in contemporary filmmaking, especially filmmaking with an English connection. As noted in chapter 3, these are films that can be understood in terms of glocalisation, in which global or at least transnational arrangements enable the development of culturally very specific, local representations (the leisured classes in southern England in the early nineteenth century), which are then circulated to audiences on a near-global scale.

This un-Englishness will often allow a certain irreverence into the films. More specifically, in the Austen films, there is a constant tension between authenticity and irreverence. They retain an affinity with traditional Austen but, on the other hand, they also 'sex up' the novels and explore social relationships from the perspective of 1990s feminism. On the one hand, the perceived cultural status of an Austen adaptation is captured by the first screening of *Persuasion* on the BBC taking place on Easter Sunday, followed by a repeat screening on Christmas Day. On the other hand, Roger Michell, the director of *Persuasion*, declared that his intention was 'to trash the hotel room of the BBC classic'.[64] Part of what is at stake here is the desire to create drama that will appeal to contemporary audiences, rather than adaptations that are 'faithful' to their source texts. Michell's goal, then, was to make *Persuasion* 'for the people who have never read a Jane Austen book and never seen a Jane Austen serial – and perhaps never seen a BBC serial'.[65] His producer felt he had succeeded: 'Roger Michell has interpreted Persuasion in a modern way, as very fresh and accessible.'[66]

This irreverent strain is most noticeable in Patricia Rozema's 1999 version of *Mansfield Park*, which I discuss in the next chapter. But even the film version of *Emma* can be seen as irreverent: on the one hand, it is a charming, tasteful and reasonably intelligent film that makes some effort to establish historical realism; on the other, the filmmakers brought in an American star, Gwyneth Paltrow, to play the eponymous heroine, while commentators noted that the film was very fast-moving and emphasised the comic aspects of the plot. Reviewers were not slow to note how this coloured the production, remarking that the director 'keeps things moving at a delirious trot', producing an 'anachronistic snap bordering on irreverence', and 'grasping the screwball possibilities' of the plot.[67]

What makes a good adaptation? Film style and meaning

In this context, what constitutes a good film adaptation of a Jane Austen novel? The obvious answer, given the various points made above, is that there are many different ways of defining 'a good adaptation'. Different interest groups will have different tastes, different expectations; each will view the film through a different frame of reference, each will mobilise a different system of values. Films become successful by appealing to as many different interest groups or taste formations as possible. The variety of ways in which a single film adaptation might be viewed can be illustrated by examining a particular sequence from *Sense and Sensibility*.

The sequence is about 13 minutes into the film, and lasts just over three minutes. It starts inside Norland Park, the grand house in which Mrs Dashwood and her three daughters initially live. The father of the family has died, and the Dashwoods have lost possession of the house, from which they must soon move, to give way to Mr Dashwood's son, John, and his wife, Fanny, who have inherited the property. Edward Ferrars, Fanny's brother, is visiting the family. In the first scene, he walks hesitantly through the house towards a room where one of the Dashwood sisters, Marianne, is mournfully playing the piano. Her elder sister, Elinor, stands listening to the music, and is visibly upset: Marianne is playing what was their father's favourite piano piece. Edward tries to comfort

Sense and Sensibility: Edward and Elinor walk in the grounds of Norland Park.

her, and they decide to go for a walk in the grounds of the house. They pass through a hallway, conversing; the conversation continues as they walk across a lawn, with the grand house behind them, in a stunningly beautiful image (see above). Their conversation continues into the next scene, where they are now on horses, riding through more of the wonderfully picturesque grounds, with sheep and a shepherd passing by.

There are many ways in which the sequence can be understood or examined. It is for instance a fascinating exercise in adaptation. There is no equivalent passage in the novel; there are no references to Marianne playing the piano; no conversation between Edward and Elinor is reported by Austen as having taken place at Norland Park; Austen does not describe either the house or the grounds in any detail. This is not then a simple visualisation of a passage in the novel, but something created afresh in the screenplay and the finished film. However, during the conversation in the film between Edward and Elinor, Edward describes his ambitions, his prospects and the desires of his mother and sister about his possible career and social status. Something very similar does appear in the novel, but as part of Austen's omniscient narration, rather than as reported speech. The ironic tone of her narrative voice is transposed in the film to Edward's speech. This is both an effective and a typical means of adapting a novel to film. The filmic characters of Elinor and Edward and their relationship in this sequence are also effective embodiments of Austen's descriptions at various points in the first few chapters of the novel.

Adaptation is often discussed in terms of what is lost in transforming a novel into a film. This example should make it clear how important it is to also discuss adaptation in terms of what is gained in the process. There is new plot material in the film sequence, but the world of the fiction is also filled out in far greater detail in the film than in the novel. Norland Park, for instance, is given a solidity it does not have in the novel, through a series of very precise visual images. While it is possible to describe this new material as 'invented' (that is, it is not strictly there in the source text), it is also possible to argue that the new material enhances what is already there, without in any way doing injustice to the source text. To adopt such an argument is also to become aware of the multiple layers of authorship at work in the sequence, as Emma Thompson's script reworks Austen's novel, and Ang Lee and his actors and production team transform that script into a carefully designed sequence of sounds and images.

It is also possible to argue that the sequence works very effectively in filmic terms. The dialogue is clearly important, and conveys a great deal of information, but plot developments and character relations are also established through audio-visual means that exceed simple dialogue. Take for instance a single 25-second shot about halfway through the sequence, as Edward and Elinor pass through the hallway of the house, deep in conversation. The camera initially picks them up in long shot in an adjacent room; they walk towards and past the camera, which pans round to follow them as they traverse the hall and exit on the other side into the grounds. They exit the space, but the camera lingers as Elinor's mother comes into shot having descended the stairs; initially in medium shot, she walks into close-up as the camera tracks away from her. A smile appears on her face, suggesting how pleased she is for her daughter, who seems to be striking up an understanding with this pleasant and eligible young man. Maintaining the sense of fluid movement, the camera then tilts up from the close-up of Mrs Dashwood's smiling face to an extreme low-angle long shot of Fanny, on the landing above, with a scowl on her face, suggesting that she is not at all happy that her brother should be establishing an understanding with the now disinherited and therefore in her eyes worthless Elinor. The smile on Mrs Dashwood's face in retrospect appears both knowing and smug, suggesting that she is aware that Fanny has also witnessed Elinor and Edward deep in evidently enjoyable conversation and is delighted at Fanny's disquiet.

In purely aesthetic terms, it is a highly pleasing shot in its complexity, with the fluidity of the multiple camera movements (panning, tracking and tilting) matching the intricacy of the character relations sketched in. Meaning is created as much through the composition of the image as through the dialogue. The formal construction of this shot is extended across the whole sequence, with the fluidity of camera movement, character movement and conversation maintained across each of the scenes. There is a powerful sense of aesthetic coherence, as the various details of the sequence are bound together into a single meaningful entity by the persistent stylistics adopted. The characters repeatedly walk towards and past the camera, which follows their movement, and the same conversation seems to continue from interior to exterior and from one time to another. The running time of each shot remains for the most part extended, with some occasional short takes providing a further sense of aesthetic richness and variety.

In the first shot, which lasts 33 seconds, Edward walks towards the camera through adjoining rooms; as he passes the camera, it pans on his movement to observe him walking towards Elinor. There is then a brief flurry of five medium-close shots, cutting back and forth wordlessly between Edward and Elinor. Edward then resumes his movement towards Elinor, the camera this time following him, in another long 37-second take. They begin to converse, and agree to go for a walk outside, prompting a brief insert medium shot of Marianne watching as the couple walk off. The next shot is the one previously described, as they traverse the hall. After that, we pick up Edward and Elinor now outside in the grounds, with the house behind; again, they walk towards and past the camera, which pans round to follow them (45 seconds). In the two final shots, Edward and Elinor are on horseback. This is clearly a new time, since there are no horses in the previous shot and Elinor wears a different outfit. But the conversation continues as if there has been no time lapse, as does the same sense of movement past the camera. The penultimate shot, which lasts only seven seconds, is an extreme long shot; the final shot is another long take, lasting 30 seconds, in which the characters initially appear in long shot and then move into medium shot as the camera slowly pans on their continued movement across the space of Norland Park.

The fluid coherence of the whole sequence is enhanced by the music that is present throughout, and that further binds together the separate fragments of conversation, the separate fragments of interior and exterior space, and the separate fragments of time. Initially, the music is clearly diegetic, as we hear and see Marianne playing the piano. But by the time Edward and Elinor are halfway across the grounds outside, the piano-playing shifts beyond verisimilitude to provide a now extra-diegetic and still very subtle romantic commentary on the scene. Shortly before the cut to the shots on horseback, the music wells up as a full orchestra joins the piano, and the shift from diegetic to extra-diegetic sound is sealed. Such stylistic touches add extra layers to the potential meaningfulness and pleasure of the sequence. We might also note the fine lighting of the interior scenes, which Ang Lee and his cinematographer carefully modelled in the style of Vermeer's paintings, and the glorious summer sunlight of the exteriors.[68] There is little sense then that this is a film hemmed in by the novel from which it is adapted; but equally, it is difficult to see the sequence as failing to do justice to Austen's intentions in that novel, in so far as we can surmise what her intentions were.

There is, however, a sense that the characters are hemmed in by their historical circumstances, and that their behaviour is to some extent defined by the kind of space they occupy and the clothes they wear. In the initial interior scenes, both Edward and Elinor are shown tightly framed by doorways and surrounded by paintings on the walls of this highly formal domestic interior. There is little room for manoeuvre, so their actions seem circumscribed by their surroundings. At one level, the architecture, the furnishings and the decor function simply as realist historical detail, filling out the world of the fiction. At another level, the *mise-en-scène*, the way that the characters operate within it and the way that the camera interacts with it help shape the meanings audiences can generate in watching the sequence.

There is another level to the images in this sequence, since they also provide a strong sense of spectacle – of costumes and interior decor, of architecture and landscape. It is a spectacle of the past; it is a spectacle of luxury; and it is a spectacle of Englishness. But if it is a spectacle of the past, it is a past that emerges out of the present, a spectacle that chimes with the interests of heritage tourism. In this context, Englishness is a brand, which can be marketed as one of the commodities one buys into through heritage tourism. Norland Park is played in the film by Saltram House, a National Trust property near Plymouth. It looks positively resplendent in this sequence, especially when viewed across the lawns, bathed in bright sunlight and surrounded by richly coloured bushes and trees. And it was carefully promoted at the time of the film's release as a property that might be admired by visitors. In a sense, the conversation between Edward and Elinor could have taken place anywhere and could have been shot in a series of close-ups – but the filmmakers have gone out of their way to film it in long shot across several different spaces, providing plenty of scope for the display of both the beautiful interior of the house and the picturesque grounds outside. On the one hand, this is a narrative space, in which conversation might take place; on the other hand, it is heritage space, a *mise-en-scène* of spectacular display, whose attractions, it might be said, are far more than are *narratively* required. In effect, Hugh Grant as Edward and Emma Thompson as Elinor take us on a tour of the interior of the house, and then the grounds.

This is not a neutral space or spectacle, however, but an ideologically loaded one: the English past on display is highly class-specific, and depends upon a complex system of exploitation. Austen's novels frequently deal with the subtleties of class and class relations at the upper end of the scale, but they overlook the role that servants, the rural poor and the working class are required to play in order to enable the upper classes to enjoy the lifestyles they do. Although the film version of *Sense and Sensibility* comments in various ways on the place of women and gender relations in late eighteenth-century England, its sense of impoverishment is confined to the still quite privileged lifestyle of the disinherited Dashwoods. The broader class system is pretty much taken for granted. As Edward and Elinor traverse the grounds at Norland Park, a couple of gardeners are briefly glimpsed in the background of one shot, followed by an anonymous shepherd in the foreground of the next shot. They become a form of 'dehumanised décor', as Andy Medhurst comments,

> dressed in all-purpose lower-orders outfits, ... simply breathing back-drops, lumped in with the meals they serve or the animals they tend. This may accurately mirror the hierarchies of the time, but it is noteworthy that [Emma] Thompson felt no need to introduce a more modern perspective here as she did with the film's sexual politics.[69]

If the sequence is in part about displaying class differences as if they were natural and unproblematic, with the upper classes as charismatic and narratively central, and the lower classes as almost part of the picturesque landscape, it is also about the spectacle of stardom. It is not only that the lower-class characters in the film are anonymous, but also that they are played by unknown actors. The upper-class protagonists, on the other hand, are played by genuine stars, Grant and Thompson. The sequence also therefore functions as a vehicle for displaying these two well-groomed, well-clad, well-spoken English stars as they walk through this mythically national landscape, laying some of the first building blocks in what will become a romantic liaison that reaches its fulfilment in the film's requisite happy ending. This of course is their pre-ordained role as stars, and they must be given space for this to happen, and dialogue and action to enable it.

This being a quiet, respectable, character-driven romantic drama, however, the action is limited to walking and some gentle horse-riding. This low-key approach to film drama is typical of the 'good taste' of the film: in effect, we are witnesses to a three-minute conversation that hardly moves the story along. In narrative terms, then, this is a very slow-moving film, driven by character and dialogue rather than action. The music playing through the sequence, meanwhile, is restrained and classical – yet it also performs a melodramatic function, bringing out the romantic overtones of the moment. Indeed, the film is awash with melodramatic ingredients, yet they are constantly downplayed. In the context of *Sense and Sensibility* as a tastefully restrained romantic drama, what Edward and Elinor actually say to each other is narratively insignificant: they do not profess their love for one another, or even intimate that this might be a possibility. The dialogue however still plays a significant role, partly because words are vital to the literate movie, andespecially the self-consciously authentic adaptation of a classic English novel. But it is also significant for the way it fleshes out character and provides further historical detail about the subtleties of class and gender in this early nineteenth-century version of upper-class England.

This latter point comes through in particular in the final two shots of the sequence:

> ELINOR: You talk of feeling idle and useless. Imagine how that is compounded when one has no hope and no choice of any occupation whatsoever.
> EDWARD: Our circumstances are therefore precisely the same.
> ELINOR: Except that you will inherit your fortune. We cannot even earn ours.

This conversational feminist critique of the system whereby women were disallowed from inheriting property, and upper-class women were positively discouraged from taking on any public role, is far sharper than a joke Edward makes earlier about the maltreatment of servants. It is typical of the way Emma Thompson as scriptwriter endeavoured to update and extend Austen's own proto-feminist commentary, and adds another layer to the possible meaningfulness of the sequence and the film as a whole. The sequence is in many ways typical of the film, not least in the space that is provided for both the display of 'English' properties and landscape, and the exposition of a feminist critique of late eighteenth-century gender relations. This is a much wordier, more dialogue-laden film than most mainstream productions.

As noted above, the filmmakers have also ensured a careful mix of analytical editing – plenty of reverse shots, point-of-view shots, close-ups and so on – and some very long takes. When Willoughby first visits Marianne at Barton Cottage, for instance, the scene is constructed around reverse shots and unusual camera angles, but it finishes with a 60-second long take outside the house, for a conversation between Willoughby, Marianne, her sister Elinor and her mother. Later, when Edward and Elinor meet in London, again there is initially a series of reverse shots, but they are followed by a long take that lasts for two and a half minutes. Such shots provide performance space, space for the delivery of Austenian speeches and dialogue – but they also demonstrate that this is a tasteful and respectable low-key, slow-moving, character-driven film that downplays *overt* melodramatics.

The complex, multi-layered quality of scenes like the ostensibly simple one between Edward and Elinor at Norland Park enables audiences to engage with the film in different ways. There is romantic drama here, and there are moments of polite comedy, philosophical speculation and social commentary; there are the pleasures of the well-made and literate film, the display of a particular version of Englishness and the English past, and the adaptation of much-loved, canonical literature. If on the one hand, films like *Sense and Sensibility* are addressed to a well-defined core audience, they are also able to address a range of other audiences and to provide scope for a range of meaningful inter-actions with what appears on the screen.

Marketing Austen to mid-1990s movie audiences

Films are never able to function as pure texts, however, for they are always produced and distributed in particular contexts, which shape the way they reach and are able to work for audiences. One of the key features of the English costume dramas of the mid-1990s, and especially the three period film adaptations of Austen novels that appeared in this phase, is that they were the products of a particular business strategy, the carefully engineered Anglo-Hollywood crossover film. The broader production trend thus represents a particular way of operating within the global film economy, drawing on English subject matter but relying on American investment and/or distribution – even if *Persuasion* was handled by a British company. And like most of the other films that emerged from this production trend, they were all low to mid-budget productions, with *Sense and Sensibility* commanding the biggest budget, thanks to the involvement of one of the major American studios (Columbia). All were carefully handled at the exhibition stage, *Persuasion* working as a traditional art-house film in the USA, but *Emma* and *Sense and Sensibility* leading double lives as both art-house releases and mainstream films. *Sense and Sensibility* went furthest into the mainstream and made the most impact at the box office, but *Emma* too was a considerable success.

The cinema/television link was an important element in the business strategy too, with television feeding Austenmania with its numerous adaptations, but also providing a more specific impetus to the film business. Thus, as noted above, *Persuasion* was made as a one-off drama by the BBC, but released theatrically in the USA, while the BBC was also later involved in the production of *Mansfield Park*. Channel 4 also of course played a vital role in supporting the development of the small-scale English costume drama on film and at the cinema, although it was not actually involved in any of the Austen films. Both the BBC and Channel 4 developed strategies of co-production and international sales to exploit to the maximum the potential of their television programmes and filmed dramas – and these strategies meshed well with those of the American film industry as it sought to engineer the crossover hit that might bring together a range of niche audiences.

There is of course a long history of BBC television adaptations of Austen's novels, and that history, as Angela Krewani has noted, as well as the history of the classic serial more generally, feeds in a number of ways into the 1990s Austen adaptations.[70] Just as previous Anglo-Hollywood heritage films paved the way for later entries in the production trend, so television adaptations of Austen in a sense prepared audiences in both Britain and the USA for the film versions that were to follow. Thus they attuned audiences to what some saw as the commercialisation of Austen and her fellow literary gods, and what others saw as a tastefully refined version of screen entertainment. In this respect, previous television adaptations and period films are as important as the Austen source texts in terms of providing an intertextual frame through which audiences might make sense of the Austen film adaptations of the 1990s.

By the start of the decade, the English costume drama production trend was well-established. What the industry attempted to do over the next few years was to finesse that trend, to refine its chances of succeeding in the marketplace, to maximise its audience share, especially in the USA and the UK. For a start, there were almost twice as many period dramas made in the 1990s as in the 1980s.[71] But it's not a question simply of quantity, it's also a question of the ways in which the production trend was exploited economically, and marketed to its potential consumers – and the period Austen adaptations that found their way into cinemas in the mid-1990s are all in their own way symptomatic of developments in this period. Indeed, the critical but especially the box-office success of *Emma* and *Sense and Sensibility* might in many ways be seen as the high point of the strategy of deliberately engineering a crossover hit. As far as the middlebrow English period film was concerned, a number of specialised American companies began to take notice when earlierlow-budget costume dramas like *A Room with a View* (1986) and *Enchanted April* (1991) reaped unexpectedly large profits at the box office. Those companies became increasingly interested in buying into this end of the market at the point of production, and then carefully milking the box-office potential of the films as they moved through the cinemas.[72]

Persuasion shares much with films like *A Room with a View* and *Enchanted April* in the sense that like them it was a small, tasteful English costume drama that was picked up by an American distributor to exploit on the specialised or art-house circuit in the USA. Indeed, both *Enchanted April* and *Persuasion* initially only aired in the UK as television dramas, but were given art cinema releases in the USA. One can see why *Persuasion* was picked up by its specialised American distributor too, given its Bergmanesque intensity and its self-consciously de-glamorised and austere *mise-en-scène*, but equally its constantly moving camera, its familiar heritage iconography and its slow-moving, character-based narrative. While there are moments of romantic comedy here, the production comes across much more as a subtle, 'adult' version of cinema – this is literate cinema, again – and it lacks the conventionally handsome romantic stars of the bigger productions. *Variety*'s verdict was that the film would 'need careful handling to find its target audience, but is sure to appeal to dedicated Jane-ites and could click in a minor way with general female aud[ience]s'.[73]

While niche art-house distribution was part of the emerging business strategy for the Anglo-Hollywood costume drama, what the American companies were increasingly interested in was those films that managed to cross over from the specialised or art-house market into the multiplexes. By the mid-1990s, the American majors had got interested in the sort of profit margins that could be achieved by such films. Such companies were prepared to invest more up front, but in return expected even more impressive returns at the box office, a strategy that did seem to make sense, given the success of more mainstream productions such as Columbia's *Little Women*. *Sense and Sensibility*, *Emma* and later *Mansfield Park* were all products of this strategy, with *Sense and Sensibility* funded by Columbia, which allowed it to benefit from a relatively high budget for a middlebrow period piece. The other two films were handled by one of the key companies involved in the development of this strategy, Miramax. Initially a relatively small independent company, by the time *Emma* was made, Miramax had become part of the Disney family, which enabled it to establish a fairly sizeable budget for such a film.

In order to make the most of their investments, Columbia and Miramax handled their films very carefully at the distribution stage. After all, the English costume drama was not everyone's cup of tea. Thus they were released into cinemas relatively slowly by comparison with the mainstream film, where the opening weekend was everything. Their releases were also carefully tied in to the Oscar season, to make the most of the publicity that Oscar nominations and awards generate. Both films were designed from the outset to win both the core audience for tasteful English costume dramas – more female-oriented and more middlebrow, middle-class and middle-aged than the mainstream – and the more youthful and downmarket general audience to whom a romantic drama might appeal. This was one of the reasons why Ang Lee was taken on as director of *Sense and Sensibility* – and why other directors from Germany, Mexico and South America had also been considered. As the producer, Lindsay Doran, put it: 'I didn't want this to be just some little English movie. I always felt it was more than that and could appeal to the whole world, not just audiences in Devon' (where it was shot).[74] Both films also enjoyed modest star casting (Emma Thompson, Kate Winslet, Hugh Grant and Alan Rickman in *Sense and Sensibility*, and Gwyneth Paltrow in *Emma*).

At the same time the core audience, the Janeites and the fans of English period films, were not to be frightened away by an overemphatic Hollywood. One of the advantages of working with material derived from Austen was that the marketing people for the films were able to rely on quality, upmarket newspapers and magazines taking such films seriously and treating them to plenty of influential column inches. They certainly came through in the case of *Sense and Sensibility*. In the USA, for instance, there was a three-page spread in the *New York Review of Books*, six pages in *Vanity Fair*, four pages in *Film Comment*, and so on.[75] The film was named 'The Movie of the Month' in *The American Spectator* (just as *Persuasion* had been the previous month but one), and 'the best of 1995' in *Time* magazine (along with *Persuasion*).[76] This wasn't just about status and prestige – it was also a marketing coup, since it meant that the film was reaching one of its target audiences. At the same time, the dominant promotional images for the film presented it as a sort of chick flick in period garb, a colourful and moving romantic drama.

Emma may have been much faster-moving and less precious, less self-consciously exclusive and refined, than, say, the Merchant Ivory films that had done so much to establish the potential of this production trend. The film may have been promoted primarily on the basis of Gwyneth Paltrow, its up-and-coming star, and the attractions of romantic comedy, hardly stressing that it was either a Jane Austen adaptation or an upmarket

Emma: will 'have no problems moving in any of your better circles'.

niche product. On the other hand, it was identified as a film from what *Variety* referred to as Miramax's 'traditional stronghold of upscale, specialised pics'.[77] Other reviewers also felt the film had the hallmarks of a quality product that did justice to its highly respectable novelistic source. As one put it, the 'speedy pacing' of the film was achieved 'without sacrificing period manners or the precision of the original language'.[78] The conclusion was that *Emma* 'has enough satirical edge to amuse audiences weary of big-screen explosions and computer wizardry',[79] that while there was plenty to keep the multiplex audiences happy, it should still 'have no problems moving in any of your better circles'.[80]

Columbia opened *Sense and Sensibility* in the USA on a modest 70 screens, which positioned it as an exclusive quality picture, and a potential Oscar contender. Even with such a limited opening, it went to eleventh place in that week's box-office charts. The film was then platformed, with the number of screens being increased at regular intervals, until it was eventually showing on more than 1,000. After reaching this peak, the number of screens gradually decreased again, although the release was widened briefly once more around the time of the nominations for the Oscars, and then again at the time of the awards ceremony. By the end of its run, this release strategy ensured that *Sense and Sensibility* had grossed an impressive $43 million in the USA, against production costs reported as $18.5m.[81] *Emma* was handled in the American market by Miramax, who started the film off on just 9 screens – a typical arthouse-type opening – but built it up over the next 7 weeks to 848 screens, enabling it to earn $22m at the American box office, against production costs reported as £6.3m.[82] It was of course this sort of box-office success, these sorts of profit margins, that attracted American companies like Columbia and Miramax to invest in such 'English' productions in the first place.

In the UK, *Sense and Sensibility* was marketed both as a period drama and as something that might appeal to more general audiences. As Jon Anderson, head of UK marketing at Columbia Tristar, observed, 'if there was any territory this film was going to work in, it was the UK', and the film was scheduled for a February 1996 release 'to take advantage of the hype from *Pride and Prejudice*', which had been a huge television ratings success on the BBC the previous autumn, and which had ensured a marked increase in sales of Austen's novels.[83] The marketing team had previewed the film with a hand-picked audience of people who had seen at least five English period films, and got an enthusiastic response. But as already noted, from the outset the film had been designed as something much bigger than a period-set literary film for the UK market, so reaching general audiences and achieving international sales was vital to its promotion – and further previews for people unfamiliar with the genre were even more positive, with audiences surprised how much fun it was but also regarding it as a prestige film.

As a result, the distributors avoided marketing that might make the film seem like just another English period film. In advertisements, quotations were taken from populist newspapers like the *Daily Mail*, which likened the film to *Four Weddings and a Funeral*, implying a populism at odds with the usual expectations of traditional period dramas. There was also a television advertisement featuring twentysomethings enthusing about the film, to try to convince younger audiences that this wasn't just another period drama. More publicity was engineered with a royal premiere, and the publication of Thompson's *Screenplay and Diaries*, the novel with promotional material for the film on its cover, and the soundtrack on Sony Classical. The publicity team further ensured that 'press articles about endowments for women would use a shot from the film or breaks in the west country would focus around it'.[84] The film was subsequently kept in the public eye with publicity designed to capitalise on its success at awards ceremonies, including the Golden Globes, the Oscars and the BAFTAs.[85]

Films that could work both as mainstream romantic dramas and as tasteful and 'authentic' Austen adaptations; films that could be exhibited at both mainstream cinemas and specialised art houses: this was what defined the crossover film. Of course, by attempting to address both the traditional audience for such films and the wider multiplex audience, the filmmakers were always running a risk. Thus for the *LA Times*, if *Persuasion* was 'the most authentically British version' of the current crop of Austens, *Sense and Sensibility* was 'the audience-friendly Hollywood version...easygoing and aiming to please'.[86] But if that risk resulted in box-office takings on the scale of *Emma* and *Sense and Sensibility* then the strategy could be deemed a success. For the companies interested in such productions, the question now became how to capitalise on the success of such films, how to exploit further the very specific cultural and economic possibilities that they represented, how to develop the Anglo-Hollywood crossover strategy.

In the case of Jane Austen adaptations, a particular problem was the very limited number of commercially exploitable titles. After all, four of the six major novels had already been produced in one form or another, and sometimes in more than one form, in 1995 and 1996 – *Sense and Sensibility*, *Pride and Prejudice*, *Emma* and *Persuasion*. But as I argued above, it would be wrong to see the Austen films in a vacuum. For the film industry, these films were always much more than Austen adaptations: they also belonged to the wider English costume drama production trend, to the genres of romantic comedy and romantic drama, and to the tradition of films with strong female characters – and all of these could be exploited further without having to rely on Austen.

The successors to the rush of Austen adaptations in the mid-1990s might then take a variety of forms. They might be small-scale art-house films such as the Virginia Woolf adaptation *Mrs Dalloway* (1997), or larger-scale Miramax productions such as the Henry James adaptation *The Wings of the Dove* – and both these films featured strong female characters. Or they might be woman-centred period dramas that weren't actually literary adaptations, but biopics of key historical figures, such as *Mrs Brown*, about Queen Victoria, or *Elizabeth*, about Queen Elizabeth I. *Shakespeare in Love* worked in a similar way; as a literary biopic, it may have focused on Shakespeare, but the female lead, played by Paltrow putting on yet another English accent, was almost as central to the film; at the same time, it played up the romantic comedy while retaining both the fascination with heritage England and the fascination with literary culture.

Another way of building on the success of films like *Sense and Sensibility* and *Emma* was to produce further female-oriented English romantic comedies, but without the period setting. From this point of view, as I suggested above, one might cite Anglo-Hollywood films such as *Bridget Jones's Diary*, which of course directly referenced the Austenmania – and especially the Darcy-mania – of the mid-1990s, and *Notting Hill*, one of whose central characters is a Hollywood actress who plays in an English costume drama adapted from a Henry James story. (And of course both films could boast Hollywood stars.)

From this point of view, it is insufficient to treat the Austen films of the mid-1990s simply as adaptations of the work of a woman writer of the late eighteenth and early nineteenth centuries. Adaptation and literary culture are certainly important intertextual frames through which to view these films, but they are by no means the only ones. To look at the details of the particular production trend to which the films belong is to suggest an additional set of circumstances that might explain why the films take the shape that they do, reach particular audiences, and generate certain sorts of debate. The films clearly do have a strong relationship to their source texts, but they also relate strongly to the other non-Austen films around them, especially culturally English films, and for the film industry, they are commodities designed to exploit a fairly clearly delineated market, and are promoted accordingly.

As already noted, the adaptations of the mid-1990s were by no means the end of Austen's posthumous involvement with screen entertainment. At the end of the decade, the appearance of *Mansfield Park* in effect acted as a coda to the Austenmania of the mid-1990s. *Pride and Prejudice* was the one Austen novel that didn't find its way onto the big screen in the 1990s; in the first half of the 2000s, no fewer than three film versions appeared, and these helped to maintain the Austen franchise as a going concern; later came the biopic *Becoming Jane*, and a new round of Anglo-American television adaptations of the Austen oeuvre. If the mid-1990s was the moment of Austenmania, for headline-hungry journalists, this was the moment of 'Austen Power(s)'. It is these developments to which I turn my attention in the next chapter.

6 The Austen screen franchise in the 2000s

Mansfield Park: 'the newest and steamiest Jane Austen adaptation'[1]

Jane Austen was kept very much at the forefront of Anglo-American popular culture for a decade and a half after the initial Austenmania of the mid-1990s. The first obvious filmic marker was *Mansfield Park*, written and directed by the Canadian feminist filmmaker Patricia Rozema, and released in the USA in 1999 and in the UK in 2000. The film is in many ways symptomatic of both Austen adaptations and the development of the Anglo-Hollywood costume drama production trend in the late 1990s, in its efforts both to do justice to the source material and its cultural status and reputation, and to open up the material to a wider range of contemporary audiences and readings. Given the success of the earlier Austen adaptations, and the involvement of Miramax, the most successful of the indie-major producers of the period, there was every reason to think this film too would be a success. In addition to the backing of Miramax, the film seemed to have all the other necessary business ingredients: a UK production company, HAL, which was run by people who had been key figures at Channel 4's FilmFour; funding from the BBC and the Arts Council's Lottery scheme; and a budget the same size as *Emma* (1996). Despite such strong credentials, the film failed at the box office in both the UK and the USA, with the combined box-office takings in those territories amounting to less than half the reported cost of the film.[2]

Like other costume dramas of the late 1990s, such as *The Wings of the Dove* (1997), *Elizabeth* (1998), *Shakespeare in Love* (1998) and *Plunkett & Macleane* (1999), *Mansfield Park* was an attempt to update and open up the period film, to make it more relevant to contemporary multiplex audiences, while not ignoring the niche art-house audience. Thus while retaining the veneer of the authentic period adaptation, the film incorporates touches of the grotesque, the Gothic and the expressionist, blatantly eroticises its themes and characters, and in various ways tarnishes the charms of the English national past. Advance publicity made much of the fact that the actor who played Austen's hero had previously played Sick Boy in *Trainspotting* (1996), while more upmarket commentators noted the extent to which the adaptation drew on feminist and post-colonial readings of Austen's novel.[3] The irreverence of the earlier Austen adaptations is thus heightened in this radically revisionist interpretation of Austen's work, which is much sharper than the earlier films in its depiction of social inequalities, including explicit references to the slave trade as the basis for the current wealth of the Bertram family.

The film was promoted in terms of this difference, and the film's cutting-edge qualities, albeit in a depoliticised form. The tagline, 'Jane Austen's wicked comedy', certainly sounded most un-Austenish, as did the sex scenes in the film itself. But the promotional strategy failed to secure a box-office hit, and by the time the film appeared on video it was being promoted primarily to the core Janeite audience – 'will delight Austen fans everywhere'.[4] Thus the very same film had become another 'faithful' adaptation, rather than the radical reading the director had in mind, or the audience-grabbing film Miramax had evidently been hoping for, or the 'bodice-ripping shagfest' that one reviewer thought some of the initial publicity seemed to suggest.[5]

At one point in the film, one of the characters makes a distinction between 'dim-witted fiction', 'trash' and 'good drama'; while the film draws on some of the pleasures of the former, it also works hard to ensure that it could still be described as good drama, as literate cinema. This is still, as a *Variety* reviewer put it, 'an upscale period piece'.[6] The filmmakers may also have updated the story in various ways, but this is no *Clueless* (1995): it is very much in the vein of Austen adaptations that attend to period detail. The process of writing is also brought to the fore. The film is credited as 'based on Jane Austen's novel *Mansfield Park*, her letters and early journals', while the protagonist of the story, Fanny, is rewritten to draw out some parallels with Austen's own life story as a developing writer. As such, the film merges the conventions of the costume film, the canonical adaptation and the literary biopic. The process of writing is there from the very first images of the film, in the shots of writing materials and a manuscript under the opening credits. Later, a young Fanny tells stories to her sister, then continues the stories in writing, drawing on Austen's own juvenile work. The final scene has Edmund, Fanny's new husband, telling her that he has found her a publisher, reinforcing the sense that this is literary filmmaking playing self-consciously with the complex process of literary and filmic authorship.

This final scene is an interesting one, in that it shows Fanny and Edmund walking into a thoroughly picturesque English *mise-en-scène*, with a quaint cottage seen across green grass. It provides the sort of tourist-heritage imagery that much of the rest of the film seems to critique. This could be read as part of an intentionally ironic happy ending, but it is also indicative of how the film tries both to present the English picturesque and suggest its darker underside. Mansfield Park, the grand house to which Fanny is sent as a child, is presented as austere, forbidding and cold, rather than luxurious or elegant, while the poverty of her own family is depicted in sharp detail. Shot at night from disturbing camera angles, Mansfield Park becomes a dark, Gothic space, in which various un-Austen-like sexual adventures are revealed. In one particularly hard-hitting, almost nightmarish sequence, Fanny discovers some grotesque and obscene drawings by her cousin Tom, depicting his father abusing slaves on their colonial plantation; later, she inadvertently bursts in on Maria, Tom's married sister, engaged in illicit and quite graphic sex with a family friend, and a former suitor of Fanny herself, Henry Crawford. The whole sequence takes place at night, the house filled with dark shadows. As one reviewer comments, the sequence 'is shocking in its deliberate rupturing of the film's predominantly genteel mise-en-scene'.[7]

This was all part of the process of updating the film, reworking the story so that it might appeal to contemporary multiplex audiences. As a spokesperson for the production company put it, this 'is not just another fluffy costume drama'.[8] One of the producers explained that 'when we are working on an adaptation of a period film, we encourage the filmmakers to treat it as far as possible as a contemporary story',[9] and Rozema herself talked of wanting to 'produce a vital work relevant to a modern audience' rather than 'a piece of archaeology. ... At the end of the day, this is not a Jane Austen movie, it is a Patricia Rozema movie'.[10] The result was controversial, with many reviewers subscribing to the view that the adaptation was 'anything but true to the novel – an audacious move that will prove as popular with some audiences as it will be abhorrent to others'. Even so, this particular reviewer proposed that 'there is little doubt that Austen still has box-office draw, and Rozema's addition of erotic fare and feminist postulating should at least pique the curiosity of arthouse audiences and Austen fans'.[11]

More conservative reviewers were inevitably offended, however, with the *Daily Telegraph* critic observing that the film has 'less refinement than the average Austen semi-colon'.[12] Earlier, that same British newspaper had attempted to create a moral panic around the film, with a headline that read 'Jane Austen film is censored for young audiences', in which it reported that the sex scene between Henry and Maria (see below) had been cut by American censors (in fact, the distributors cut the scene to ensure the film received a child-friendly rating, which was deemed important in box-office terms).[13] The fact that a very similar story appeared in the *Times*, the *Evening Standard* and the *Guardian* on the same day suggests that the distributors of the film had deliberately tried to engineer a bit of publicity for the production.[14] It certainly allowed battle lines to be drawn between modernisers and purists, as journalists assembled quotations from both filmmakers and self-confessed Austen experts and guardians, such as the honorary secretary of the Jane Austen Society.

Even some of the more populist commentators were surprised by the radical departures in the production. *Empire* magazine's reviewer, for instance, suggested that 'seldom has a film played quite so fast

A graphic sex scene ruptures the polite world of Austen in *Mansfield Park*.

and loose with an enduring literary work in the dubious cause of seeming "accessible" and "relevant"'; 'if Jane Austen gets wind of this adaptation…she will be turning in her grave'.[15] At times, the attachment to the literary source material leads to an oddly protective reading of fiction, where revisions to the story, such as these sex scenes, can be described as 'totally invented'.[16] The implication is that the fiction – the invented drama – of the novel is somehow an objective truth.

One of the issues that was at stake here was a traditional image of Englishness, as embodied by conservative readings of Austen and all that she seemed to represent. For Rozema, this image was too 'twee' and in urgent need of revision.[17] As Claudia Johnson points out, this 'prettified Austen' has been 'purveyed in the market place of middlebrow culture since the late nineteenth century', but there are other versions, other readings of Austen that see her fiction and the world she describes in very different terms.[18] It is no surprise that the radical vision of Austen in this film version is the product of an outsider perspective, courtesy of Rozema's Dutch-Canadian background (while Frances O'Connor, who plays Fanny, is Australian).

The marketing of *Mansfield Park* was played out differently in the USA and the UK. In the USA, it was given the sort of limited release usually reserved for art-house films, opening on just 8 screens, moving up to 30 in week two, and 148 in week seven, from when it gradually tailed off, a release strategy that yielded only $4.8 million.[19] Having failed to take off in the American market in the way that Miramax had obviously expected, the film was handled in a different way in the UK. Its potential as a crossover film was underlined by its inclusion in a deal struck between the British Film Institute and the Odeon cinema chain to ensure that at least one screen at the mainstream Odeon cinemas was given over to an art-house film.[20] This was the basis for a fairly wide multiplex release, but without the publicity that such a release needs to succeed, and the film rapidly disappeared from UK screens, having taken only just over £500,000, a paltry sum for a film with a £6m budget.

Why did the film fail at the box office? One of the reasons, I would suggest, was that it fell between audiences. On the one hand, it was not Austenish enough, too radical, and too overtly eroticised for the Janeites; it was also too knowing, too revisionist in its approach to the past, too austere, without the traditional period clutter for the costume drama aficionados. On the other hand, it lacked the big stars, the fast-paced narrative and accomplished storytelling, and the lavish spectacle necessary for multiplex success. More generally, so many companies had tried so hard to get onto the crossover bandwagon that by late 1999 the market was saturated, with even the majors producing films like *American Beauty* (1999), while the success of *Shakespeare in Love* and one or two other films around the same time made it very difficult for similar films to secure sufficient audiences. In effect, too many indie films had been produced, too much had been spent on them, and they were all competing for the same screen time. This was then partly a problem with the Austen adaptation, partly a problem with the market for costume dramas more generally, and partly a problem with the even broader category of the specialised indie film designed to have crossover potential.

The moment of *Pride and Prejudice*

It was a few years before another period adaptation of an Austen novel appeared on the big screen, but that did not halt the development of the Austen franchise. In the early 2000s, *Pride and Prejudice* returned to the big screen for the first time since 1940, this time in a variety of guises. The first of the Bridget Jones films appeared in 2001, with strong Austen references for those who wanted to pick them up. Then came three more explicit adaptations of the novel, *Pride and Prejudice – A Latter-Day Comedy* in 2003, *Bride and Prejudice* in 2004 and *Pride and Prejudice* in 2005. In the meantime, Austen's novels sold copiously, as too did the Bridget Jones books and Karen Joy Fowler's *The Jane Austen Book Club*. In 2003, *Pride and Prejudice* was voted into second place in the BBC Big Read survey of the UK reading public's favourite books; in 2004 it was voted by female listeners to the BBC radio programme *Woman's Hour* as 'their top "watershed" book; that is, the book that most made women change the way they view themselves'; and in 2007 it came top of another British poll, this time of books 'we cannot live without'.[21] Between the Austenmania of the mid-1990s and the Austen Power(s) of the late 2000s was the moment of *Pride and Prejudice*.

The full title of *Pride and Prejudice – A Latter-Day Comedy* is an important clue to the nature of this particular adaptation of Austen's novel, for it is an updated version, set amongst the Mormon community – or, to give them their full name, the Church of Jesus Christ of Latter-day Saints (LDS). A low-budget independent production, the film was made by Mormon filmmakers and primarily for Mormon audiences, although it was hoped the film might also break out to reach wider markets. Part of an emerging 'LDS genre' of films, it was admired by some viewers because it was 'clean' – while the *Salt Lake Tribune* suggested that 'Austen would be pleased'.[22] Following in the footsteps of *Clueless* as a modern-day romantic comedy, *Pride and Prejudice – A Latter-Day Comedy* relocates Austen's characters and plot to the campus of Brigham Young University in Provo, Utah. Elizabeth is an aspiring novelist concerned about her love life, in a context in which the expectations of the Mormon community concerning women and dating reproduce some of the restrictions faced by women in Austen's world. The status of the film as an adaptation is overtly signalled in on-screen quotations from the novel between sequences, but for most reviewers, the low-budget origins of the production were all too obvious, and the film failed to achieve the sort of exposure that had evidently been the goal.

As noted in chapter 3, Gurinder Chadha's *Bride and Prejudice* reworks Austen's story through the lens of an 'all-singing, all-dancing' Anglo-Bollywood production, with the Bennet family becoming the globe-trotting Bakshis of Amritsar.[23] The Bridget Jones films meanwhile present the exploits of a hapless thirtysomething single woman living in London and working in the contemporary media business. Her experiences in various ways parallel those of Elizabeth Bennet in Austen's *Pride and Prejudice*, not least in her relationship with a certain Mark Darcy, named after Darcy in Austen's novel, and played by Colin Firth, who had famously played Darcy in the 1995 BBC adaptation of the novel. It would be difficult to describe these various modern-day versions of *Pride and Prejudice* as self-consciously literary works. At the same time, none of these contemporary romantic dramas is reticent about its Austenian genealogy, while the Bridget Jones films are also adaptations of Helen Fielding's novels, and Elizabeth in *Pride and Prejudice – A Latter-Day Comedy* is a novelist. Reviewers and commentators also frequently compared the films with Austen's novel, ensuring that the literary connection was never far from view.

Even so, the contemporary reworkings of Austen's novel that appeared in the early 2000s are best understood as mainstream, or would-be mainstream, romantic comedies, closer to *Clueless* than to period Austen adaptations. Such reworkings go out of their way to appeal to diverse contemporary audiences, and especially the younger multiplex audience. There is no attempt in *Clueless* or *Pride and Prejudice – A Latter-Day Comedy*, the two American-set films, to present an authentic English cultural identity or history; this is then a much more radical strategy for ensuring the exportability of a strongly indigenous source text than those adopted in the audience-friendly period adaptations of *Emma* and *Sense and Sensibility* in the 1990s. By transposing the setting to the contemporary USA, the films are stripped of all those aspects that might seem exotic to the mainstream American youth audience. Englishness plays a much more important role in the Bridget Jones films and in *Bride and Prejudice*, but historical England makes only a fleeting appearance, while contemporary Englishness becomes ambiguous and troublesome – and in any case filtered through the American star of the Bridget Jones films and the British-Asian characters the Bakshis meet in London in *Bride and Prejudice*. Rather than presenting us with an 'authentic' version of Austen, these films use some of Austen's plotting and characters to comment on the nature of contemporary cultural identity, with the Bridget Jones films adopting a post-feminist perspective and Chadha's *Bride and Prejudice* a post-colonial perspective.

There was a great deal of interest in *Bride and Prejudice* before its release. The huge success of Chadha's earlier film about young female footballers in multicultural London, *Bend It Like Beckham* (2002), meant that Chadha herself was always going to be newsworthy, especially given her status as both a British-Asian filmmaker and a female film-maker. For the film business, the interest focused on the production of a film that might succeed both in Western markets and in the enormous Indian market, in a context in which Hollywood was increasingly targeting Asian markets. For others, the interest was in the cross-cultural storyline, and the attempt to mix together Austen and Bollywood. Chadha's interest in the project lay in part in the parallels she saw between the situation of arranged marriages in Indian society and the nature of the family and the plight of women in Austen's world. As she worked on the script, she reported, 'It became clear that even though Jane Austen was writing in 1790s England, everything she was saying morally and culturally fitted contemporary small town India.'[24]

Chadha presented her film in interviews as a potential crowd-pleaser that was both irreverent and true to the spirit of Austen. 'I quite like the mischievousness of taking one of Britain's great institutions and Indianising it',[25] she explained, adding in another interview that she wanted to 'make a truly diaspora film'.[26] At the same time, she suggested that the film was still 'very true to Jane Austen and the spirit of the book'.[27] And if the film 'nods to Bollywood and to Hollywood and elements of it feel like the movie Grease', she was also adamant that 'it is actually a very British movie'.[28] This Britishness was, however, one that was dependent on the new global circumstances in which the film emerged, but which also become elements in the storyline of the film itself. As noted in chapter 3, the film benefited from British, American and German funding – while the narrative explores the impact of American capital on Indian development. The cast and crew were from a variety of backgrounds: the British-Asian Chadha co-wrote the script with her Japanese-American husband, while the cinematographer, the choreographer and the musical director were all Bollywood veterans, and the cast were drawn from India, the UK, the USA and New Zealand. The story too mixes characters from different cultural backgrounds, with various relationships developing between the resident Indian, white English, British-Asian and American characters. This cross-cultural romancing depends on the transnational journeys undertaken by the various characters, which in many ways mirror the globetrotting of the filmmakers themselves.

Once released, the film was not particularly well received by reviewers in the UK, the USA or India, with few being convinced by some of the lead performances or by the musical sequences. For those attached to the subtleties of Austen's novels, there was also dismay at what many saw as the bluntness of the adaptation. The box-office takings were disappointing, and nothing like those enjoyed by *Bend It Like Beckham* (*Bride* took $25m worldwide, *Bend It* a spectacular $77m – even though the former had a budget about three times the size of *Bend It*). That the film managed to make it to the top spot in the UK box-office chart on its opening weekend probably owed as much to the success of the marketing campaign as to the film itself. That campaign had sought to create a sense of international celebrity around the Indian star Aishwarya Rai: although already very well known to Indian audiences, as a former Miss World and a star of several Bollywood films, she was an unknown to most UK audiences. The marketing for the film plastered Rai's image across thousands of London buses, and nearly 100 billboards nationwide. In addition, the leading London tourist venue Madame Tussauds was persuaded to create a waxwork model of her, whose unveiling became a media event, and was part of a Bollywood-themed *Bride and Prejudice* attraction. The website and trailers for the film meanwhile downplayed the musical/Bollywood elements and played up the romantic comedy of the film, focusing on Rai and her male lead.[29] While reviews invariably discussed the Austen connections, the marketing in this respect was minimal – although a special, and by all accounts reasonably successful, screening of the film was arranged for the Jane Austen Society in Bath.

Even if the film was not in the end a major success, it represents a bold attempt to rework Austen's characters, storyline and themes in a contemporary setting. In the process, the representation of England and Englishness is radically transformed. Austen's focus on an enclosed, white Anglo-Saxon community in a highly specific locale, where social interaction takes place only among the gentry and the aristocracy, is replaced by a global and multicultural community, where interaction takes place across continents, and across ethnic and national divides. England, or at least London, is no longer a solely white space, and is presented as the unquestioned home of a well-established British-Asian community, albeit one with its own status hierarchy. The depiction of 'ordinary Englishness' effectively shifts from the white, upper-middle-class Bennet family to the lower-middle-class British-Asian families that are briefly seen enjoying a barbecue in suburbia.

The 2005 version of *Pride and Prejudice* was a very different sort of production, which took audiences back into the world of period drama and what many saw as a more authentic version of Austen, directed by white Londoner Joe Wright, and starring two white English actors, Keira Knightley and Matthew Macfadyen. It was again designed as a film that might work for a range of audiences: for dedicated fans of Austen, but also for dedicated fans of Knightley; for lovers of English literature, but also for lovers of romantic costume drama; and for those who visit art-house cinemas, but also for those who prefer the multiplexes. It was also another Anglo-Hollywood film, made by the British company Working Title in collaboration with its main funder and parent company, the American studio Universal. Once again, it provided a very interesting take on Austen, cross-breeding her refined world with the rather different sensibilities of Emily Brontë on the one hand and Henry Fielding on the other. It is more dirty realist than picturesque, with the Bennet household a carnivalesque and bawdy place, far from the sense of decorum usually associated with Austen – and that sense of the carnival is even stronger in the vigorous and sweaty ball sequences. It thus very much follows in the tradition of English period films of the previous few years, extending some of the concerns already raised by earlier Austen

Pride and Prejudice: a dirty realist version of Austen.

adaptations, especially *Persuasion* (1995) and *Mansfield Park*, and offering a less safe and less pretty version of the modern English past.

The director, Joe Wright, was an unusual choice for a romantic drama, given his penchant for social realism, and especially the films of Alan Clarke and Ken Loach. But for Wright, Austen 'was one of the first British realists ... I wanted to treat [*Pride and Prejudice*] as a piece of British realism rather than going with the picturesque tradition, which tends to depict an idealized version of English heritage as some kind of Heaven on Earth. I wanted to make *Pride & Prejudice* real and gritty'.[30] At the start of the film, for instance, Elizabeth Bennet walks through some fairly non-descript grassland; as she approaches the family house, she crosses a makeshift bridge across a very muddy moat, then weaves her way through a jungle of washing hanging out to dry. This is not genteel England, but very much a dirty realist domestic space, in which farmyard animals seem to roam freely; indeed, at one point, a huge pig sporting a giant pair of testicles is led through the house itself. But if this is not genteel England, Elizabeth is reading a book as she walks, so it is still very much literary England; and if this is a dirty realist version of Austen, it is also heavily coded and promoted in terms of romance, romantic drama and romantic comedy. This was certainly the dominant image used to promote the film, its difference from other images in the film underlining the extent to which contemporary cinema constantly develops hybrid products that might draw in a range of audiences.

For some reviewers, the film's realism was to be applauded. The magazine *Jane Austen's Regency World*, for instance, proposed that 'it's almost as if, for the first time ever, we are actually witnessing Austen's work come to physical life. Gone are the picture-perfect, slightly-too-clean Regency tableaux familiar from the BBC mini-series. Instead ... we are treated to the sight of muddy pigs, squawking chickens, puddles, unshaven men and, most unusually, practically make-up free women. ... It's Austen as you've never seen it before.'[31]

If the setting was more bucolic than Austen is usually imagined to be in film and television adaptations, many reviewers still saw the adaptation as 'faithful' to the novel,[32] and, despite the muddy-hem realism, 'not obviously daring or revisionist', and with none of the 'great textual variations or interpretative liberties' some reviewers had come to expect – or fear – of Austen adaptations.[33] Of course there were changes from the novel, but there was 'nothing remotely outrageous about [this] latest Austen adaptation', which instead 'cheerfully satisfies the traditional demand for the conventions of bowing and bonnets and breeches and balls' set amidst 'swoon-inducing countryside'.[34] In other words, for some reviewers, the realism either enhanced the pleasure of the adaptation or failed to detract from the traditional picturesque of the English period drama – and the filmmakers certainly made the most of their locations. But for more purist commentators, the impression of realism was a problem, since it 'loosen[ed] the strings of the era's decorum' which was so important to the way that the novels worked and to the representation of the characters.[35]

The film was pitched as something that would appeal to mainstream young filmgoers as well as the core costume drama/Austen adaptation audience. A British trade reviewer saw it as 'the ultimate chick-flick romance', 'more commercial than previous big-screen Austen adaptations', suggesting that 'the arthouse isn't within hailing distance here – despite gorgeously faithful period sets and costuming'.[36] The film was thus able to become a more modern romantic drama, even if it eschewed the blatant eroticism that marked the much more self-consciously revisionist *Mansfield Park*. And if Joe Wright could suggest that 'for a film with not a single kiss in it, there's a lot of sex in there', the intimations rather than graphic realities of sex were perfect for a film that was expected by reviewers to play well, 'even to audiences who may be more used to watching the latest Meg Ryan romance than a Regency love story'.[37] In fact, in some versions of the film, there is a kiss: the filmmakers originally included a scene at the end of the film in which Darcy and Lizzie are evidently married and very much in love, and build up slowly to a very romantic kiss. This was eventually cut from the UK release prints, but retained for the American version. Inevitably, some members of the Jane Austen Society of North America expressed their disappointment with this final Hollywood kiss, with Elsa Solender, former president of the society, reported as saying that 'It has nothing at all of Jane Austen in it, is inconsistent with the first twothirds of the film, [and] insults the audience with its banality.'[38]

The debate about Austen, here as elsewhere, was also in many ways a debate about Englishness, pitching an ideal vision of traditional English morality, behaviour and social relations against what was presented as a more modern, realistic vision, but experienced by some as immoral and immodest. On the one hand, this new vision provided a reinterpretation of the English past; on the other, it pandered to what were perceived as the expectations of contemporary mainstream audiences about the world in which they lived and the way people should behave. Either way, England and Englishness has not changed a great deal: it is still white and Anglo-Saxon; the divisions between genders and between classes are still marked; propriety and good manners are still valued; romantic fulfilment can still resolve most problems; and England is still pre-industrial and picturesque, even if the picture is a little muddy round the edges. For this was a vision of England that could readily be sold in the global marketplace, and especially in the Anglophile sections of the American market: it did not in that respect need changing.

That this debate was conducted between English filmmakers, corporate American financiers, Jane Austen fans, both American and British, and film audiences around the world underlines once again that Englishness – or at least this particular vision of a traditional ideal Englishness – does not necessarily belong to the English; rather it is a global brand, a sensibility, that can be appropriated by producers and consumers almost regardless of national identity. Austen's world cannot be reduced to this vision of Englishness, however, for it is also a carefully gendered world. That is to say, once again, that her work and the various film and television versions of it appeal in particular to female readers and audiences. If some of the adaptations of Austen's work were conceived self-consciously as feminist, there was hardly anything new about this, since Austen's novels already construct female-centred worlds, value feminine pleasures and concerns, and comment on the plight of women in a patriarchal society. Again, it might be said, not much has changed.

This female-centred world was evidently regarded as one worth investing in, with *Pride and Prejudice* costing some $28m to produce. Even before its release, however, it was already regarded as 'one of the hottest British movies of the year', and it duly went straight on to a wide release in the UK, opening on 397 screens and securing the top spot in that week's box-office chart. Two weeks later it was on 412 screens, and by the end of its 16-week run it had taken $26m. Despite the predictions of some in the trade press, it did in fact show in art houses as well as multiplexes – and was classified as an art-house release in *Sight and Sound*. In the USA, it was treated slightly differently, opening on a fairly modest 215 screens, and only going wide in its third week, when it was showing on 1,300 screens; at the end of its run, it had taken $38m.[39] By the time worldwide box-office ($121m in total) and DVD sales are factored in, this suggests an impressive return on the investment in the film. But it was always going to be much more than just a film: as a newspaper article about the multi-million-pound 'Jane Austen spin-off industry' observed shortly before the film was released, what was at stake was 'a literary sensibility that makes solid financial sense'.[40]

One of the ways in which the adaptation had a life beyond the screen was in the form of *Pride and Prejudice*-related tourism. The Visit Britain website, for instance, encouraged visitors to 'Tour Pride and Prejudice Country', as Derbyshire and the Peak District were rebranded, and follow in the footsteps of both Austen and the film's stars, while the official movie website had a link to a similar promotion, complete with short breaks, a movie map, a 50 per cent discount on entry to various *Pride and Prejudice* movie locations – and 20 per cent off car hire, so visitors could actually reach the locations.[41] The National Trust later promoted a themed visit to various of its properties that had featured in *Pride and Prejudice* and other recent film and television adaptations of 'Jane Austen's ageless novels': 'Ever wished to take a peek inside "Netherfield", or admire "Pemberley" from across the lake? It's easier to follow in the footsteps of Lizzy and Darcy... than you might think'.[42]

Several of the stately homes used as locations in the film reported an upturn in business, including Chatsworth House, which stood in for Pemberley. At Basildon Park, 'over 100 coach tours were sold on the back of the film, a 76% increase', while there was a 40 per cent increase in visitors in late 2005 and 20 per cent the following year, with nearly a third of the visitors reporting that their trip was inspired by the film.[43] Where *Bride and Prejudice* and the Bridget Jones films offered a vision of modern, or even postmodern metropolitan London, with traditional England glimpsed only momentarily in the background, the Working Title version of *Pride and Prejudice* saw the film business and the tourism business working hand in hand to reinforce the enduring brand image of England as a picturesque, historical place.

If this was one way in which the Austen franchise embraced more than just the films themselves, another way involved various heavy-weight newspapers again churning out celebratory articles about the complexities and pleasures of the great literature that Austen produced, using the adaptation of *Pride and Prejudice* as the springboard for their commentaries, which yet invariably managed to diminish the film itself. The *Observer* newspaper's literary editor, Robert McCrum, for instance, was given most of a broadsheet page to examine Austen's 'enduring appeal'.[44] In some ways, then, the business of creating populist versions of Austen simply underlined the core English literary qualities of the source text.

'Austen Power'

The success of Working Title's film version of *Pride and Prejudice* in 2005 was one of the drivers behind the second Austen boom, prompting ITV to put together a Jane Austen Season, which appeared on British television screens some 18 months later.[45] The season included three new television dramatisations, *Mansfield Park*, *Northanger Abbey* and *Persuasion* (all 2007), all of them done as period pieces, followed by a repeat screening of their 1996 serialised version of *Emma*. 'What, more Jane Austen? It seems we can't get enough of her', observed the *Radio Times*.[46] 2007 also saw the release in cinemas of the biopic *Becoming Jane*, a period drama that aimed for a certain historical realism, and the contemporary drama *The Jane Austen Book Club*, about a group of mainly women in present-day California who set up a reading group to discuss Austen's novels, and end up playing out various of the characters and plots. The ITV adaptation of *Northanger Abbey* was scripted by the ubiquitous Andrew Davies, who also wrote the screenplay for a BBC period adaptation of *Sense and Sensibility*, which appeared on British television screens in 2008, as did another biopic, *Miss Austen Regrets*. Later that same year another ITV mini-series was screened, *Lost in Austen*, which subjected Jane Austen to time travel, with a modern-day Londoner obsessed with Austen finding her way back into the historical plot and diegetic world of *Pride and Prejudice*. Finally, in 2009 the BBC produced a four-part serialised version of *Emma*, with yet another script by Davies. Austen-related audio-visual material now also had an impressive fan-generated presence on YouTube.[47]

The press and publicists had a field day with so much Austen material appearing at the same time. 'Austen-mania is stronger than ever', concluded one journalist,[48] while the three ITV adaptations in 2007 were heralded by a rash of predictable 'Austen Power(s)' headlines.[49] The BBC was not to be left out either, since they scheduled a broadcast of the 1996 film adaptation of *Emma* for the evening before the ITV *Mansfield Park*. The description of the film in *TV Times* leaves little doubt as to how the attractions of such Austen adaptations were perceived; thus *Emma* was 'a beautiful romantic drama', 'a stunning Regency romance', about 'girls dreaming of love'.[50] That same week, the rival and slightly more upmarket TV listings magazine *Radio Times* went to town with Austen.[51] The banner on the cover read 'Austen Power: the nation's favourite novelist is back – big time', accompanied by a full-page photograph of Billie Piper, Sally Hawkins and Felicity Jones, who played the heroines of the three new ITV dramatisations. Inside, Austen appeared on nine separate pages. There was also a review of *Becoming Jane*, already doing the rounds in British cinemas – and on the same page as the review, readers were invited to purchase audio CDs of all six of Austen's novels.

The general line in the publicity was by now familiar: 'Jane Austen gets a fresh look'.[52] That was certainly the case in the photograph of a sullen, pouting Billie Piper that appeared all over the place: she might have been in period dress, but her posture and facial expression, and her hair dyed a different colour from her eyebrows, suggested a very contemporary young woman. The image was confirmed by the *Radio Times*, which might have featured Piper and her two ITV season co-stars on the cover in period dress but inside had them wearing jeans in almost the same pose.

Elsewhere, it was reported that *Mansfield Park* 'has a more modern feel than previous Austen adaptations, with the characters adopting less stuffy manners'.[53] This was clearly the preferred line. The *Radio Times* also observed 'a more contemporary, robust and passionate version than we've been used to in previous incarnations. It's a bold way of approaching Austen...',[54] while the *Times* prepared readers to 'expect tight breeches and heaving bodices, but also a modern chick-flick tone to entice a new generation of viewers'.[55] A headline in the *Sunday Telegraph* proclaimed 'Jane Austen to be the latest teenage sensation'. The article continued: 'Step aside Britney Spears. Movie moguls, television producers and publishers believe this year's teen hit will be the 19th-century "lit girl" Jane Austen.'[56] It was also announced that Penguin would be bringing out new editions of Austen's novels, 'with covers designed to appeal to teenagers'.[57] Andrew Davies, the screenwriter who had done so much to rebrand Austen for modern screen audiences with his 1995 adaptation of *Pride and Prejudice*, expected all these Austen products to create 'a Jane Austen frenzy. The stories are absolutely contemporary. They are about sex and they are about money.'[58]

There was something very familiar about this 'revved-up Austen';[59] if the programme-makers were 'jazzing up Jane Austen for the 21st century', they were doing so in a way that had already been well-rehearsed in the 1990s, with almost all the same ingredients. The purpose, however, was to address a new generation who had yet to experience Austenmania, and for whom even the 1999 film adaptation of *Mansfield Park* might now seem dated. There was nothing new either about cultural commentators wondering whether Austen herself would have approved of the way her works were being reimagined, with one headline writer suggesting that she 'might have had a fit of the vapours at ITV1's radical new vision of her fiction'.[60] For programme-makers, the goal was to impress viewers, not authors, however, so how would viewers respond? 'Austen fans will notice some changes from the book, while newcomers will delight in its freshness and stellar cast', suggested the *TV Times*.[61]

ITV's goal was twofold: to build up their reputation for so-called quality drama, and 'to bring Austen to a whole new generation'.[62] Nick Elliott, ITV's Director of Drama, explained that 'every generation does [Austen] in its own style' and 'we wanted ours to be very 21st-century, so it seemed a good idea to have the heroes and heroines played by actors who are ... young and fresh enough to appeal to viewers who don't usually want to watch Jane Austen'.[63] Asked how the new version of *Mansfield Park* differed from previous versions, one of those actors, Billie Piper, explained, 'it's shot with handheld cameras, so it feels really alive. Also the director wanted us to be contemporary in the way we moved. It's tempting to be stiff and starchy when you do period drama, but the characters are still human – they bitch, gossip and fall in love.'[64] Elsewhere, it was noted that 'Billie Piper isn't your usual Jane Austen heroine ... rather than being ladylike and reserved, she tumbles across the screen with unkempt hair and carefree laughter ... "It's not like your average costume drama," admits Billie.... "We wanted it to feel natural and very real." '65

The co-producer Suzan Harrison explained the thinking of the programme-makers: 'I don't think our youthful audience – or, indeed, many of our audience – would understand or relate to the overly pious Fanny Price of the novel.'66 Hence the independent-minded, strong young woman that Piper plays, but also the appearance of the other characters. 'All of us were keen not to be corseted by the decorum of the time...This is a story about first love – it's messy and a bit raucous', suggested Piper's co-star, Blake Ritson, who plays Edmund. Sex, of course, was never far away, either: 'It's all about sex!' ran another headline.67 In fact, it wasn't *all* about sex; it was also in part about making television that could compete with other drama showing at the same time on the small screen:

> Maggie Wadey's dramatisation rips through Austen's stateliest novel at a rate of knots. 'It's a very young cast and the camera needed to keep up with the pace of the kids,' explains...Harrison. 'We have audiences now who are familiar with American drama series such as *Lost* and *24*, where everything moves very fast. And that's great for us, because the audience gets it quickly – you don't need to labour things to get them to understand the nuances.'68

The *Radio Times* confidently concluded that 'this is about as fresh an approach to Jane Austen as it's possible to get'.69

But the debate is actually again very similar to the one about the earlier Austen cycle of the mid-1990s: as previously, historical authenticity is contrasted with irreverence, period detail with attempts to appeal to contemporary audiences in terms of contemporary mores. The kiss at the end of the 1995 version of *Persuasion* and the eroticisation of Austen's characters and the graphic sex scenes in Rozema's 1999 version of *Mansfield Park* had already prepared the way very thoroughly for the 2007 *Mansfield Park*, and the rest of the ITV season. And of course the 2005 film version of *Pride and Prejudice* had also been heralded as a modern and realistic take on Austen's times. Perhaps there was a more concerted effort to attract younger, more street-savvy viewers, with the ITV website encouraging visitors 'to find your perfect match, send a flirtmail, join our seduction survey and much more'.70

In the USA, Masterpiece Theatre put together what they called 'The Complete Jane Austen' on PBS for the first four months of 2008. This began with the three new ITV adaptations of *Persuasion, Northanger Abbey* and *Mansfield Park*, followed by the BBC biopic *Miss Austen Regrets*. Then came repeat screenings of the 1995 BBC adaptation of *Pride and Prejudice* and the 1996 ITV adaptation of *Emma*, with the season coming to a conclusion with the new BBC adaptation of *Sense and Sensibility*. The mix of BBC and ITV productions in the same season may from a British perspective seem surprising; from an American perspective it is much less so, because all of the new programmes, whether made by BBC or ITV, were co-productions with the American company WGBH/Boston (WGBH had presented Masterpiece on PBS since 1971), while the two repeat screenings were both co-productions with another American company, A&E Television Networks. Likewise, four of the adaptations, two from the BBC (*Pride and Prejudice* and *Sense and Sensibility*) and two from the ITV stable (*Emma* and *Northanger Abbey*), were scripted by Andrew Davies.

It was certainly a coup for PBS to be able to show high-quality period adaptations of all six of Austen's completed novels, with the biopic as a bonus. The season was promoted very much in terms of quality, with little of the emphasis on innovativeness or modernity that had been such a feature of the British promotion of these same programmes. 'True love' still features prominently, but the other key aspects noted in the PBS press release are the Austen connections, the picturesque English period settings, and the status and reputations of the scripts, the writers and the actors: 'For the first time on television, Austen fans can…sit down to a weekly feast of all of her immortal plots…in beautifully acted, lavishly set and gorgeously costumed adaptations.' No effort was made to attract the young audience that was the target for the new ITV adaptations; and if in Britain there was a perception that the shows needed to be more like the fast-moving American drama to which audiences were now accustomed, for the American viewers of PBS the key intertextual references were to be found in quality British television adaptations of period fare, and in Austen: 'There are six transcendently satisfying scenarios, as told in a half-dozen enchanting novels by Jane Austen – one of the most beloved writers in all of literature.'[71]

There was also a strong educational tie-in with the Masterpiece season, with a comprehensive website, including an extensive bibliography and guide to internet resources relating to Austen, her novels and the historical period in which she was writing, and a 26-page *Complete Guide to Teaching Jane Austen*, available as a downloadable booklet. This guide again included material on the novels and the historical period, but it gives as much time to the adaptations, and to the process of adaptation. While its *raison d'être* is that Austen is a great novelist whose work deserves to be studied and whose own biography is therefore of interest, it also proposes another crucial layer of authorship, asserting that 'an Andrew Davies screenplay has a distinctive signature'. The overall tone of the booklet is quite different from the discourse of 'Austen Power', despite being organised around the same productions. It is still of course a form of marketing, a means of enlarging the audience for the Austen adaptations and increasing the sales of related DVD products, but it plays out a quite different relationship to the literary Austen, the cultural status of her novels and the English world they depict.

In effect, in the promotional discourse around the new Austen boom in England, Englishness is taken for granted; the period setting is necessary but unremarked, thereby coming across as banal, mundane. Transposed to the USA, however, the period English setting becomes remarkable, exotic, one of the selling points. Once again, it appears that this particular vision of England and Englishness is a highly marketable brand image within a certain sector of the American marketplace.

Austen biopics: *Becoming Jane*

The fact that two Austen biopics appeared as part of the moment of Austen Power, one on film (*Becoming Jane*) and the other on television (*Miss Austen Regrets*), is indicative of the extent to which film- and programme-makers were keen to exploit the possibilities of both the Austen industry and the market for literary cinema and television – and more generally, the market for 'traditional' English drama. *Becoming Jane* also needs to be seen in the context of the long run of literary biopics produced by the Anglo-Hollywood film industry in the 1990s and 2000s, and it is typical of that strand of filmmaking in the way it casts an American actress to play an English icon, in its endeavour to appeal to mainstream audiences attuned to the Hollywood star system. In *Becoming Jane*, Anne Hathaway plays Austen; in *Shakespeare in Love*, Gwyneth Paltrow plays Shakespeare's muse; in *Finding Neverland* (2004), Johnny Depp plays J.M. Barrie; in *Miss Potter* (2006), Renée Zellweger plays Beatrix Potter. Add to this the Australian stars who play Queen Elizabeth I in the two *Elizabeth* films (Cate Blanchett, 1998, 2007), Virginia Woolf in *The Hours* (Nicole Kidman, 2002), and Austen's Fanny Price in *Mansfield Park* (Frances O'Connor), as well as Zellweger's turn as another sort of

English icon in the Bridget Jones films, Kidman's role as Mrs Coulter in *The Golden Compass* (2007), and Paltrow's performance in *Emma*, and the strategy looks both concerted and extensive.

One of the taglines used to promote *Becoming Jane* proposed the film's storyline as 'the inspiration behind Jane Austen's greatest love stories'. In so doing, it captured the dual appeal of the film: on the one hand, this was a serious literary film, part of the Austen cycle; on the other hand, it was a love story, another romantic drama. The production was designed from the outset to work in these complementary contexts. Initially developed by the producer Tony Garnett, for Sony, with Natalie Portman lined up to play Austen,[72] the film was subsequently handled by the British company Ecosse Films, with funding from the UK Film Council and the Irish Film Board, the BBC and various other investment sources, while the post-Weinstein version of Miramax bought the North American distribution rights. With funding, distribution deals and pre-sales from a variety of European and American sources, the package was typical of modestly budgeted cinema addressed to crossover audiences, with the goal of attracting both a youthful mainstream audience and a more mature audience interested in 'literate films'. Ecosse had established a decent reputation in this field, notably through their success with *Mrs Brown* (1997), another biopic about a prominent English icon, in this case a queen, Victoria, rather than a canonical author, while Miramax had engineered a big hit the previous year with another 'English royal' film, *The Queen* (2006), and hoped to do something similar with *Becoming Jane*. Ecosse had also worked with *Becoming Jane*'s director, Julian Jarrold, on his first feature film, *Kinky Boots* (2005).

With a budget of around £9m (or $16.5m), and with two emerging stars in the lead roles (Anne Hathaway and James McAvoy), there were high hopes for *Becoming Jane* as a modest but 'star-studded' film that had the right ingredients to do well.[73] The British trade paper *Screen International*, for instance, predicted that the film would 'hold an irresistible appeal to global audiences who swooned over big screen adaptations of *Pride and Prejudice* and *Sense and Sensibility*',[74] and that 'the chemistry between [the] co-stars … and their combined marquee value should position *Becoming Jane* as a potent middlebrow, mainstream attraction, especially in the UK'.[75]

In fact the film did not fare as well as expected at the box office, despite the fact that Miramax, by now Disney's specialty division, had a strong track record for dealing with relatively small films that seemed to balance 'the refined and the commercial'.[76] The initial plan was to release *Becoming Jane* in the USA in June or July of 2007, through a strategy known as counter-programming, whereby so-called small, intelligent, quality films would be released in the same week as one of the big summer blockbusters. Previously, the specialty distributors had left the major Hollywood studios to their own devices in the summer months, and tried to release their own films when they would not be swamped by the tentpole productions released at that time. Now, however, 'the strategy is to aggressively court restless adults',[77] addressing the demographic groups left aside by the tentpole films.

As the head of distribution at Warner Independent, Steven Friedlander, put it, 'our audience feels neglected or even dissed in the summer, as if their money is inconsequential to the studios, so they actively search out stuff to support.... If you are over 35 and educated, there are [weeks] with nothing for you to see.'[78] This was the gap that *Becoming Jane* was expected to fill. It was also seen as 'a seven-day movie' – that is, not one that relies solely on the opening weekend of its release for the bulk of its income, but the sort of film that would play well throughout the week, and gradually build up audiences as its run developed.[79]

If *Becoming Jane* was perceived in part as a small-scale, intelligent and literate film that might appeal to 'restless adults', it was also a romantic comedy-drama with up-and-coming young stars, and was therefore also expected to play well to more mainstream audiences. Following a disappointing performance at the UK box office in March 2007, the film was in the end released in the USA in August, opening on 100 screens in its first week, moving to 601 screens in the second week, and eventually reaching 1,210 screens, a release pattern by now well-established for modestly budgeted crossover films. The film eventually grossed $18.6m in the USA, and the same amount in other territories, with another $8.2m coming from DVD sales in the USA.[80]

This dual address, to both those that want a literate film and those that prefer a romantic drama, was central to the way the film was conceived and put together. In a scene at the start of the film, for instance, it is early morning and Jane (Hathaway) is writing; she is delighted when she conjures up some choice words, but her elation awakens the whole house and causes some consternation. Her mother's response is precise: 'That girl needs a husband.' Thus from the outset, both the literary and the romantic are carefully signalled. The mother's response triggers a

Becoming Jane: revisiting Austen's genteel world in the guise of the bio-pic.

typically Austenian storyline about romance, subtle class differences and the problems of inheritance.

Jane's parents want her to marry a Mr Wisley, who expects to inherit a large fortune. Jane's preferred beau, after initial doubts, is Tom LeFroy (McAvoy), a boisterous young man who frequents London high spots and lives a life of excess and dissipation, against which his uncle, a judge, preaches restraint – and duly sends him off to spend time with some other relations 'deep in the country'. Here he meets Jane, whose family are clearly of modest means, but mix with much richer families. Jane and Tom fall in love, and eventually elope, until Jane thinks better of this plan and returns home to become a writer. A tear-jerking finale has Jane and a now married Tom meet again 15 years after they separated; the scene is marked by a sense of romantic loss, but also of literary achievement, as Jane reads to Tom's young daughter, also named Jane.

In the end, then, this is a tale of desire against the odds, followed by selfless renunciation to ensure the well-being of others. But it is also a biopic about a canonical English author. At one level, then, this was another Austen film, a quality English period drama, not quite a literary adaptation, but certainly designed to make the most of its proximity to such films. It thus tapped into a cultural vein with a certain contemporary prominence and thereby sought to engage with a sizeable pre-established audience. Productions such as this thus carefully signal the literary Austen, the iconic Austen, using that as a lure for certain audiences – but then find ways to address other audiences as well. They thus both engage with and disengage from the literary Austen.

Becoming Jane clearly engages with the literary Austen from the outset, and images of Jane writing become a key motif of the film, along with scenes of her reading the stories she has written, defending her writing and her interests, and discussing the relationship between writing and experience. One scene is set in the grand library of a country house, where Jane meets Tom, who encourages her to read *Tom Jones*, which they later discuss. In another scene, Jane visits the Gothic novelist Mrs Radcliffe, who encourages her to use her imagination, but who also explains that 'To have a wife who has a mind is considered not quite proper. To have a wife with a literary reputation nothing short of scandalous.' The sentiment is underlined by Lady Gresham, Wisley's wealthy aunt, played by an imperious Maggie Smith; she notices Jane writing, and asks 'Can anything be done about it?', as if a woman writing were a woman with a serious ailment. Fortunately, Jane perseveres with her writing, and we witness her blending her experiences and observations into an early draft of *Pride and Prejudice*, with Tom played out in the film as a model for Darcy. Like *Bridget Jones* and *Clueless*, but also indeed all the more 'authentic' adaptations, the film has fun playing with Austen's characters and plots. But it is also very much about the literary process, about the experience of literature and about the difficulties of female authorship.

This engagement with literature and especially with the literary Austen can also be found in the study guide produced by Young Minds Inspired (YMI) in association with Miramax to accompany *Becoming Jane*'s DVD release. Designed for teachers, with ideas for classroom activities, the objectives of the guide were 'to generate student interest in Jane Austen and her work through the upcoming film Becoming Jane' and 'to motivate the reading of Jane Austen's novels'.[81] The literary connection was thus paramount. If *Becoming Jane* was described in the guide as 'a timeless romantic comedy', it was also

> imaginatively based on the life of one of the most influential and revered novelists of the early 19th century … This film provides a uniquely engaging introduction to Austen's novels for new readers and a revealing

back-story for current fans. ... Like the movie Becoming Jane, the activities introduce students to Jane Austen and her world, setting the stage for enjoyment of her novels through hands-on lessons that reinforce language arts, literary analysis, and critical thinking skills.[82]

The producers of the film had already stressed the film's historical credentials – 'It is taken from research, culled from a lot of biographies'[83] – and drawn attention to the fact that the script was based on one particular biography, *Becoming Jane Austen: A Life*, whose author, Jon Spence, was employed as a historical consultant on the film.[84] The star of the film, Anne Hathaway, also claimed in several interviews to have researched her part carefully, including 'reading every one of Austen's letters in the British Library'.[85] Her co-star, James McAvoy, elsewhere claimed 'we wanted the production to have some integrity and not just be a British rom-com in tights'.[86] The fact that this most English of stories was shot in Ireland was also explained in terms of historical authenticity, with the producers arguing that it was easier to find authentic eighteenth-century landscapes and buildings in Ireland than in modern England – 'In Ireland, one really did find that one was entering a Jane Austen landscape.'[87] Of course, the fact that there were encouraging financial incentives to shoot in Ireland at the time clearly helped shape this vision of the film, and indeed of historical England.

Jarrold's stated aim as director was 'to bring Austen up to date by roughening her up a bit', arguing that Austen adaptations were too often 'a little bit picture-postcard and safe and nice and sweet. I want more life and energy and fun.'[88] If an effort was made to establish a sense of historical authenticity and deal with the familiar, there was also therefore a concern to ensure a modern spin. 'We wanted to bring [an] element of modernity to Becoming Jane', explained co-producer Robert Bernstein.[89] 'It is young love. It is Jane Austen in love, something you've never seen before, a complete departure from the usual oblique portrait of her as a spinster.'[90] Like his producer, Jarrold felt that audiences other than Austen purists would be put off by the traditional image of the author as 'a middle-aged spinster obsessed with manners and propriety. That's one of the things that attracted me – that one is able to breathe a little life into it.'[91]

This of course was hardly a new way of thinking about Austen; indeed, it was very much a rerun of the debates about *Persuasion*,

Emma and *Mansfield Park* in the 1990s and the new ITV adaptations that appeared around the same time as *Becoming Jane*. But if the production was to develop a new, more modern image of Austen, it was to be a more restrained modernity than the one embodied by Billie Piper in the ITV adaptation of *Mansfield Park*, or Alicia Silverstone in *Clueless*, and it is less shockingly erotic than Patricia Rozema's version of *Mansfield Park*. 'The film is not titillating or gratuitous', assured Douglas Rae, of Ecosse Films; on the contrary, 'It's very chaste! There is only one kiss!'[92] If the film was to be as intimate as possible, that intimacy would be hemmed in by the constraints of late eighteenth-century customs: 'There is a lot of passion in the film, but it is passion across the ballrooms and the soirées and walks with other people.'[93] There was then a careful balancing act going on around the figure of Austen. On the one hand, as Rae explained, 'what we've tried to do is convey the intelligence and energy and humour of the woman – to keep the integrity and spirit of Jane Austen'; on the other hand, '[we've tried to] make her story and her passion more accessible'.[94]

The casting of Hathaway and the focus on Austen's early adulthood were central to this strategy of creating a new image of Austen. 'I wanted to get away from the old-fashioned, nostalgic, chocolate-box English period drama thing', explained Jarrold. 'Having an American, or someone from a different background, a different way of acting, seemed kind of interesting.'[95] What Jarrold wanted to establish was an image of the young Austen as 'feisty...full of energy', instead of the usual 'prim and proper' image, someone 'that anyone could relate to'. 'There was something very interesting', he suggested, 'about looking at her before she became an iconic image'.[96] The discourse is again very familiar: these were exactly the terms on which *Elizabeth* had been conceived a decade earlier. And of course, the idea of presenting a 'modern' Austen accessible to contemporary mainstream audiences had been central to the Austen project since at least the mid-1990s.

Hathaway's presence was vital in this respect. Where *Clueless* had re-imagined Austen's *Emma* as a high-school romantic comedy for teens, *Becoming Jane* sought to tap into this same vein through the casting of someone who had made her name in the two *Princess Diaries* films (2001, 2004), Disney's young teen and pre-teen comedy-dramas, in which Hathaway plays an American girl who discovers she's actually European royalty: 'We went with Anne because we know she will bring a young teen audience with her to the film. Many of the 11-year-olds who fell in love with her in The Princess Diaries are now just turning 15. They are the right age for Austen.'[97] By the time *Becoming Jane* came out, she had also done the much edgier teen flick *Havoc* (2005), as well as more adult roles in *Brokeback Mountain* (2005) and *The Devil Wears Prada* (2006) (as well as another earlier fantasy film, *Ella Enchanted*, 2004). Such roles would of course only extend the potential appeal of Hathaway in *Becoming Jane*.

Austen purists were not impressed, and there was a predictable outcry among Janeites on the internet; this was picked up by the mainstream press, which reported that Austen fans were 'livid' that Anne Hathaway, a beautiful American woman, was 'playing their beloved authoress'.[98] The tension between passion and restraint made for good journalistic copy, with both *Empire* film magazine and the *Daily Telegraph* – unlikely bedfellows – adopting a phrase that had a certain popular currency at the time, describing 'a pacy, even "sexed-up" take on Austen'. The *Empire* journalist encouraged readers to 'watch out for one of the year's hottest screen snogs', and noted that *Becoming Jane* might also be 'the first Austen-related film to boast a clear reference to cunnilingus' (Jane's father, the Reverend Austen, and his wife appear to indulge in this activity in a bedroom scene).[99]

Given the carefully contrived dual address of the film, this 'Brit lit costumer'[100] was taken up in a variety of ways by reviewers. At one level, they saw it as yet another quality English period drama, somewhat against expectation: it was 'less fluffily contrived than you'd expect', its themes were 'handled with thoughtful decorum',[101] it had 'an especially eloquent, witty screenplay', and it enjoyed 'pretty locations and attractive cinematography'.[102] If the pacing seemed 'a little measured at times...that pays off in the richness of the storytelling and a downbeat denouement that is genuinely moving'.[103] In the words of the *Daily Express*, this was 'a touching, well-made tale that should be the next triumph for great British film-making'.[104] The film opens with a delightful picturesque 'English' rural scene, a 'typical' late eighteenth-century improved landscape, with rolling parkland, hills and trees. The camera cuts in to a closer image of an old church and a grand house tucked in among the trees, which gives way to a montage of little details – including shots of Jane writing. Immediately, the film is situated as a tasteful 'English' period drama (despite, or perhaps because of the Irish settings), with the usual delightful costumes, period decor, and splendid properties surrounded by green countryside.

Of course there is also the by now predictable effort to dirty this delightful vision, which is rarely bathed in the sunlight so favoured by earlier Merchant Ivory productions. As one reviewer noted,

> Becoming Jane certainly looks different from most other Austen productions. It is still a period picture, with magnificent country houses and carriages, and a Wordsworthian rapture for fields, but the air is cold and wet, the colours are earthy... and there is a wintry feel draped over the proceedings. For once you hear the squelch of mud and the sound of crows and pheasants rising out of the mist. Even the costumes seem oddly casual.[105]

The literary connection was obviously important to a lot of reviewers. This was 'a beautifully crafted biography',[106] about the 'quintessential English author Jane Austen',[107] 'The story of Jane Austen's life done as if it was an adaptation of one of her books'.[108] For others, though, this was a disappointingly middle-of-the-road, middlebrow film, 'a pleasant, picturesque if pedestrian biopic... solidly directed' but overall 'bland and... too much like Sunday night telly'.[109] The *Sight and Sound* reviewer also found the film dull – and fanciful: 'the biographical nonsense wouldn't matter so much if the film worked as a standard-issue period romp, but unfortunately it can't decide whether to pander to the prettified heritage industry or strain for some serious point about the genesis of the female novelist in the 18th century'.[110] The film is certainly rather insipid, dull and lifeless, lacking the vivacity of some of the Austen adaptations and other English period dramas. It was also seen by some as predictable: 'it is a picture whose mannerisms have been learned from other Austen adaptations'.[111] Certainly many of the characters, plot developments, relationships, desires, conversations and settings seem overly familiar. Of course, in part, this was intentional: the film had to try to recreate the sorts of attractions that had worked in previous period films and literary adaptations; and it was also deliberately drawing parallels between the imagined biography of Austen and the plots and characters of her subsequent novels.

If one approached the film with a different mindset, the experience might be more amenable: 'Many were expecting an Oscar caliber period piece when what you really got was a romantic comedy. Still, it is effective for a romantic comedy and those going in with the right mindset should be pleased.'[112] Others agreed with this assessment: 'As literary biography it's about as tenable as Shakespeare in Love. But as a romantic comedy-drama for those who like big frocks and stately homes, it's wittier than most Austen film adaptations.'[113] It was all about what was expected of the film and how it could be used by its audiences:

> Feminist critics might take exception to the idea that the inspiration for Austen's success stemmed from a stymied heart, while literary scholars may bleat about liberties taken and history imagined. But for thousands of love-hungry couples seeking a mutually agreeable reason to cuddle up at the flicks, it's terrific – eye candy for blokes and girls alike, with a smartly sneaking sense of the reality of relationships.[114]

One woman's magazine confidently declared 'You absolutely must not miss this bright, funny romantic, heart-breaking triumph',[115] while a film magazine described it as 'a warm, charming, bittersweet romance – destined to make a thousand dates'.[116] 'Guys, take her to see this one', proposed an American television reviewer: 'She'll love you for it!'[117] If it was an ideal romantic dating movie, it was also a female bonding film: released in the UK just before Mother's Day, a banner in a newspaper advertisement proposed to readers that they should 'make a date with your mother'.[118]

For some, though, the film was clearly strong enough to be 'more than just a handsomely mounted chick-flick or a Mother's Day treat'.[119] It was enjoyed because it 'seems true to the period yet is also fresh and accessible to a modern audience and studiously avoids the anachronistic'.[120] In this respect, there was a minor tussle between those described as Austen purists, the Janeites, on the one hand, and on the other hand those who wanted to create a more accessible, modern Austen – a tussle which the press tried to turn into a newsworthy debate. The modernising tendency saw the film 'tak[ing] risks in doing what it pleases with an obscure period in Austen's life', admitting that 'it certainly won't be for everyone',[121] but enjoying what they perceived as its revisionist historicising: 'Becoming Jane certainly is a fresh departure – Jane Austen kissing! – but the filmmakers have been careful to base the love affair on the truth as they see it.'[122] The Jane Austen character is frequently described in reviews as 'feisty'.[123] This meant that 'Rather than sainted Jane of Austen, the tea-sipping spinster of the popular imagination, this spirited costume drama depicts Austen as a hot-headed young woman who flirted, danced and drank, and, most importantly, fell deeply in love.'[124] Of course, this upset the defenders of the Janeite faith, but they had been up in arms ever since the too pretty and too un-English Anne Hathaway had been cast in the central role.

Becoming Jane was in many ways typical of both the Austen adaptation and the modestly scaled literate film that yet addressed mainstream

Foregrounding romance in *Becoming Jane*.

audiences hungry for a romantic comedy-drama. Its dual address was carefully strategised, and it was designed well enough for audiences to decide whether they wanted to engage with or disengage from the literary Austen. Perhaps it was too typical, too familiar, too predictable to be a major box-office success, but it still worked reasonably well within the niche reserved for films of this ilk. The film made it possible to renew and extend the Austen franchise, which had proved to be such a potent aspect of culturally English filmmaking (and television programme-making) in the 1990s and 2000s. The transnational production arrangements and the literary connections of *Becoming Jane* were typical of the way in which canonical versions of Englishness reached the screen in this period.

The Austen franchise as a whole straddled both contemporary romantic comedies and more reverential heritage dramas; both versions in their different ways speak to contemporary audiences and feed into and feed off contemporary debates, with the heritage versions of Austen playing an important role in the branding of England as a historical nation. The English past is represented in many different ways on film. The period dramas that invoke the iconic heritage Austen play a pivotal role in defining the limits and possibilities of these representations. It is to this wider field of representations of the English past that I turn in the next two chapters.

7 Intimate and epic versions of the English past

Introduction

Representations of the past play a vital role in establishing images of identity – and indeed, identities of both place and people. The relationship between the past that is represented and the present when the film is produced and received is complex. Some films are designed to play self-consciously on this relationship; others do so more obliquely; some audiences are keen to explore that relationship; others are more interested in the narratives of romance or adventure offered by these films, or by the attractions of period detail or star images. Some films play on the exotic otherness of the past; some stress similarities with the present: in either case, historical distance has to be both established and negated, so that audiences can embrace difference without losing the comforts of familiarity.

England and Britain have long and well-documented histories, and filmmakers have explored those histories since the beginning of cinema. In recent decades, in England as elsewhere in Western culture, the past has been a major source of fascination, manifested above all in the growth of the so-called heritage industry. Cinema has participated in this cultural shift in all sorts of ways, particularly in the case of films about the English or the British past. (As in other chapters, there is the problem of nationalist terminology, but here the problem is exacerbated, since Britain and England mean different things at different moments in history. While I have been as careful as I can be in how I use this terminology, a certain looseness or ambiguity will occasionally be necessary.)

Films about the English past have also played a key role in establishing and reproducing the brand image of England as a historical place, and American capital has ensured that this brand image circulates globally. At the same time, filmmakers working with historical subject matter have also been keen to ensure that the resulting films appeal to contemporary audiences, and in many cases the relatively young multiplex audience. The effort to make the past seem relevant to such audiences produces films that are often self-consciously contemporary in feel; in this sense, films about the past have also ironically in various ways participated in the rebranding of Britain as a modern, vibrant place, as the 'Cool Britannia' of the late 1990s and beyond. The introduction in 2007 of the Cultural Test for determining the Britishness of films for official purposes played into this dual temporal engagement. It encouraged filmmakers to engage with the country's cultural heritage on the one hand, and on the other to adopt a creative and distinctive approach. In this chapter and the next, I examine some of the ways in which filmmakers have handled English historical subject matter in the 1990s and 2000s.

A great many different periods of English history have been presented on film in the 1990s and 2000s, but in terms of the numbers of films produced, some periods have been preferred over others. Between 1990 and 2009, there were some 220 films set in the past and either located in England or Britain, or dealing with English or British characters – that is, around 12 per cent of the UK films in this period.[1] Of those films, around 30 were set in the medieval period, just under 20 in the period between 1500 and 1800, and some 50 in the recent past (that is, since the Second World War) – which means that the vast majority (around 120) were set between 1800 and 1939, in what I am calling the modern past. The most popular period for filmic representations proved to be the seventy-odd years between 1870 and the Second World War, embracing some 75 films.

My concern in this chapter and the next is with the ways in which these different pasts are presented to contemporary cinema audiences, for by no means do all these films engage with the English past in the same way, regardless of the period in which they are set. I am therefore interested in the extent to which filmic representations of the Middle Ages, the period between 1500 and 1800, the modern past and the very recent past are distinctive and historically specific, but also the extent to which they draw on well-established conventions for representing the past, regardless of period. How is a medieval sensibility invoked, for instance, in the films set in the Middle Ages? What makes the modern past seem modern?

Different aesthetic and ideological traits, different cultural traditions and identities, are adopted to represent different pasts, and to appeal to different audiences. As with all films, there is a certain reliance on stereotypes, but different sorts of stereotypes apply to each period represented on screen. Consequently, the nation is constructed and projected differently in films about different pasts. In examining the differences and similarities between films and the representations and pleasures they offer, I will focus on the period in which they are set, but will also consider the scale, scope and genre of the films, where they are positioned in the marketplace, and the audiences to whom they are addressed. As will be clear from previous chapters, different films offer different sorts of pleasures to different audiences. Different sorts of productions rely on stereotypes in different ways. And only certain sorts of narratives and dramas will attract funding and secure distribution – so what sorts of films get made and shown, under what circumstances, and why?

In exploring these issues, I will examine the various modes of film practice adopted for representing the English/British past, from the blockbusting, star-laden historical adventure to low-budget art-house fare. I will suggest on the one hand that filmmakers frequently blur the boundaries between different historical periods, but on the other hand that there is something specific about the way different pasts are represented. This specificity, I would argue, owes as much to generic convention and the audience address of the films as it does to histories of the period depicted. To some extent we can identify two extremes.

King Arthur: epic history for boys.

At one end are the historical epics about medieval heroes (*King Arthur*, 2004, for instance), which tend to adopt a more populist, youthful and masculine appeal. At the other end are the numerous intimate costume dramas set in the nineteenth and early twentieth centuries, which tend to adopt a more middlebrow, middle-aged and feminine mode of address (*Ladies in Lavender*, 2004, for instance). These latter films include the period adaptations of Jane Austen's novels, and make up the heritage costume drama trend which I discussed in chapter 5.

As in previous chapters, I will be dealing with films from a range of production contexts – and while some of them might be designated as English films, others were made and funded solely by American companies, and many more were international co-productions, at least at the level of funding. These films embrace a variety of modes of film practice that can be differentiated from each other in terms of production context, production values and budgets; film style, generic convention and star presence; and promotion, exhibition and reception. Given the vagaries of the marketplace, it is not surprising that some of the smaller-budget films ended up impacting only minimally on both critics and the box office, while others – *The Madness of King George* (1994), for instance – were both critically acclaimed and took far more at the box office than is normal for a film of that scale. Equally, at the other end of the scale, some of the big-budget epics – *Braveheart* (1995), for instance – captured the popular imagination, while others, including *King Arthur*, left critics cold and were comparative box-office failures (even if they actually sold many more tickets than smaller-budget films!).

A key concept in this discussion will be the sensibility of the films in question – the way in which a film is pitched to its audiences, the particular assumptions that are made by filmmakers about how a film might address its target consumers, what it can and cannot say, the ingredients that are assumed to be attractive and acceptable in terms of style, theme and subject matter. For reasons that will become clear, I draw a broad distinction between films that deal with the modern past and those that deal with what I will call the pre-modern past. Broadly speaking, pre-modern films adopt a different sensibility from those depicting the modern past, although there are always exceptions to the general trend. I argue that the modern past in culturally English films starts around 1800 – and is in effect ushered in by the various period adaptations of Jane Austen's novels. Its end point is, strictly, yesterday – but I also argue that films that deal with the very recent past – from around the time of the Second World War to the present – develop a sensibility that is distinct from films set in the nineteenth and early twentieth centuries. In film terms, the pre-modern British past comprises what in common parlance is often described as the Dark Ages, the medieval period and what historians refer to as the early modern period, and is generally presented as a much more dangerous, bawdy and primitive time, compared to the refinement, respectability, sophistication and safeness of the modern past.

In this chapter, I survey the range of films made in the 1990s and 2000s that depict the English past, and draw some broad distinctions between pre-modern films and those that depict the modern past. I then focus on some of the differences between large-scale action-adventure films in epic mode, and the more intimate costume dramas associated with representations of the modern past. One of the distinctive features of many of the films dealing with the pre-modern past is the extent to which they adopt what I will call a dirty realist mode of representation: the pre-modern past is not only dangerous, it is also frequently dirty. The modern past, by contrast, is frequently both more picturesque and a safer, more civilised space; representations of the very recent past, on the other hand, tend to be defined more by their attention to the details of consumer culture and the pervasiveness of a popular culture mediated above all through television and music. This is not to suggest that films set in earlier times fail to embrace contemporary consumer culture, for the ways in which they have been taken up by the heritage and tourism industries clearly indicates otherwise.

Having established some of the parameters within which films about the English past operate in this chapter, in the next chapter I explore some of the ways in which those parameters are challenged and different historical periods and modes of representation merge into one another. I note two things in particular in this respect. First, I note some of the ways in which the ideal Englishness often associated with costume dramas about the modern past is deliberately tainted in some productions. Second, I note the historical myopia of the film business, which leads to a blurring of the boundaries between markedly different historical periods. Yet at the same time, films about the past are often discussed in terms of realism, and I examine in more detail some of the claims made about their historical authenticity, and the various strategies used by filmmakers to establish a period patina. Realism, of course, is about creating an illusion that audiences will find credible; to that extent, it depends as much on convention as on literal accuracy, on what is accepted at any one time by audiences and critics as an apt and adequate means of representing the past. Finally, I reflect on the versions of England, Englishness and English heritage displayed in these various films about the English past.

Surveying the past

As noted above, around 30 films released in the 1990s and 2000s offered some version of the British medieval past or sought to represent British medieval heroes. (The distinction is important, since some of the heroes associated with medieval literature and folk tales lived before the medieval period.) The heroes represented have for the most part been very familiar, from centuries of storytelling. Thus in the early 1990s there were two *Robin Hoods* within a year of each other, a relatively low-budget British version, *Robin Hood* (1990), and an American blockbuster, *Robin Hood: Prince of Thieves* (1991), starring Kevin Costner; shortly after, Mel Brooks's spoof of the legend appeared, *Robin Hood: Men in Tights* (1993). More recently, there was a film version of *Tristan + Isolde* (2006), and two of the Beowulf story, the first epic poem to be written in English, an Icelandic version, *Beowulf and Grendel* (2006), and an animated version, *Beowulf* (2007). Another 11 films engage in some way with the Arthurian legend, although they all have their own takes on the tale, their titles often indicating their particular focus, as with *Guinevere* (1994), *First Knight* (1995), *Merlin* (1998) and *King Arthur*. Several more reworked Mark Twain's 1889 fantasy *A Connecticut Yankee in King Arthur's Court*, with a twentieth-century figure returning in some way to Arthurian times – from the children's film *A Kid in King Arthur's Court* (1995) to Sam Raimi's horror fantasy *Army of Darkness* (1992) (sometimes the time travel worked the other way round, with Arthurian elements emerging in the present, as in *Merlin – The Return*, 2000).

As with several of these films, the setting, even if it is in some vague sense Britain/England, is often mythical; elsewhere, medieval heroes are occasionally situated beyond the borders of England, as in the case of *Braveheart* (1995) and the Crusader story *Kingdom of Heaven* (2005). Several more films were adapted from an assortment of other literary sources, from the medieval to the postmodern. Medieval poems and letters and the plays of Shakespeare and Marlowe accounted for *The Wanderer* (1991), *Anchoress* (1993), *Macbeth* and *Edward II* (1991), for instance, while *A Knight's Tale* (2001) was loosely inspired by Chaucer. There were also adaptations of more recent novels by writers as diverse as Barry Unsworth (*The Reckoning*, 1991) and Vera Chapman (*The Magic Sword*, 1998). We might add to this list the pseudo-medievalism of the *Lord of the Rings* trilogy (2001–3). There were also a handful of other films made from original scripts, including a semi-pornographic film about sexual activity within an enclosed religious community, *Sacred Flesh* (1999), and a less exploitative low-budget horror film about the plague in fourteenth-century England, *Anazapta* (2001).

One might also note a tension between the Romantic mythology of heroic knights in shining armour, which is there to some extent in *First Knight*, and the demythologising brand of dirty realism and historical authenticity, which is where *King Arthur* situates itself. But at any moment, both the romantic and the dirty realist can be undercut by tongue-in-cheek comedy or outright parody – whether it is the archly camp villains of the otherwise realist *Robin Hood*, *King Arthur* or *Kingdom of Heaven*, the postmodern anachronisms of Derek Jarman's *Edward II* or *A Knight's Tale* (2001), or the full Mel Brooks treatment of *Robin Hood: Men in Tights*. Each of these modes of expression, and especially the frequent confusion or tension between them, owes much to the Monty Python brand of medievalism in *Monty Python and the Holy Grail* (1975) and *Jabberwocky* (1977).

The early modern period in England, from the end of the fifteenth century to the end of the eighteenth century, was represented in fewer than 20 films produced in the 1990s and 2000s. England's monarchs play a key role as protagonists in most of these films, indicating the extent to which filmmakers rely on well-known and familiar figures. *Elizabeth* (1998), the sequel *Elizabeth: The Golden Age* (2007) and *The Other Boleyn Girl* (2008) deal with the Tudors, while Queen Elizabeth also appears in *Shakespeare in Love* (1998). *To Kill a King* (2003) charts the rise of Cromwell and the demise of Charles I, while *Restoration* (1995), *Stage Beauty* (2004) and *The Libertine* (2005) are all set in the Restoration period, with Charles II playing a more or less significant role in each; *The Madness of King George* (1995) brings this royal cavalcade up to the late eighteenth century. Then there is *Orlando* (1992), adapted from Virginia Woolf's novella, which romps its way from the first to the second Elizabethan era, with three sequences set in the early modern period.

Several of the representations of the early modern period were, like *Orlando*, adaptations of novels or plays, including the historical adventures *Rob Roy* (1995), from Sir Walter Scott's novel, and *The Last of the Mohicans* (1992), from James Fenimore Cooper's novel. *Restoration*,

The Madness of King George, *Stage Beauty*, *The Libertine* and *The Other Boleyn Girl* were all versions of much more recent novels or plays, while *The Duchess* (2008) was based on a recent biography of the eighteenth Duchess of Devonshire. Adaptations of work actually produced in the early modern period include *Moll Flanders* (1996), *The Clandestine Marriage* (1999) and *A Cock and Bull Story* (2005), from Laurence Sterne's *Tristram Shandy*, which tries to be faithful to the source text by being us much about the making of a historical film and the self-consciousness of its leading protagonist as about the story itself, so that the illusion of a recreated eighteenth century is hardly present.

Shakespeare or his writing figure in several films, including *Shakespeare in Love*, *Stage Beauty* and *The Libertine*. There are various other adaptations or reworkings of Shakespeare's plays, which could perhaps be included in this list but for various reasons have not been. Several of the recent adaptations of those plays that are actually set in early modern England were updated to a much later setting (for example, the 1995 adaptation of *Richard III*, updated to the 1930s, or Al Pacino's *Looking for Richard*, about staging Richard III in present-day New York). The plays set outside England may be central to English culture, but the absence of any English characters or settings in the films adapted from them hardly suggests they belong in this discussion. Perhaps a case could be made for including Peter Greenaway's *Prospero's Books*, but it would be difficult to make a case for Kenneth Branagh's *Much Ado About Nothing*, shot in Tuscany, or Baz Luhrman's *William Shakespeare's Romeo + Juliet*, set in a postmodern California. Films set in the early modern period and made from original screenplays were few and far between, and invariably deal with well-documented historical events, from the two *Elizabeth* films and *To Kill a King* to *Chasing the Deer* (1994), a low-budget film about the lead-up to the Battle of Culloden, *Plunkett & Macleane* (1999), about a pair of notorious eighteenth-century 'gentlemen highwaymen', and Terence Malick's *The New World* (2005) – like *The Last of the Mohicans*, dealing with the colonial exploits of the English in America (and, in this case, the story of Pocohontas).

As the above demonstrates, it is possible to identify shared themes and characteristics across the various films set in the medieval or early modern past and released in the 1990s and 2000s. Even so, it would be difficult to make a convincing case for a sustained cycle of either medieval or early modern films – productions are too sporadic and too different for that, and the medieval and the early modern are not really categories of filmmaking used by the film industry. Clearly there's an ongoing fascination with the Arthurian legend, Robin Hood, the Tudors and Shakespeare, but it is hardly specific or unique to the 1990s and 2000s. In terms of sheer numbers of films, it is actually the modern past, and especially the late nineteenth and early twentieth centuries, that has provided the richest terrain for contemporary filmmakers wanting to make period films with English settings or characters.

The modern English past begins to emerge on film around 1800, in the various period adaptations of Jane Austen's novels, from the 1995 version of *Sense and Sensibility* to the 2005 *Pride and Prejudice*. By this, I mean that, while there is no denying the distance of the past, or that the characters wear 'funny clothes', Austen's characters as they appear on film seem very modern by comparison with those in films set in earlier times. Their language, their concerns, interests and anxieties (especially their romantic interests), their modes of behaviour, all seem very famil-iar. This recognition effect is clearly not absent from films set in earlier times – indeed, filmmakers work hard to ensure their period characters appeal to modern audiences – but arguably it is stronger in the Austen films, and in a line of further films stretching up to the present.

The 120 or so films that cover the period from 1800 to 1939 can be categorised in various ways. Literary adaptation, for instance, is again a key feature. The range of adaptations with period settings was already noted in chapter 4, but it is worth rehearsing here. Some of the adaptations rework the novels of classic nineteenth-century authors, from Austen, via the Brontës (*Wuthering Heights*, 1992; *Jane Eyre*, 1996) and Charles Dickens (*Nicholas Nickleby*, 2002; *Oliver Twist*, 2005), to Thomas Hardy (*Jude*, 1996; *The Woodlanders*, 1997). There are versions of some of the most canonical late nineteenth- and twentieth-century writers, from Henry James (*The Portrait of a Lady*, 1996; *The Wings of the Dove*, 1997) and E.M. Forster (*Howards End*, 1992; *Where Angels Fear to Tread*, 1991) to Virginia Woolf (*Orlando* again, and *Mrs Dalloway*, 1997), D.H. Lawrence (*Lady Chatterley*, 2006) and Evelyn Waugh (*Brideshead Revisited*, 2008). There are children's classics (*The Secret Garden*, 1993; *Black Beauty*, 1994), and middlebrow best-sellers (Dodie Smith, *I Capture the Castle*, 2003). And there are reworkings of more recent 'quality' writers, from Kazuo Ishiguro (*The Remains of the Day*, 1993) and Ian McEwan (*Atonement*, 2007) to A.S. Byatt (*Angels and Insects*, 1995) and Peter Carey (*Oscar and Lucinda*, 1997). Writers and other cultural lumi-naries are also of course the subjects of several biopics, from *Bright Star* (about John Keats, 2009) and *Topsy Turvy* (Gilbert and Sullivan, 1999), via *Finding Neverland* (J.M. Barrie, 2004) and *Chaplin* (Charlie Chaplin, 1992), to *Carrington* (Dora Carrington and Lytton Strachey, 1995), *Tom and Viv* (T.S. Eliot, 1994) and *Miss Potter* (Beatrix Potter, 2007).

A good many of the literary adaptations dealing with the modern English past focus on the privileged, the wealthy and the titled, including the Austen films, the Forster and James adaptations, and three versions of Oscar Wilde plays – *An Ideal Husband* (1999), *The Importance of Being Earnest* (2002) and *A Good Woman* (2004, a reworking of *Lady Windermere's Fan*). Merchant Ivory's versions of *Howards End* and *The Remains of the Day* very much set the tone here, although *Mrs Brown* (1997), about Queen Victoria, was also a considerable success. In the 2000s, there has been a particular fascination with privilege in the 1930s, a period usually associated with economic depression, with some 14 films set at least partly in this period, including *Gosford Park* (2001), *I Capture the Castle*, *The Heart of Me* (2002), *Ladies in Lavender* (2004), *Atonement* and *Brideshead Revisited*. Poverty is by no means ignored in films about the modern English past, however. Even the Austen adaptations are in part about the relative impoverishment of their central protagonists. More obviously, Victorian poverty is addressed in the two Dickens adaptations, as well as *The Fool, Jude* and *Black Beauty*, while something similar is done for the 1930s in *Keep the Aspidistra Flying* – but even in films that deal with varying degrees of poverty, romance and the picturesque are never far away. Another recurring fascination of films about the modern past is the foibles of the English abroad, where stereotypes of national identity are often tested. Such films include *Enchanted April* (1991), *Sirens* (1994), *The English Patient* (1996) and *Tea with Mussolini* (1998).

Atonement provides a useful bridge between depictions of the modern past and those of the very recent, often postmodern past, since its narrative begins in the 1930s, covers the war years, and then leaps to the present. Inevitably, the divisions I make between different periods are to some extent arbitrary. My final category, films dealing with the recent past, begins with the Second World War, even though clearly for some audiences this is no longer the recent past, but something quite distant and unknowable, except through media representations. Indeed, for all audiences, films set in the recent past are still very much period films. By proposing that the recent English past begins on film with the Second World War, I am arguing that the more than 50 films set in this period again have a relatively distinct sensibility, and often feel very

The privileged upper-class English world of the 1930s in *Atonement*.

different from films set before the war. There are a number of reasons for this: they do not deal with mythical heroes of the stature of those represented in the medieval films, for instance; they rarely deal with the highly privileged world of royalty or the aristocracy that is present in so many of the early modern films; they do not even very often steep themselves in the perhaps slightly less privileged milieux of the upper classes, or the upper middle classes, that populate so many films set in the late nineteenth or early twentieth centuries. If they deal with the rich and famous, they are generally those who have made their names, rather than inherited them: musicians, for instance, from rock stars, in *Stoned* (2005) and *Control* (2007), to classical performers, in *Hilary and Jackie* (1998); and film stars, as in *The Life and Death of Peter Sellers* (2004). Even the biopics about writers, like *Shadowlands* (1993), *Iris* (2001) and *Sylvia* (2003), deal with authors less well known than Shakespeare or Beatrix Potter, or less notorious than Wilde.

Indeed, the protagonists of films about the very recent past tend above all towards ordinariness. *Atonement* sets the tone here: its representations of conditions at the front and in a London hospital during the Second World War are markedly different from the privileged world of the 1930s at the start of the film. *The Remains of the Day* does something similar, with its 1930s sequences set in the heyday of the country house that is at the centre of the narrative, but the 1950s sequences exploring a much more mundane *mise-en-scène*. A similar vision of a world without privilege, or a world inhabited by characters stripped of privilege, is present in other films with wartime settings, from *Chicago Joe and the Showgirl* (1990) to *Charlotte Gray* (2001) and *Enigma* (2002). But strong characterisations of working-class people can appear in a range of settings, from the war period (*The Land Girls*, 1998), via the 1950s (*Vera Drake*, 2004), to the 1980s (*Trainspotting*, 1996, and *Billy Elliot*, 2000).

The English past also finally becomes a multicultural space, in films such as *Young Soul Rebels* (1991), *East Is East* (1999), *Anita and Me* (2002) and *Brick Lane* (2007). The living conditions in *Land Girls* may seem almost pre-modern at times, but the representation of relative poverty in these films generally feels different to the medieval poverty of *Anazapta* or the Victorian poverty of the recent Dickens adaptations, *Nicholas Nickleby* and *Oliver Twist*. One reason for this is surely that films set in the very recent past lack the distancing qualities of even the films set in the 1930s, and deal with events that are familiar through media representations or even living memory, rather than through folk memory, official history or formal education. The way that films like *Sixty-Six* (2006), *Velvet Goldmine* (1998), *24 Hour Party People* (2002) and *Trainspotting* embrace aspects of modern, and indeed postmodern, popular culture also distinguishes them from films set in earlier times. And the world depicted often in some way engages with the world of consumerism. Of course, there are films that challenge these generalisations: *The Queen* (2006), for instance, is set in the very recent past (the 1990s), and deals with the royal family and the Prime Minister – but it is also very much about the impact of postmodern media culture on the queen and her relatives, who seem almost untouched by consumer culture – and at the same time, rather ordinary.

Capturing the popular imagination: the medieval epic vs the modern costume drama

One fact that becomes clear from this survey is that there are far more films about the modern past than about the pre-modern past: less than a quarter of the period films released between 1990 and 2008 deal with the medieval period or early modern England. On the one hand, then, filmic representations of the more distant past have hardly dominated the representation of English history in the last two decades. On the contrary, in terms of the numbers of films produced, it is the much more numerous, relatively small-scale and intimate costume dramas set in the late nineteenth and early twentieth centuries that have dominated. On the other hand, a good proportion of the films about the medieval period were relatively big-budget productions about very familiar medieval heroes or stories, which made an impact at the box office in a way that few of the films about the modern past did. Films such as *Robin Hood: Prince of Thieves, Braveheart, First Knight* (1995), and more recently *King Arthur, Kingdom of Heaven* (2005) and *Beowulf* all established a considerable box-office presence. To this list, one might again add the *Lord of the Rings* trilogy, as large-scale, blockbusting films with a medieval-style setting and medieval-style heroes. To this extent, one could argue that the few action-adventure epics depicting the medieval past or featuring medieval or medieval-style heroes have had far more of an impact on the popular imagination than the far more numerous but smaller-scale costume dramas about the modern past. It is worth noting that most of the films set in the early modern period were also relatively small-scale and enjoyed only a limited release.

It is tempting to construct a neat set of binary oppositions, with the medieval action-adventure epic at one end of the scale and the intimate, romantic costume drama of the modern past at the other end. These two extremes offer distinct attractions and different ways of engaging with audience expectations. At one level, this is a question of the gendered appeal of different film genres, since the historical adventure film is addressed more decisively towards male audiences, while the romantic costume drama is geared more towards female audiences. The latter offers a much more intimate and conventionally feminine version of history, closer to the woman's film: to some extent, this is history for girls. The films are thus characterised by comparatively mundane narratives of politeness, restraint and refinement, in which relatively little happens – but what does happen tends towards romance, affairs of the heart and domestic drama, and characters are less heroic but psychologically more complex.

The historical adventure film offers a much more epic and conventionally masculine version of history for boys, characterised by dramatic narratives full of consequential action, in which strong masculine hero figures are defined precisely by the actions they undertake, and where passions are raw and more overtly threatening. Film titles can be revealing: several of the costume dramas depicting the modern past have as their title the name of a woman – *Emma* (1996), *Mrs Brown* (1997), *Mrs Dalloway* (1997), *Miss Potter* (2007) and *Young Victoria* (2009), for instance. Several of the

Mrs Brown: intimate history for girls.

films dealing with medieval heroes, on the other hand, carry masculine names; thus *Robin Hood*, *First Knight*, *King Arthur* and *Beowulf* all identify their core target audience in terms of gender in their titles.

The opening of *King Arthur* establishes the scale and sensibility of the film. First there are vast vistas across open land. Shortly after, and still within a few minutes of the start of the film, an epic battle takes place, a bloody, vicious and dramatic battle, between the Woads, led by Merlin, and the Romans and Arthur's Sarmatian knights. The battle takes place in a primeval landscape, flanked by a dark and mysterious forest, while mist swirls around the combatants. At the end of the battle, the ground is littered with fallen bodies. In effect, though, this is just a taster, to whet the appetite, and the film builds up to a climactic confrontation in another primeval landscape, across which Hadrian's Wall stretches. This time, the battle is between hordes of Saxons, stretching across the widescreen image, and Arthur's knights, this time fighting on the same side as the Woads. Everything here is on an enormous scale, with the skies full of hurtling arrows and firebombs, and the ground a swirling mass of smoke, knights on horseback, and foot soldiers slugging it out. It is spectacular, noisy and awe-inspiring, with the camera moving between close-ups of one-to-one combat and soaring crane shots that capture the impossible magnitude of the battlefield.

If anything, *Kingdom of Heaven* is even more epic in scale, the massed armies for the battle scenes even larger than the Saxons in *King Arthur*, and equally impressive crowd scenes in Messina and Jerusalem, both teeming medieval cities. The landscapes are again spectacular, with widescreen long shots from on high emphasising the scale of the image, the contrast between the cold, windswept mountains of central France and the deserts of the holy land demonstrating just how much money was lavished on the film. In both *King Arthur* and *Kingdom of Heaven*, there are also romantic and passionate moments, and both films end with an ideal heterosexual couple being established. Even so, the love interest is a very minor element of the films, with the violent and aggressive exercise of power the main attraction, and a very conventionally masculine attraction it is too.

The core female audience was wooed to the costume dramas of the early modern and modern past not just through titles, but through casting, storylines and marketing. Many of them had female protagonists, from *Elizabeth*, *Moll Flanders*, and *Sense and Sensibility* to *The Wings of the Dove*, *I Capture the Castle* and *Charlotte Gray*. By definition, many of them featured fine costumes. Some of the source material was written by female authors (Austen, the Brontës, Woolf, Rose Tremain's *Restoration*). Romance was a frequent narrative motivation, from *Shakespeare in Love*, via *Pride and Prejudice* to *Atonement*. Indeed, *Shakespeare in Love* was sold above all as a romance, with promotional taglines including 'Love is the only inspiration' (in the USA), 'your perfect date' and 'a comedy about the greatest love story almost never told' (in the UK). The film may also have been widely discussed in the so-called quality press – in both newspapers and magazines, and in reviews, think pieces and news items – as an interesting take on Shakespeare, in which questions of period authenticity might be considered. But this was less about promotion and more about leaving the quality press to generate a debate about the film to bring in the upscale segment of the audience. In fact, *Shakespeare in Love* was rarely marketed as a period movie, or an authentic representation of the late Elizabethan period: it was not the historical setting that sold the film to a mainstream audience, but the romantic comedy.

The distinction between epic medieval adventures and romantic costume dramas of the early modern and modern periods is not simply about the differently gendered appeal of different genres, however; it is also to some extent about class, cultural capital and taste, and the difference between popular and middlebrow versions of film culture. Thus the medieval adventure belongs above all within the realm of popular cinema, while most of the costume dramas about the early modern and modern past inhabit the university-educated middle-class niche market for small-scale, quality films, the point at which the art-house sector crosses over into the mainstream. The medieval adventure is more likely to be funded by a major Hollywood studio, to operate within the economy of the blockbuster and to address multiplex audiences square-on. The intimate costume drama of the modern past is more likely to be an independent production – or if it has the support of one of the Hollywood studios, it will be through their specialist, boutique label for smaller-scale, quality fare. Such films are defined, discussed and distributed in terms of prestige, they get shown at film festivals and they win awards – all of which is important in terms of how they are sold to audiences.

The British distributor of *To Kill a King*, for instance, identified the core audience for the film as 'older, more discerning cinemagoers who hanker after upscale period fare such as *Mrs Brown*', thereby neatly identifying both the planned market position for the film, and the links between films about the early modern and modern pasts.[2] Another early modern film, *Stage Beauty*, was described by reviewers as 'intelligent and entertaining',[3] 'the sort of thoughtful, well-crafted movie intelligent film-goers yearn for'.[4] At stake here is the well-worn distinction between the serious and the popular, with *To Kill a King*, *Stage Beauty* and *Mrs Brown* being identified as intelligent filmmaking, distinct from the, by implication, trivial blockbuster cinema aimed at the young people that dominate the multiplex audience. This is once more *literate* cinema – a description bolstered by the number of films set in both the early modern and the modern past that were adapted from novels or plays. One might also note the use of playwrights and novelists as screenwriters; thus the playwrights Alan Bennett, Tom Stoppard, Jeffrey Hatcher, Stephen Jeffreys and David Hare wrote the screenplays for *The Madness of King George*, *Shakespeare in Love*, *Stage Beauty*, *The Libertine* and *The Hours* respectively, while the novelist Ruth Prawer Jhabvala wrote the screenplays for *Howards End*, *The Remains of the Day* and *The Golden Bowl*, and Deborah Moggach scripted *Pride and Prejudice*. The medieval films, by contrast, while they often draw on literary sources, rarely have the same relationship to contemporary literary culture (nor indeed do many of the films set in the very recent past).

The different ways in which these various films circulate in the marketplace can be indicated through box-office performance. *King Arthur*, for instance, opened on 3,086 screens in the USA, taking $22m on its first weekend, and on 400 screens in the UK, taking $6m – and despite taking $64m overall in the USA and the UK, and more than $200m worldwide, was regarded as a box-office flop! *Braveheart* opened on 2,035 screens in the USA, and 289 in the UK, and took nearly $100m in the two markets combined. The box-office champion among medieval films was *Robin Hood: Prince of Thieves*, which took over $200m in the USA and the UK combined. *Mrs Brown*, about Queen Victoria, was widely considered a significant success for a middlebrow costume drama, but its box-office takings seem paltry next to these medieval epics – just $14m worldwide. In the USA, it opened on just six art-house screens, gradually building up to 432; in the UK, it opened on 149 screens – a lot for a film of this type, but minimal compared to *Braveheart* or *King Arthur*. There may have been plenty of middlebrow critical debate about *Mrs Brown*, and it may have appealed much more to discerning, middle-class audiences – but its hold on the popular imagination was far less secure than even a relative box-office flop like *King Arthur*, with its $120m budget and epic canvas.[5]

Among the films that depict the early modern period, *Orlando* was a solid art-house success, grossing $5.3m in the USA alone, although that was still some way short of its £6.6m budget; *Stage Beauty* took only $1.65m in the USA and the UK combined. Even *Emma*, a relatively high-profile costume drama, could only manage £5.3m at the UK box office and $22.2m in the USA, while just over a decade later, *The Duchess*, heavily promoted on the back of the star presence of Keira Knightley, was unable to muster more than $29m worldwide, less than 14 per cent of the takings of *King Arthur*, where Knightley's presence was supplemented by several other up-and-coming and established stars. In box-office terms, as in many other respects, then, there are important differences between the blockbusting epic and the smaller-scale costume drama. Of course all these films also have lives on terrestrial, cable and satellite TV, on video and DVD, and in other ancillary markets, but even so it would be difficult to claim in general that the smaller films routinely appeal to more than a niche audience.[6]

From the picturesque modern past to the dirty realism and dangers of the pre-modern past

In terms of cinema the medieval is much more than a loosely delineated historical period. On the one hand, as I've indicated, the medieval emerges in the generic conventions of the epic historical adventure, which give the medieval a sense of drama, a sense of danger and a sense of scale that is rarely present in the films set in the modern past. To this extent, one might say that the medieval is more a genre than a period. On the other hand, the medieval emerges precisely through a contrast with the modern, regardless of the actual period in which the films are set. The modern past obscures danger and drama behind a veneer of refinement, respectability and safeness; the medieval is about stripping away that veneer. Medievalism is thus very often as much about a sensibility and a *mise-en-scène* as it is about a historically specific period.

One of the key characteristics of the modern English past as represented in costume dramas, as I have demonstrated elsewhere, is the display of heritage spectacle, in terms of landscape, architecture and interior design.[7] The high point of this heritage spectacle can perhaps be found in the 1990s adaptations of the novels of Forster, including *Where Angels Fear to Tread* and *Howards End*, and Austen, especially *Sense and Sensibility* and *Emma*. What characterised those films was on the one hand the politeness and restraint of the characters and the storylines, and on the other hand the surface prettiness, the delightful picturesque images of a traditional, semi-rural, semi-cultivated southern England apparently untouched by industrialisation or urbanisation.

The modern past in such representations is thus an idealised version of historical England; the landscape for instance is modern enough to have been partly cultivated and enclosed, but it is still protected from modern technology and the city; and while it remains a pastoral landscape, it is a green and pleasant land, not the windswept, untamed landscape of so many of the medieval films. It is generally a geographically specific landscape too, the gently rolling hills of the Home Counties, rather than moorland, forests or mountains. In this definitively picturesque landscape are the stately homes and grand cottages of the privileged classes, with their comfortable, domesticated interiors – above all, the genteel, carefully furnished drawing rooms. The inhabitants of this *mise-en-scène* again adopt a veneer of polite respectability. If by the beginning of the twentieth century they start to travel about in motor cars, those cars are of such gleaming, vintage quality, such models of craftsmanship, that they appear glamorously old-fashioned, indicators of taste and wealth, rather than symbols of a modern, speeding, fluid and technological world.

Occasionally, this picturesque space is threatened by storms, which form the backdrop to a troubling narrative incident, as happens twice in *Sense and Sensibility*, for instance. In *Ladies in Lavender*, set in Cornwall, a charming, sunlit opening scene establishes setting, character, period and sentiment, but is replaced by stormy seas, and the barely alive body of a stranger is washed up on the beach. Calm seas and clear skies soon return, and there is some glorious scenery in the film, from the ladies' cottage with its pretty flower garden, nestled in trees with a view down to the beach below, to rolling cliff-top vistas. Charles Dance, director of the film, explained that he wanted 'Cornwall to look its best'.[8] Cornwall at its best, of course, is a little more craggy than the Home Counties, and the settings occasionally seem wild and remote. Indeed, the film as a whole is a slightly odd romantic drama, with the central romance involving an elderly woman feeling like a romantic teenager in the presence of the young stranger she and her sister have found on the beach. The genteel charm of the ladies is also matched by the rather more rough, bucolic working-class community in the village. Even so, the overall tone is the picturesque.

The medieval *mise-en-scène* is different, dramatically heightening the rough touches, moving towards the sublime and away from the picturesque, revelling in landscapes that are much more wild, uncultivated and often bleak than anything *Sense and Sensibility* or *Ladies in Lavender* can offer. The dwellings are different too, with the relative intimacy of the drawing room and the country cottage replaced by vast stone castles and cavernous spaces – or by peasant huts surrounded by mud. The peasant huts notwithstanding, the *mise-en-scène* is often on an epic scale, where one is struck by the awesome magnitude of both the landscapes and the castles. Where rolling grassland is green and pleasant in the modern past, in the medieval past it is a bloody battlefield. In the modern past, the sun often shines; in the medieval past, it is more likely to rain or snow – and if it doesn't, then at least it is cloudy and grey: light in so many respects is replaced with darkness. There are two quite different regimes of spectacle at work in the costume dramas of the modern past and the films with a medieval sensibility, one characterised by surface prettiness and a modest scale, the other playing more on feelings of terror and astonishment. Clothing too is different, the pretty dresses of the modern costume drama replaced in the medieval past by armour for the boys and chastity belts (in *Anazapta*) or bondage-style leather strapping (in *King Arthur*) for the girls.

In *King Arthur*, there are numerous spectacular wide shots of bleak, windswept hills, with grey clouds above and knights on horseback galloping in silhouette in the distance. The uncultivated grass may be a vibrant, fertile green, but the landscape is frequently swirling with mist, and the sun rarely shines. Lighting generally is gloomy, with heavy clouds preferred for daytime exteriors, occasional scenes in dark forests, and other scenes shot at night; interiors are invariably gloomy. Here, and in *Braveheart*, the mountainous landscapes of the Celtic fringes are even more awesome.

The *mise-en-scène* of *First Knight*, the glossy 1995 Hollywood version of the Camelot story, is far less consistently wild and dramatic, because it hangs on to the mythical dimensions of Camelot, which is here a gleaming white citadel, a Christian democracy, ruled over by a noble and fair King Arthur and set in a virgin pastoral landscape. It is a place of chivalry, a place for romance and fine costumes. Lancelot, on the other hand, is a solitary wanderer, a medieval cowboy who lives by the sword rather than the gun, and who is associated with the untamed natural countryside, green hills and woods. Somewhere between the city and raw nature, and closer to the dirt of so many other medieval films, are the peasant villagers, while Malagant is associated with darkness, and with a ruined, damp and inhospitable fortress. Feuding between Arthur and Malagant means that the past, for all its chivalry and romance, is still a highly dangerous place, affording plenty of action scenes for the boys.

The *mise-en-scène* of what historians call the early modern period appropriately falls somewhere between the picturesque modern past and the awesome and dangerous medieval past. From the Tudor period to the eighteenth century, the costumes and wigs are spectacular. So too are the many fine and impressive locations, but the castles and palaces, from the *Elizabeth* films to *The Madness of King George*, are often also stern and uncomfortable places, the great halls too cavernous to feel homely. *Elizabeth: The Golden Age* is designed ostentatiously as a crossover film that mixes the aesthetics and sensibilities of the medieval and the modern pasts, but also of the epic historical adventure and the romantic costume drama. The epic qualities are there from the outset in the splendours of Philip's court in Spain, and the huge crowd below the palace that waits to greet Philip and his daughter, with mountains beyond the palace walls. England too has its spectacular castles and palaces, huge, forbidding stone structures, with monumental columns and cavernous interiors that dwarf all human perspective. The sense of awe and magnitude is underlined by the frequent towering bird's-eye camera shots looking down at the protagonists from above.

There are spectacular landscapes in England too: Elizabeth and Walter Raleigh gallop across gently rolling, brightly sunlit green hills that fill the widescreen image of the film. Studded with oak trees, this is 'England' on display, and it is the same 'England' that must be defended at the end of the film when the Spanish armada threatens. On land, Elizabeth, clad in shining, almost delicate armour and on a white horse, like some mythical knight, addresses her massed troops on yet more rolling green hills. At sea, there is the spectacle of the armada itself. Individual ships are impressive enough, but when the partly computer-generated armada fills the screen, we know we are momentarily in the realm of the epic. Action becomes the defining aspect of the drama in this moment, and Raleigh in particular becomes an action hero in a historical adventure, with Clive Owen masquerading as Douglas Fairbanks or Errol Flynn, torching a fire ship, swinging from a rope, diving into the raging seas. On board the ships, we see the effects of the attack, cannon balls ripping into the timber and the men themselves, one ship ploughing into another, explosions, fires, mutilation, fear and death.

If the drama is in part organised around the threat of the Spanish enterprise to Elizabeth's throne, a drama on a national and indeed international scale, there is another more intimate drama taking place within Elizabeth's palaces. This drama is precisely organised around the tension between Raleigh, the handsome, rugged pirate, adventurer and explorer, always pushing the boundaries, and the palace-bound queen, frozen in so many tableaux of spectacular costumes, wigs, interior decor and architecture. One travels abroad, the traditional hunter-gatherer; the other stays at home, the traditional home-maker – except that there is little homely about the vast spaces of the palaces she occupies; she is then a nation-maker rather than a mere home-maker. Raleigh represents what Elizabeth cannot have and cannot do, and becomes an object of desire, around whom romance develops. The camera gets very close to Raleigh, closer than to any other character in the film, his handsome face is weather-beaten, and he wears a permanent half-smile and a glint in his eyes; he has been cast, framed, posed and lit as the conventional romantic male lead. The camera keeps a reverential distance from Elizabeth, on the other hand, framing her in a rich tapestry of colour and texture, presenting her as the dominant feature within a formal vision of beauty. Where Elizabeth is always visually in context, the big close-ups of Raleigh rarely show anything else except a vague blur: he is a larger-than-life character, who leaps off the screen.

But this is also very much a film about the private life of a monarch, and we see Elizabeth off-guard, too, as it were, her finery stripped away, and she shares several intimate scenes with Raleigh, and with her young ladies-in-waiting, especially her favourite, Bess. If Raleigh is an action-adventurer, he is also a courtier, a lover and a family man, and if Elizabeth is at times a mythical knight and at times magisterial in her regal finery, she is also above all a woman, who is worried about ageing and desperate for romance and more. A romance does develop: the queen and Raleigh are clearly attracted to each other, they are together in private, they discuss love, they share one passionate kiss. But if the romance is real, the queen cannot allow it to develop, so she tries to play it out at arm's length, through Bess. Cue Elizabeth recalling her own youthful affair with Dudley, in a flashback to the previous film, *Elizabeth*; but cue also Raleigh and Bess becoming more involved than Elizabeth had intended. The final scene of *Elizabeth: The Golden Age* shows Elizabeth cradling the baby of Raleigh and Bess, the handsome young couple together in their relatively modest house: it is a modern image of family and home, Elizabeth the doting grandmother; it is also a fitting end to an intimate and romantic costume drama, the more epic historical adventure having been resolved a couple of scenes earlier.

The film then clearly draws on the conventions of both the historical adventure and the period romance. It also has touches of the medieval. Behind all the spectacle of majesty, the fine costumes and the stunning locations, a much murkier, nastier world exists, one that is violent, vicious and gruesome. Spanish and Catholic English conspirators plot to unseat the queen, cutting the tongue from a traitor in their midst, then shooting him at point-blank range; Walsingham spies on the conspirators, throwing those he catches into foul dungeons, brutally torturing them, and eventually hanging them. At the centre of the plot is Mary Stuart, Queen of the Scots, imprisoned in a medieval fortress, a stark stone edifice amid forbidding mountains and lakes, grey clouds gathering above – in contrast with the sunlit green hills of 'England'. Trapped by Walsingham, Mary is beheaded for treason against Elizabeth. A threatening figure to Elizabeth's vision of English nationhood, we only ever see Mary in gloomy semi-darkness, while Philip of Spain is forever clad from head to foot in black, and the armada is defeated in darkness. Walsingham's dungeons and torture chambers are places of darkness too – and as the threat of the Spanish enterprise increases, even the interiors of Elizabeth's world seem to become darker.

For England to be secure, it must emerge from this medieval darkness, and regain the sunlight and the green hills. Indeed, as news of the defeat of the armada reaches the queen, we see her wandering barefoot, in a white gown, at dawn, the light coming up on the green grass at the top of the sea cliffs, the sea crashing against the borders of the island nation below. It is a spectacular, mythical image of England and its queen, but also a very intimate moment, the queen vulnerable in her flowing night-dress. Again, the film successfully mixes a range of different attractions.

As in films from other periods, there is often a tension between the desire for spectacle and the concern for historical realism. One reviewer described *Restoration*, for instance, as 'A sumptuous heritage costume drama', in which 'a lot of effort, research and money' has been invested. 'The viewer is bombarded with enjoyable visual information about the seventeenth century.'[9] The problem is how that heritage spectacle is used, the function it serves in the films, with historical complexity often overwhelmed by the surface allure of the image. Thus Lizzie Francke describes *Orlando* as 'a romp through English history, which it presents as richly textured spectacle'. This, she suggests, produces an 'overladen visual style [which] perversely turns the film into a celebration of the cultural heritage' which the spectator 'can only look at with wonder', but which Orlando, the character, must reject at the end of the film.[10] In an effort to avoid this sort of problem, the makers of the first *Elizabeth* film chose Northumberland as one of the key locations because of its 'bleakness': 'We wanted to get away from the "chocolate box" feel so many period movies have,' explained producer Alison Owen; 'Northumberland is beautiful, but in a very stark way.'[11] At the same time, for several reviewers, 'the real scene-stealers are the locations',[12] with much of the action 'set among stunning shots of Merchant Ivory-type heritage locations such as Haddon Hall and Durham Cathedral'.[13]

If the picturesque *mise-en-scène* of the modern past is overwhelmingly pretty and charming, the world of the pre-modern past is frequently both sublime and dirty and disgusting. In both cases, there is a realist sensibility at work; it is simply that the authentic pre-modern past is imagined through the lens of dirty realism. This is particularly evident in the medieval films, but the medieval again lingers long into the early modern past, so that if the costumes in the films set in the sixteenth, seventeenth and eighteenth centuries are often fabulous, once their wearers step outside, they must also frequently tread carefully through mud and worse. Andy Medhurst establishes the appropriate tone here, writing about *Restoration*: 'Its image of the past is a world away from the gentilities of Jane Austen, preferring instead to depict...a past caked in filth, a past that teems, a past that stinks.'[14]

There is then a sharp contrast at the level of the image between, on the one hand, the permanently sunny picturesque of a *Howards End*, the manicured, domesticated gardens and streets, and the gently rolling hills of the Home Counties beyond; and on the other hand, gloomy, grey, often wet weather, the filthy lanes, and the wild landscape beyond in so many medieval and early modern films. Another aspect of this dirty realism in the early modern period is the exploration of the teeming, bustling early modern metropolis. Thus *Shakespeare in Love, To Kill a King, Restoration, Stage Beauty, The Libertine* and *Plunkett & Macleane* all play out their dramas in part in and around London, which is rarely in such films presented as a pretty place. Where costume dramas set in the nineteenth and early twentieth centuries often seem horrified by the city, the early modern films seem fascinated by its awful otherness.

The aesthetic of dirty realism is not simply an iconography but embraces a fuller sense of *mise-en-scène*, lighting and cinematography: as reviewers noted of *To Kill a King*, the drama unfolds 'in gloomy debating chambers and draughty castles',[15] there is a 'lived-in look [to] the production and costume design', and a 'bleak, wintry look and subdued colors' in the cinematography.[16] Of all the recent early modern films, it is perhaps this one that is most concerned with its sense of historicity. Thus the filmmakers have chosen numerous period locations that in another

The dirty realist *mise-en-scène* of *To Kill a King*.

film might have been exploited for their visual splendour as much as for their ability to authenticate the fiction. In *To Kill a King*, however, the camera rarely lingers on the period buildings, nor are they lit or framed for splendour. Exteriors of grand houses, castles and palaces are often shot either at night or in gloomy or overcast conditions – a far cry from the surface prettiness of the Merchant Ivory brand of costume drama. In *Orlando* too, if the past is spectacular, the exteriors in the three seventeenth-century sequences are again almost always shot either at night or in the frozen winter, so creating a bleak rather than picturesque effect.

As the costume drama meets the historical adventure genre on the one hand and looks towards medievalism on the other, it is not simply that the landscape becomes bleaker, the dwellings more austere, and the streets, lanes and villages filthier. England/Britain generally becomes a far more dangerous space to inhabit; it is closer to nature, more primitive, less civilised. Life is lived in its raw state, passions are less restrained and much more overtly threatening. As Philip Kemp puts it, reviewing the medieval film *Anazapta* (2001), a film awash with mud, foul weather, disease, gore and eroticism, this is a 'full-throated rejection of the decorous conventions of "heritage cinema" '.[17] Except of course that the medieval is still part of the national heritage: it is in this instance the swamp from which modernity must emerge.

Genteel living and polite society begin to emerge in the spectacular costumes of the early modern period, in the courts of Henry VIII, Elizabeth I, Charles II and George III, but these courts are still dangerous places, with plotting a-plenty, the torture chambers of Elizabeth's castles only gradually giving way to primitive medical practices that seem equally torturous in *The Madness of King George*. There is little domestic about these spaces – although George and his queen, Charlotte, begin to seem domestic in the way they address each other in private as Mr and Mrs King, and their final expressed ambition is to become a model family to the nation. They are certainly a long way on from Bors, the rough and uncouth knight of *King Arthur*, who has a mistress and a dozen unruly and dirty children, but no evident home to speak of. But it is not until later, well away from the medieval period, and away from the early modern court too, in the Austen adaptations, that a semblance of modern family life really becomes established. It is notable that when we return to the monarch in the modern past and the very recent past, in *Mrs Brown* and *The Queen* respectively, a bizarrely mundane domestic family life is the overwhelming sensibility of the films.

The early modern films are again positioned somewhere between the raw austerity of life in the medieval period and the refined and domesticated world that is presented in the costume dramas of the modern past. They are generally less populist and less epic productions than the medieval adventures, aspiring more to the serious, artful, intelligent and literate cinema of the costume dramas of the modern past. But they are still far less polite than those later costume dramas, frequently indulging in bawdy and decadent behaviour. There is a rudeness and lewdness at the level of performance, characterisation and action; there is also often a carnivalesque irreverence towards the past and especially towards figures of authority; and there are far more life-threatening dangers at the level of narrative incident. Passions can still be unrestrained, and violence is frequent. All this is behaviour that might perturb or trouble the modern sensibilities of the characters at the heart of the period adaptations of novels by Austen or Forster or plays by Oscar Wilde.

One of the attractions of the medieval and the early modern historical films, therefore, is that they provide a legitimate and respectable space in which certain modes of behaviour can be played out, modes of behaviour that are currently considered unrespectable or decadent, outmoded or primitive. In other words, the 'unmodern' setting of these films is used as a licence to project taboo images and actions – particularly around the body and what might be done to it, or done with it, or how it might be displayed. The unmodern setting thus legitimates what now seems socially or culturally transgressive, what might otherwise be considered censorable representations. Note for instance the numerous post-Peckinpah depictions of violence in medieval films, from *Braveheart* to *King Arthur*. Note the sexual licentiousness and general debauchery, whether in the low-budget exploitation aesthetics of *Sacred Flesh* (1999), a pornographic film of sexual fantasies in a medieval convent, or in the various more upmarket Restoration dramas or *Shakespeare in Love*. Note too the element of cross-dressing, ambiguous genders, uncertain identities and social mobility or inter-class mixing in *Robin Hood*, *Orlando*, *Shakespeare in Love* and *Stage Beauty*. And note the dramatic effects of illness, disease and injury in *Kingdom of Heaven*, *To Kill a King*, *Restoration*, *Stage Beauty* and *The Madness of King George*.

Anazapta, a Hammer-style horror about the Black Death, with its 'rich, reeking mix of shit, mire, pus and gore', as Philip Kemp puts it, has almost all of the unmodern ingredients I've identified.[18] There is mud, rain and bruised flesh aplenty. There are grossly mutilated and diseased bodies and splendidly bad teeth. There is a gang rape, masturbation through a chastity belt, erotic drawings and an utterly depraved bishop. If England is occasionally green, it is always bleak and desolate, and the sun never shines; indeed, even when a cloudless blue sky is visible, the cinematography makes the scene look gloomy. Moving on to the Restoration period, *The Libertine* presents us with a very muddy London, sordid violence, a disease-ridden hero and frequent scenes of debauchery and sexual licentiousness – an orgy in St James's Park, lewd imagery in a stage performance, erotic drawings and more. *Plunkett & Macleane* establishes the tone it is to adopt from its utterly gruesome and disgusting opening sequence depicting a violent robbery, complete with a close-up of an eye being gouged out; the second sequence shows worms crawling through the face of a dead body; in the third sequence, the city streets are presented as filthy, the site for pigs to roam, fights to take place, bodies to be hung, and crowds to teem about. The settings may include some grand buildings, but they also include a quite revolting prison, and the sewers under the city streets.

Several of the early modern films, from *The Other Boleyn Girl* to *The Madness of King George*, offer the spectacle of majesty, but they also frequently go behind closed doors, penetrating the inner sanctums of the kings and queens of England, laying bare their private lives – and in so doing, they often debunk the monarchy. The films set in the seventeenth and eighteenth centuries in particular adopt a highly irreverential attitude towards the monarchy – Charles I is beheaded in *To Kill a King*; Charles II is shown with his mistresses in *Restoration* and *Stage Beauty*, and openly mocked by Lord Rochester in *The Libertine*; along with a shocked court, we witness George III's eccentric and often very crude behaviour during a period of illness in *The Madness of King George*. Admittedly we also explore the private lives of two more recent monarchs, in *Mrs Brown* (about Queen Victoria) and *The Queen* (about Elizabeth II) – but the aristocracy in the modern past is rarely as depraved as it is in *The Libertine* or *Plunkett & Macleane*.

At the same time, the early modern setting is constructed as on the cusp of 'true' modernity, and the films are used to dramatise the emergence of late modern identities and modes of behaviour and morality – modern gender identities and expectations in *Orlando*, the modern Shakespearean legacy in *Shakespeare in Love*, modern naturalistic acting in *Stage Beauty* and *The Libertine*, a modern sense of the self in

Stage Beauty, a modern English moral schema and political constitution in *To Kill a King*, a modern understanding of madness in *Restoration* and *The Madness of King George*, and so on. On the one hand, then, these films explore the emergence of modernity; on the other hand, they seem collectively to celebrate the pleasures and possibilities, but also the dangers and risks of a pre-modern social space.

This reading of the early modern films as in some ways at odds with the polite decorum of English modernity is by no means universally adopted. This is hardly surprising, of course, given that the success of several of these films is bound up with the possibility of identifying them as intelligent, respectable, literate, upmarket commodities. For the conservative *Daily Mail*, for instance, the success of *Shakespeare in Love* in 1998–9 (along with a Monet exhibition at the Royal Academy, the Classic FM radio station, and Ted Hughes's *Birthday Letters*) was cited as evidence of the strength, pervasiveness and resilience of a morally righteous middlebrow culture: 'The triumph of this wonderful and witty film stands in grim contrast to the continuing wave of sleaze which washes across our TV screens.'[19] As evidence of such sleaze, the *Daily Mail* offered Channel 4's then new American import *Sex and the City*, and an arts documentary about 'a naked, gay, Latin American dancer':

> in contrast to this myopic focus on the sordid and the second rate, I believe that large parts of the public hold onto a much higher set of values, such as those embodied in the screenplay of *Shakespeare in Love*. Rather than following the lead of our nihilistic programme-makers, many British people actually prefer the stimulus of great art and high culture. ... Desperate to be controversial, terrified of accusations of 'traditionalism', fixated with ideas about class and race, this army of cultural commissars ... want us to wallow in all that is tawdry and squalid, as long as it can be covered with the cloak of modernity. But this is not what the public wants. Far from succumbing to this arrogant degeneracy, people are moving in the opposite direction.[20]

The general argument is very familiar, contrasting as it does a tastefully done version of English heritage and the national past with a 'sordid', 'squalid' version of the sort of complex, contemporary cultural formation that has for long upset the conservative *Daily Mail*. It is a contrast that implies a nostalgia for an England or a Britain that was once great, and a set of moral values that were apparently both more acceptable and more stable. The details of the argument need to be looked at more closely, however, for the tastefully done version of English heritage that is *Shakespeare in Love* actually delights in the queen's bad teeth, the dung in the streets and the general bawdiness of everyday life. As to the 'much higher set of values … embodied in … *Shakespeare in Love'*, this is a film that, like so many other English costume dramas, presents adultery and extra-marital sex as fun, and finds pleasure in cross-dressing and other forms of masquerade and deceitfulness. All of which seems to escape the attentions of the *Daily Mail*, which prefers to celebrate the film as culturally 'proper' and uplifting.

Shakespeare in Love is one of those films that playfully insert historical anachronisms and present-day references into their ostensibly historical settings. These sorts of references suggest not the difference but the parallels between past and present. When a director like Antoine Fuqua, associated with contemporary action films, is brought in to direct *King Arthur*, or 1990s dance music is used in *Plunkett & Macleane*, the extent to which the past is *like* the present is underlined still further, suggesting that barbarism and a primitive sensibility have not disappeared, but live on in the present-day world. If films set in the pre-modern past are in some ways a licensed space for representing the transgressive and the taboo, there are plenty of films set in the present that seem to operate with the same licence.

There is clearly plenty of mileage to be gained from contrasting the medieval epic with the more intimate early modern and modern costume drama – and one conclusion that we could draw from this discussion is that different generic conventions are adopted for the depiction of different historical periods. But as with any such critical construct, this neat binary opposition between two generic modes is far too rigid to represent accurately the range of films I am discussing, and there are all sorts of crossovers, exceptions and hybrid developments that muddy the waters. I begin the next chapter by considering some of these developments.

8 Blurring boundaries: historical myopia and period authenticity

Generic hybridity and market crossovers: changing visions of the past

The central argument I developed in the previous chapter depends upon a binary opposition between representations of the pre-modern and the modern pasts in recent cinema. Inevitably, of course, the divide is far less clear-cut than this. Thus, by no means all of the films set in the Middle Ages are framed in an epic mode or adopt the conventions of the historical adventure. The art-house film *Anchoress* (1993), for instance, tells the story of a young girl who has visions of the Virgin Mary, and devotes her life to God, enclosed in the walls of her village church, while the low budget for *Anazapta* (2001) effectively offset any pretensions the filmmakers might have had towards presenting this macabre and horrific tale on a more epic canvas. Such low-budget films thus occupy a space on the very edge of mainstream cinema. Modes of exhibition and box-office figures are again revealing. *Anchoress* had an exclusively art-house release, similar to that given to another low-budget medieval story, *Edward II* (1991); despite the fact that the latter was directed by Derek Jarman, a recognised auteur, neither showed on more than 16 screens in the USA, and their combined takings in the USA and the UK were less than $1m. *Anazapta*, meanwhile, was hardly shown at all until it reached the DVD market. The American blockbuster version of the Robin Hood story, *Robin Hood: Prince of Thieves* (1991), given a predictably wide release, opening on nearly 2,400 screens, was a box-office winner of suitably epic proportions, taking more than $390m worldwide; the much more modestly budgeted British version of the same story, *Robin Hood* (1990), could manage only $600,000 in the UK, and wasn't even released in the USA.[1]

If all of these films about the pre-modern past work in one way or another with a dirty realist aesthetic, the claims they make for the

Anazapta: a low budget, macabre version of the Middle Ages.

authenticity of their historical representations are varied, and hardly differ from the sorts of claims made about films about the modern English past. Later in this chapter, I consider the debate about historical realism in more detail. First, however, I want to look at some of the other ways in which the distinctions between films about different versions of the English past are blurred.

If *Anchoress* and *Anazapta* are in no sense epic productions, they also eschew some of the conventions of the action-adventure film, and in various ways seem closer to intimate dramas of the modern past. They are for instance among a small number of medieval films that feature a woman as protagonist, with others including *Guinevere* (1994) and *The Midwife's Tale* (1996). It would be foolish, too, to ignore the romantic elements of some of the big-budget pre-modern adventures, such as *King Arthur* (2004) and *Kingdom of Heaven* (2005), which also construct their protagonists along modern lines, as psychologically complex, brooding characters. Both *King Arthur* (in its casting of Keira Knightley as a feisty, 'girl power' version of Guinevere, who eventually weds Clive Owen's Arthur) and *Tristan + Isolde* (2006) (in its mimicking of the title, not to mention the storyline, of that key romantic teen hit of the mid-1990s, *William Shakespeare's Romeo + Juliet*, 1996) also attempted to extend the audience appeal of the historical adventure by addressing young female viewers. Even so, with its violent battle scenes, its lack of decorum, and its often wild and primitive sensibility, *King Arthur* is a quite different experience from most costume films about the modern past. Love and romance are very much side issues, while domesticity is hardly possible. On the contrary, the film is powerful, exciting, dramatic.

We might approach the equation from the other end as well, for if the medieval adventures tend to be more obviously epic in scope, sometimes the intimacy of the more refined modern costume dramas is overwhelmed by an epic dimension. Thus the romantic costume drama of the modern past comes up against the conventions of the blockbusting disaster movie in *Titanic* (1997), while Shekhar Kapur's version of *The Four Feathers* (2002), set in the late nineteenth century, situates its romance in the context of an action-adventure film. Large-scale action or adventure is also the *raison d'être* of *Master and Commander: The Far Side of the World* (2003) and *Around the World in 80 Days* (2004), which were again set in the modern past. There are also a small number of action-adventure films set in the early modern past, including *Chasing the Deer* (1994), *Rob Roy* (1995), *Plunkett & Macleane* (1999) and the blockbusting Disney *Pirates of the Caribbean* films (2003–7). But most of the films set in the early modern past, from *Orlando* in 1992 to *The Duchess* in 2008, were pitched at the lower-budget, but more upscale, art-house end of the market. Given the nature of the contemporary film business, however, none of these films could survive by being distributed only in the art-house sector. To this extent, they are typical of the lower-budget costume dramas of the 1990s and 2000s in that they were designed as crossover films that might appeal both to the core specialised or art-house market and to the mainstream or multiplex end of the market and achieve a wider appeal: only such an exhibition plan could justify the £13.6m budget for *The Duchess*, for instance.

Three of the most successful early modern films of the 1990s and 2000s, *The Madness of King George* (1994), *Elizabeth* (1998) and *Shakespeare in Love* (1998), were all in part successful because of this market strategy. *Shakespeare in Love*, for instance, had a budget of £15m, modest by Hollywood standards, but went on to take an enormous $100m in the USA, and another $189m worldwide, including a very impressive £20.8m in the UK.[2] The film was identified from the outset as much more accessible than most such period dramas. Thus the leading British trade paper proclaimed, quite rightly as it turned out, that 'the picture is a sure-fire crowd-pleaser which should break out of the specialised market and become a crossover hit'.[3] The *News of the World* agreed, applauding 'a movie that will have you shaking with laughter. For the stuffy old period drama has been dusted off and polished until it sparkles in *Shakespeare in Love*. ... With its hot performances and hilarious comedy, this movie has reinvented the big screen period drama – and we should all be grateful for that.'[4] Or as a journalist from the more upmarket *Observer* put it, *Shakespeare in Love* 'is to be celebrated as a costume drama that has nothing to do with the heritage industry; it has too much life and wit for that'.[5] The implication is that museum culture, the period drama and especially the Shakespearean drama were generally considered to be of limited appeal, too dry to be of real interest to a mass audience. The cranking up of the romantic comedy in *Shakespeare in Love*, however, had enabled the filmmakers to re-energise the genre, to create something that would appeal to a wider audience. The crossover film must by definition appeal to a range of markets, a range of audiences, and part of the success of *Shakespeare in Love* was that it could work very effectively both for a highly educated and culturally discerning middle-class audience and for a mainstream romantic comedy audience that was discerning in a different way.

Tainting the modern past

The distinction I made in the previous chapter between representations of the pre-modern English past and the modern past identified as its turning point the period around 1800, with the adaptations of Jane Austen's canonical novels heralding the arrival of a fully-fledged modern sensibility. At one level, there clearly is a difference between the epic historical adventures depicting medieval heroes and the intimate historical romances of the period Austen films, just as the dirty realism and the bawdiness of several of the films set in the 16th, 17th or 18th centuries contrasts with the picturesque aesthetic of the mid-1990s adaptations of *Sense and Sensibility* (1995) and *Emma* (1996). At another level, though, the ideal vision of the modern past that the division depends upon is tainted by characteristics otherwise associated with the pre-modern past.

One of the ways in which the pre-modern past is associated with lewd, debauched behaviour, for instance, is through the explicit representation of sexual activity. In the medieval-set *Anazapta* a bishop covets erotic, pornographic drawings; in the seventeenth-century drama *The Libertine* (2005), Lord Rochester covets similar artwork. Yet, as was noted in chapter 6, in the UK period Austen adaptation *Mansfield Park* (1999), Fanny's cousin Tom also indulges in such drawings – and there is later a momentary glimpse of a graphic scene of illicit sexual intercourse.

In another indication of the difference of the very distant past, in both *King Arthur* and *Kingdom of Heaven*, the heroes confront versions of serfdom. Again, things are not so very different in the apparently more civilised world of *Mansfield Park*, where the wealth of the family depends upon slaves working on their plantations in the West Indies. This is hardly the polite Austenian England presented in *Sense and Sensibility*, *Emma* and so many other representations of the modern past.

The boundary between the pre-modern and the modern past is also blurred in the 2005 version of *Pride and Prejudice*, which draws on the dirty realist aesthetic as much as the picturesque, and presents some often quite bawdy and indecorous behaviour. As was again noted in chapter 6, the director of the film, Joe Wright, approached the film 'as a piece of British realism rather than going with the picturesque tradition', aiming for a 'real and gritty' look. And indeed, while there are numerous pastoral images of the countryside in the film, they generally depict rough and ready spaces and are rarely straightforwardly pretty. The author of the film's screenplay, the novelist Deborah Moggach, called the film 'the muddy-hem version' of Austen.[6] It is an apt metaphor: in one scene, for instance, Elizabeth Bennet travels to Netherfield, the neighbouring country estate, to visit her sick sister, and has to walk through thick mud to get there. Significantly, when she arrives in a now dirty dress, one of the other characters remarks that she looks 'positively medieval'. Again, then, the medieval insinuates itself into the modern past, deliberately muddying the picturesque image of heritage England. Even so, despite the gritty realism of certain aspects of the film, it remains resolutely charming, light-hearted and romantic.

Adaptations of the work of other nineteenth-century writers such as Dickens and Hardy also provide a rather less idealised and idyllic version of the modern past. Thus there are images of the teeming and often filthy metropolis in *Nicholas Nickleby* (2002) and *Oliver Twist* (2005) – but one can also find a heavily overdetermined representation of the picturesque semi-rural English past, and it is clearly the latter to which we are encouraged to aspire. A very similar sensibility, with an exaggerated pastoral England set against scenes of poverty, hardship or austerity, is established in two other costume dramas of the modern past addressed to children, *Black Beauty* (1994) and *The Secret Garden* (1993). A more challenging dirty realism can be found in Michael Winterbottom's Thomas Hardy adaptation *Jude* (1996), and in a different way in Tim Burton's thoroughly gory, filthy and horrifying version of *Sweeney Todd* (2007).

The difficulty with adapting Dickens is the different levels on which his novels work, or the different modes of representation that they adopt. If his work offers a realist depiction of poverty and hardship, he is also a caricaturist, and filmmakers have been keen to capture both aspects of his writing. Indeed, with *Oliver Twist*, Roman Polanski wanted to create a film that would delight children, a film that was 'bigger than life' and exaggerated its characterisations, colours and emotional pull.[7] So the filmmakers made strenuous efforts to establish authentic period detail, and almost all the features of the dirty and dangerous pre-modern past are here: disgustingly muddy streets; dreadful conditions in the workhouse and in the slums of London; murky interiors, and foggy, rainy night scenes; and a bustling, teeming metropolis. All this represents the world from which Oliver must escape; the problem comes when it is contrasted with the ideal world in which he finds refuge. Here it is sunny, the colours are rich and vibrant, and the inhabitants are irredeemably charming (Fagin and his motley crew may be kind, but there is always another side to their kindness). Momentarily we enter a more familiar world for costume dramas of the modern past, a world of rolling green hills and golden cornfields, of picturesque country cottages – and, when Oliver is taken in by Mr Brownlow, a genteel, tastefully furnished town house, but one that is right on the edge of the city, with a pastoral, sunlit garden. In film terms, two rather different genres or modes of representation are awkwardly bracketed together.

Films such as *Jude*, *Mansfield Park*, *Pride and Prejudice* and the Dickens adaptations are representative of a wider trend in English period films, one that set out to offer a less safe and less pretty version of the modern past, one that blurred the boundaries between different versions of the English past. The 'classic' heritage film of the 1980s and 1990s, the Merchant Ivory frock flick or the *Emma / Sense and Sensibility* version of Austen, did not disappear, it diversified. It moved back in time and cross-bred with the conspiracy thriller in *Elizabeth*, and the historical adventure in the sequel, *Elizabeth: The Golden Age* (2007); it cross-bred with the musical in *Mrs Henderson Presents* (2005) and *Sweeney Todd* and the whodunnit in *Gosford Park* (2001); or it simply settled in the 1930s, in *Bright Young Things* (2003), *Becoming Julia* (2004), *Atonement* (2007) and several others. But if the charming, picturesque costume drama of the modern past diversified, there were always enough elements of the classic model to keep the core heritage film audience happy.

For the Second World War sequences in *Atonement*, for instance, the filmmakers made a considerable effort to depict the harsh realities of war, which of course look very different from the idyllic vision of England in films like *Howards End* (1992) and *Emma*. *Atonement* offsets the war image, however, with its eloquent evocation of upper-class, country-house living in the 1930s sequences. There is plenty of scope for a transgressive and troubling drama in *Mrs Henderson Presents*, too, with its London settings and its tale of well-to-do characters confronting first the poverty of the Depression in the 1930s and then the dangers of wartime life, all bound up with the fortunes of a theatre that specialises in presentations of female nudes. But even here, there are snippets of pastoral England, and the *mise-en-scène* and performance of high society – especially the brilliantly realised upper-class eccentric that is Judi Dench's eponymous character. The nudity and the heterosexual male gaze that it invites is also presented as tasteful and artistic, while the overall tone is again light-hearted and charming.

Historical myopia: blurring the boundaries between different periods

The blurring of boundaries between different historical periods is in many ways typical of how cinema deals with the English past. When the trade paper *Screen International* considered the market potential of *Stage Beauty* (2004), set in the mid-seventeenth century, it compared the film to *Shakespeare in Love*, which deals with some very similar themes, and is set in a period not too far removed. But it also compared the film to *The Madness of King George*, set in the late eighteenth century, and to the director Richard Eyre's previous film, *Iris* (2001), set in the late twentieth century. The same paper also compared the Civil War drama *To Kill a King* (2003) to the Victorian drama *Mrs Brown* (1997).[8] What these comparisons suggest is that for some audiences and for some in the film industry, a period film is a period film: that is to say, it doesn't really matter in which period the film is set, since the pleasures on offer tend to be the same. In this respect, we are bound to find a blurring of the distinction between the medieval and the early modern, for instance, and we are bound to find that filmmakers don't get the costumes 'right', as expert audiences invariably point out. This sort of historical myopia is partly a function of the desire to produce entertaining and commercially successful films, and it can be seen at work in the way that star images and generic conventions are mobilised for the representation of the past.

Filmic history, for all the claims that filmmakers make about period authenticity, tends to be fuzzy around the edges. There is as a result no clear break between the Dark Ages, the Middle Ages and the early modern period in film terms, which all to some extent occupy a generic pre-modern space. In some ways, this is productive, since it refuses the rigid categorisations imposed on historical development by conventional history-writing, but in other ways, all 'distant' pasts blur into the same pre-modern vision. The epic historical adventure may as a genre of the English past be associated above all with representations of the medieval period and medieval heroes, but the same generic conventions can be used to represent quite other historical periods. Films such as *King Arthur* and *Kingdom of Heaven* thus share as much with other recent historical epics about classical times, or the early modern or modern past, as they do with other representations of the Middle Ages. The producer Jerry Bruckheimer, for instance, made *Pearl Harbor* (2001), about the Second World War, *Pirates of the Caribbean*, set in the eighteenth century, and *King Arthur*, set in Roman times, in the epic mode; the director Ridley Scott made both *Gladiator* (2000), set in ancient Rome, and the Crusader film *Kingdom of Heaven*; David Franzoni scripted both *Gladiator* and *King Arthur*; and Bruckheimer produced Scott's *Black Hawk Down* (2001), set in the very recent past. Regardless of the period or location in which they are set, the iconography, the sensibility and the pleasures on offer in these films are similar. The medieval in this sense is simply a vehicle for another version of the historical epic, the historical adventure as blockbuster, pitched somewhere between *Alexander* (2004), *Troy* (2004) and *The Passion of the Christ* (2004) on the one hand, and *Pirates of the Caribbean*, *Gangs of New York* (2002) and *Pearl Harbor* on the other.

In a similar process, when films such as *Rob Roy*, *Pirates of the Caribbean* and *Plunkett & Macleane*, set in the early modern period, and *Master and Commander* and *The Four Feathers*, depicting the modern past, draw on the conventions of the historical epic, the implication is that aspects of the medieval linger on in later centuries. The Harry Potter films (2001–10) might be included here too, as large-scale family adventure films that inhabit a hybrid past/present, moving effortlessly between something like the present day, and a mock Gothic past that embraces the Victorian public school tradition and the notional wizardry of the Middle Ages. One conclusion we might draw from such examples is that filmic representations of the past are always caught between generic convention and historical specificity. *King Arthur*, for instance, was promoted in part as a historically accurate film, which 'tells the heroic true story behind one of history's greatest legends', and much was made of the discourse of authenticity and historical realism, in advance publicity, in the opening titles of the film itself, and in the 'making of' documentary on the DVD.[9] The film, then, was in part conceived and presented as historically authentic. On the other hand, history is telescoped and legend reworked in order to produce an engaging story and a familiar filmic experience for the contemporary multiplex audience. Thus, alongside the discourse of authenticity, the same promotional material heralds 'an immensely thrilling adventure epic', a 'spectacular motion picture', which 'fuses historical grandeur with edge-of-your-seat action'.[10] It is no surprise then that one of the film's main selling points was that *King Arthur* was 'from the producer of *Pearl Harbor*'.[11]

Historical myopia and the desire to make commercially successful films are also embodied in the star system and the ways stars are cast in period films. Some stars, it would seem, are perceived as regal – or perhaps it is that if an actor has successfully portrayed one monarch, that actor is able to carry monarchical connotations over into other roles. Thus Rupert Everett can play Charles I in *To Kill a King*, Charles II in *Stage Beauty* and the Prince of Wales in *The Madness of King George*; in *Shakespeare in Love*, however, he is merely a writer (Christopher Marlowe). Helen Mirren, on the other hand, could play both Elizabeth I, in the 2005 television series of the same name, and Elizabeth II in *The Queen* (2006). Such casting blurs the boundaries between historical periods, and it is by no means infrequent. Thus Cate Blanchett could present herself as both Elizabeth I in *Elizabeth* and its sequel, on the edge of medievalism, and as a Second World War spy, in *Charlotte Gray* (2001); and Clive Owen could move effortlessly between the Dark Ages of *King Arthur*, the Tudor period in *Elizabeth: The Golden Age* and the 1920s of *Gosford Park*. Keira Knightley does something similar, appearing in *King Arthur*, *Pride and Prejudice* and *Atonement*. Orlando Bloom on the other hand blurs the boundaries between the 'real' Middle Ages of *Kingdom of Heaven* and the mock medievalism of *The Lord of the Rings* (2001–3).

This blurring of historical specificity can be seen also in the way that the meaning or sensibility of a particular period changes over time as well. In the 'gaslight melodramas' of the 1940s, and in David Lean's adaptations of Dickens's *Great Expectations* (1946) and *Oliver Twist* (1948), it is the Victorian period that is horrendous and threatening, and against which true modernity can be defined. But in many of the refined costume dramas made in the 1990s and the 2000s, this relatively recent past was more positively valued. Representations of the Middle Ages have moved in the opposite direction, however. In the early 1950s, in films like *The Knights of the Round Table* (1953) and *Ivanhoe* (1952), the medieval period is a Romantic past, a time of chivalry and pageantry. More recently, it has become a period of terror and uncivilised passions.[12]

Questions of realism and authenticity

Despite – or perhaps because of – this blurring of historical specificity, much of the debate about period films tends to be about how accurate they are in terms of historical detail. One newspaper, trying to account for the wide appeal of *Shakespeare in Love*, sought out the views of Stanley Wells, chairman of the Shakespeare Birthplace Trust and Emeritus Professor of Shakespeare Studies at the University of Birmingham, who was quoted as complaining that the film was not 'intellectually or emotionally challenging'; worse, it was 'easy history. Some people will think they're getting history, but there are some purely fictional characters in the film. Perhaps there should be a warning before the film.'[13] Or as another commentator put it, 'it's fluff, it's Shakespeare-lite'.[14] Films like *Shakespeare in Love* were good entertainment, it was being suggested, and good for bringing new audiences to Shakespeare, making his work more accessible – 'as long, of course, as they don't believe it's all true'.[15]

The problem was that even if the historical accuracy of the film could be challenged, and even if the film was blatantly and deliberately playful about the past, it still had an aura of authenticity:

> It's a jovial demystification of English history … [but] despite all the efforts to puncture the bubble of historical accuracy, this is absolutely mainstream costume romance. Every last codpiece is given the pains-taking period look; the muddy streets feel researched to the last wisp of straw. The earnestness that invariably attends such re-creations only stifles the humour. … What we get is an all-out attempt to dazzle us with English Heritage prestige.[16]

This is not just about English Heritage prestige, however: it's also about the cinema industry's idea of prestige, with the spectacular displays of fine costumes and impressively constructed sets of *Shakespeare in Love* 'show[ing] the Elizabethan era to its best advantage'.[17]

What comes through in such debates is the issue of what is deemed to be appropriate in the representation of a particular period. In some

Shakespeare in Love: 'it's fluff, it's Shakespeare-lite'.

ways, whether or not a film is historically accurate is of less interest than the sorts of devices and strategies used to establish a sense of historical realism or authenticity, the ways in which a credible sense of historicity is established for the audiences of these films. One of those strategies of course is to adopt a conventional representation of the past – one that is familiar from previous films, and therefore seems credible to audiences, regardless of whether it actually matches the demands of historical scholarship.

Some commentators distinguish between apparently more factually based *historical* films, so-called, and the more knowingly fictionalised *costume drama*. In fact what we might call history effects or authenticity effects play a similar role in both sorts of period cinema. Thus the historical film is invariably in some way fictionalised and presented as entertainment, while the costume drama, however frivolous, generally makes some effort to authenticate its fiction, to achieve a sense of verisimilitude, through vaguely appropriate costumes, settings and so on. In other words, some films and filmmakers work to historicise fiction, while others are more concerned with fictionalising history, but in both cases, the credibility of the film with its audiences depends in part on its deployment of history effects, and in part on adhering to established conventions for representing a particular period.

The makers of *To Kill a King* went to great lengths to present the drama as authentic and historical, but even this film has a statement, admittedly right at the end of the credits, tucked well away from view, that reads: 'This film is based on history; however, certain characters and events have been combined and/or fictionalised for dramatic purposes.' In fact, several of the period films of the 1990s and 2000s are actually quite playful with the idea of historical representation, either adopting a self-consciously postmodern approach to reimagining the past, or simply playing on historical anachronisms for comic effect. Michael Winterbottom forcefully played the postmodern card in *A Cock and Bull Story* (2005), his adaptation of *Tristram Shandy*, but also in *24 Hour Party People* (2002), a film set in the very recent past; in both films he comments self-referentially on the process of representing the past. Derek Jarman adopted an equally challenging perspective in his much earlier adaptation of *Edward II*, meshing together in perverse fashion both historical detail and contemporary cultural clothing, idioms and references.

Orlando is another film that is deliberately playful with history, not least in the conceit of a character who lives through 400 years of English history but does not age. And while there is a sense of authenticity about the representations of, say, seventeenth-century life in the film, the past in these sequences is constructed as rich and strange, spectacular, but also mannered, extraordinary, perverse. This sense of strangeness is achieved in part through casting, with various actors cross-dressing for their roles: thus Quentin Crisp plays Queen Elizabeth, and Tilda Swinton in the early stages of the film plays a male Orlando (Orlando later becomes a woman). The strangeness is further enhanced by the highly mannered performances and the decidedly episodic nature of the narrative, with scenes played out as tableau-like snatches of drama.

The creators of *A Knight's Tale* (2001) and *Plunkett & Macleane* also had fun with historical anachronisms, to much more raucous effect, especially in the use of contemporary rock and dance music. Rebecca, in the latter film, also betrays a very modern media consciousness, plastering her bedroom wall with press cuttings about the eponymous highwaymen. *Shakespeare in Love* too is cavalier about the past, littered as it is with comic, postmodern anachronisms. As one reviewer put it: 'You note the history, but feel the contemporary pull.'[18] In these cases, the goal is to render the past as of interest to a contemporary mainstream audience. *A Knight's Tale* in particular is wonderfully irreverent about period authenticity, blending together rock musical, medieval jousting drama, sports film, romantic comedy and Chaucerian pastiche: 'Rarely has a period costume picture been quite so craven in courting a young audience ... [I]ts deliberate anachronisms ... will deeply divide audiences; traditionalists and older viewers in general will scoff, while pop culture addicts will no doubt go with the flow, enough so to give Sony a hit'.[19]

Sweeney Todd presents the past through the lens of both the musical and Tim Burton, who set out not to establish a precise historical verisimilitude but a deliberately fantastic and ambiguous version of the past. There is thus a sort of generalised nineteenth-century template at work, which provides a Grand Guignol, Dickensian version of London. *Robin Hood: Men in Tights* and *Stiff Upper Lips* (1998), meanwhile, parody some of the conventions for representing particular pasts (with the latter spoofing the Merchant Ivory version of the costume drama). An enhanced sense of theatricality is also occasionally used to underline the sense of masquerade, dressing up, impersonation and ambiguous identities that is involved in any costume drama or period film: this is evident in *Shakespeare in Love*, *Orlando*, *Stage Beauty* and *Restoration* (1995), among others.

Other filmmakers sought to provide what they saw as a fresh take on the period film, one that might attract the attention of more mainstream audiences. Thus the producers of *Elizabeth* proclaimed that they wanted to create 'a "modern" film about a historical character', and were less concerned with establishing historical accuracy in the unfolding of the narrative than with imaginatively interpreting that history for contemporary audiences.[20] Their approach is neatly summed up in one of the taglines used in publicity for the film: 'Forget About Pulp Fiction – Anyone For A Slice Of Pulp Fact...'

It is clear from the promotional material for *Stage Beauty* that something similar was envisaged for it. On the one hand, there was a commitment to achieving an authentic representation of the Restoration period; on the other hand, there was a quite deliberate and self-conscious attempt to blur the boundaries between the past and the present, to take licence with history. As Richard Eyre, the director of the film, put it, 'all of our present-day sensibilities are applied to this story', further explaining that 'what I'm trying to do is yoke the past and the present together', rather than allow the film to become 'a prisoner of period'.[21] Both Eyre and his production designer, Jim Clay, talked about wanting 'to make Restoration London seem as vivid and contemporary as New York's East Village'[22] – to which end they note that one of the key visual influences was the work of the contemporary New York photographer Nan Goldin, whose work depicts a twilight world of transsexuals and transvestites.[23] So much for an authentic English seventeenth century. Even so, *Stage Beauty* could still be recognised as fulfilling audience expectations of the period, with one reviewer noting that the film was 'satisfyingly full of all that we have come to expect of the rackety, glamorous Restoration: double-edged quips and the whiff of debauchery, fops, wigs and lashings of rouge'.[24]

Andy Medhurst, commenting on different versions of British costume drama, makes a distinction between those films that indulge in 'a genteel commitment to period verisimilitude' and those that celebrate 'the romping joys of frocking about'.[25] It certainly seems to be the case that a po-faced commitment to period verisimilitude is much more common in films about the modern past, whereas the more playful approaches to the past have tended to depict a pre-modern past. Even so, there are still plenty of conventional markers of authenticity deployed in films about the medieval and early modern periods: dates appear on the screen, introductory titles explain something of the historical context, period locations are carefully incorporated, websites explain the lengths to which cast and crew go to achieve historical accuracy with costumes, accents, interior designs, food and so on. These and other similar devices are of course designed to create the impression of historicity, to authenticate the drama on display.

Kevin Loader, the producer of the Civil War drama *To Kill a King*, professed to being 'shocked how little people know about this fascinating period'[26] – and the film is clearly in part an effort to rectify this situation. The film adopts many of the most familiar devices for establishing the authenticity of its vision. It opens with a series of informational titles providing historical detail and context, which are presented in stark white text on a black screen, and run for all of 24 seconds, with no musical accompaniment. Immediately, this establishes a sense of sombre concentration, and an almost educational feel. After a highly stylised title sequence, reminiscent stylistically of *Elizabeth*, we move into a very low-key opening scene, the camera lingering on Fairfax as he reminisces in voice-over about the Civil War and about his friend Cromwell. The understatement of this speech is typical of the deglamorisation of the film as a whole, and the avoidance of showy effects. The next scene shows the dreadful aftermath of battle, and further establishes the characters of Cromwell and Fairfax – and while there is plenty of incidental detail, none of it is prettified.

Several of the scenes are shot in period locations that include Dorney Court, Dover Castle, Ham House, Hampton Court, Hatfield House and Midhurst – but as with the costumes and interior designs, one gets a sense less of the *mise-en-scène* being presented as spectacle and more of all this detail providing an authentic backdrop to the action. There are also of course plenty of references to and renderings of historical documents, events and characters. Reviews of the film noted the difference of the production. As one critic put it, *To Kill a King* is 'a powerful throwback to a period of costumers – that effectively ended 30-odd years ago – when discourse, ideas and dialogue were more important than visual effects'.[27] Another suggested that the film was very much not 'history in the heritage mode', but 'a rare historical movie that focuses on politics rather than spectacle' and which is 'calculated to arouse serious discussion'.[28] It is in that sense 'a sober, serious-minded tale', 'a history lesson propelled by ideas rather than action'.[29]

Another strategy adopted by the filmmakers in an effort to achieve a sense of historical authenticity was the decision not to cast American actors to play English characters. But by adopting such a rigorous line, the producers made it very difficult for themselves to raise the necessary finance for the film. The focus on realism, and often a very dirty realism at that, and the concomitant absence of glamour, and especially the absence of glamorous American actors, clearly frightened off the financiers, with the production twice going bankrupt. But it clearly also put off distributors – I have found no evidence that the film was ever released in the USA, for instance; and perhaps it put off audiences too, since the film flopped at the UK box office. Commenting on these difficulties, the film's producer complained 'there is a perception that to make a British period movie it has to be like Merchant-Ivory...This was not: it was a piece of mainstream historical storytelling.'[30] Or perhaps, if we are more honest, it was neither glamorous nor epic enough to work as mainstream cinema, nor pretty enough to secure the Merchant Ivory crossover market.

One of the key strategies filmmakers use to establish an authentic historical world is informational titles at the start and end of the period film, titles that can sketch in the historical context. Such titles are rarely used in films with an entirely fictional basis; they are much more likely to be used in films whose dramas are organised around real historical characters. Thus, none of the adaptations of novels by the canonical nineteenth- and early twentieth-century writers, from Austen to Forster,

feature such titles, but many of the films with real historical monarchs
do, from *Kingdom of Heaven* to *The Libertine*. Narratively, these titles
are usually redundant, since the films are designed to work as self-
contained dramas that can be understood by audiences with little or
no historical knowledge: they are historical adventures or romances in
period costume, and they follow conventional paths for playing out their
adventures and romances. If the world of Austen can be understood
without informational titles, there is no real reason why the world of
Elizabeth I can't be too. What informational titles do provide is a sense
of historical context, whether accurately or not, and whether narratively
necessary or not. They also in effect say: 'This is a historical film; we, the
filmmakers, have taken the past seriously – and we invite you, the spectators, to do the same.'

Of course other strategies can be used to achieve the same effect. In
most of the more upscale literary adaptations set in the nineteenth and
early twentieth centuries, it is above all the attention to period detail in
costume, architecture, interior design and so on that is used to establish
the serious historical credentials of both film and filmmakers. In other
films, there is an attention to what may be called art-historical realism,
where costumes, buildings or whole tableaux are based on paintings or
engravings from the period being depicted.

In the 2005 version of *Oliver Twist*, for instance, the art historical
model for realist detail is Gustave Doré's engravings of London streets
and London's poor. One such engraving is seen under the credits at the
start; the engraving is replaced by a similar black and white scene, which

The teeming metropolis: bringing Gustave Doré's engravings to life in *Oliver
Twist*.

comes to life, the colour slowly bleeding in. It is as if the drama of the film has come to life from a real historical image. More engravings are shown under the end credits, but more significantly, many of the film's images of life in the streets of London are based closely on Doré's images. On the one hand, the filmmakers have used the engravings to provide them with a historical model for recreating period detail (and it was very much a case of recreating detail, since the film was shot almost entirely on a specially built set on the backlot of a Prague studio); on the other hand, they also draw attention to the use of the engravings, through the end credits sequence, and through promotional material, again as a way of proclaiming the authenticity of the representation.

A familiar tension thus arises between realism and spectacle: in order to capture Doré's images of teeming London streets, the filmmakers have created a spectacular vision, with scores of horse-drawn vehicles and hundreds of carefully dressed extras. And it is a vision that for some reviewers was too pretty, too clean, too polite, for all the carefully laid mud and impoverished interiors: 'despite the pain and fear, the hangings and the beatings, there is always a nagging disquiet that what Polanski thinks he is giving us is basically a much-loved children's classic…a handsome repro edition…lightly sprinkled with the picturesque movie dust of Old London Town'.[31]

Filmic representations of the past are designed to serve particular functions, within film culture but also within contemporary culture more generally. Clearly one function is that such films are seductive and entertaining dramas capable of providing a great deal of pleasure to a range of audiences; they thus offer a particular set of attractions, and are designed to tap into entertainment markets that appreciate such attractions. Among those attractions are the spectacle of the past and the discourse of authenticity. The discourse of authenticity is thus in part a selling point, a means of attracting certain audiences to a film – but at the same time there is a tension between the discourse of authenticity and the desire to produce profitable entertainment, which often dictates that a representation or a narrative is reshaped for the purposes of drama rather than to achieve a heightened sense of historical accuracy. Historical authenticity may be one selling point, but it may also then come into tension with other selling points.

Thus the producers and distributors of *King Arthur* may have proclaimed that the film was historically accurate, but the look of the film was also clearly caught up in a more modern sensibility, with the costume designer Penny Rose explaining that they wanted Arthur and his knights to come across as 'fifth-century rock stars'.[32] This is even more blatant in *A Knight's Tale*: 'so thoroughly does the driving force behind [the film] feel like a marketing strategy rather than an impulse to tell a story that the character of the film is entirely summed up by its ad campaign tag line: "He will rock you."'[33] It is clear, too, from the promotional material for *Kingdom of Heaven* that there was a certain commitment to achieving an authentic representation of the Middle Ages in the film, but Ridley Scott also admitted that the film was intended as 'a terrific story from a dramatic age – not...a documentary'.[34] At the same time, this is a story chosen for its ability to address current concerns. The filmmakers thus use a version of medieval history in *Kingdom of Heaven* to address twenty-first-century tensions between East and West, Islam and Christianity. Ironically, they managed to invoke the wrath of conservatives in both camps. On the on the one hand, they received death threats from Muslim activists who saw any revival of the Crusader stories as dangerous and anti-Islam.[35] On the other hand, right-wing Christians were incensed by the representation of Salah al-Dīn (Saladin) as a tolerant Muslim.[36]

Alberto Sciamma, the director of *Anazapta*, underlines the problems of balancing period realism and entertainment; having decided to make a film about the plague in mid-fourteenth-century England, a film that would blend in the supernatural, the horrific and the metaphorical, he and his co-scriptwriter undertook extensive historical research – 'we needed a certain amount of credibility'. The task of raising funding from people who wanted to see a return on their investment proved far more difficult – 'a medieval film about boils wasn't particularly the most appealing thing to financiers' – and in the end, the film was made on a very small budget.[37]

The different interests and aspirations at work in any film production inevitably lead to compromises. In the case of films about the past, the representation of England and Englishness will always be mediated by budget, genre and the accepted discourses of authenticity and entertainment. Many of the films about the English past are of course transnational co-productions, in which context the national often functions as a means of distinction in a crowded marketplace, a marketable brand image. As history becomes entertainment, the successful film is one that can market its wares to a range of audiences, and that is at the same time able to meet audience expectations, in terms of genre, star presence and the spectacle of the past.

One of the arguments running through this and the previous chapter is that one can draw a line between representations of the modern English past and representations of the period 'before modernity'. But if films often play on a generic vision of a pre-modern past, it is clear that any boundaries between periods are vague and ineffective. There is a much clearer distinction between the epic historical adventure and the intimate costume drama, but even the smaller-scale medieval films offer rather different pleasures from the much more numerous middlebrow period films set in the England of the nineteenth or early twentieth centuries. The chivalry of *First Knight* and the spectacular costumes of the early modern films with royal or aristocratic settings notwithstanding, the decorum of the modern past tends to be displaced by much wilder and more threatening versions of the past in the dirty realist pre-modern film. Aspirations to historical accuracy may characterise some of these representations of the past, but the medieval in particular is in the end defined as much by generic convention, and generic distinctions between the pre-modern and the modern.

From the national past to contemporary England

In chapter 2, I described the terms of the Cultural Test introduced by the UK government in 2007 to determine the Britishness of films seeking official support in the form of tax breaks or Lottery funding. One way in which filmmakers could attract funding was by concentrating on what was defined in a loose sense as 'Britain's cultural heritage'.[38] The argument was that screening aspects of that cultural heritage could help UK audiences develop their understanding of British national identity and a collective national memory. Filmmakers were in effect encouraged to participate in the process of maintaining a shared national sense of cohesion by focusing on the nation's history.

Looking at the range of representations of the English past in films of the 1990s and 2000s, it is clear that filmmakers needed little encouragement to focus on subject matter that might be read in terms of a national cultural heritage. The English past often functions simply as a setting for a more or less familiar story, however, a narrative space in which a drama is allowed to unfold. The 'national' setting, in other words, is often merely a banal background, afforded little significance in the human drama that is the *raison d'être* of the film, the drama of families and relationships, of individual ambitions and their fulfilment. Just occasionally, some of the films function more self-consciously as national epics, mythologising the construction of the nation. Thus the two *Elizabeth* films and *The Other Boleyn Girl* (2008) in various ways dramatise the emergence of England under the Tudors as a modern powerful and Protestant nation in the sixteenth century, one that is further shaped by the debates and developments of the Civil War period as depicted in *To Kill a King*.

In a similar vein, *King Arthur* takes us back to Roman Britain in an effort to tell us the 'true story' behind a canonical medieval narrative. Camelot, of course, has long been exploited as a symbol of democracy; while the radical revisionism of this film means there is no Camelot as such, and while it purports to go behind the Arthurian mythology, the film still manages to mythologise the emergence of both a British nation and the semblance of a democracy. To this extent, this US/UK/ Ireland co-production again functions as a national epic, about nation-building, about achieving national sovereignty, about the founding of an independent Britain, about fulfilling national destiny, and about a very American concept of 'freedom' (justified here as freedom from the external authority of Rome). There is a fascinating tension in and around this film, then, between the national and the transnational, between 'authentic' history and cultural appropriation.

Like the *Elizabeth* films, and notwithstanding the concerns of some cultural commentators, *King Arthur* is also about an already highly mythologised 'national' monarch and national hero; but again like *Elizabeth* it is about the making of the legend, the mythologising of the hero: it is about how its eponymous character *becomes* a ruler, how he attains mythic status (which is not to deny that both films at the same time mythologise their characters!). With its Woads (Picts), its Sarmatians, its Romans and its Saxons, ethnicity is also very much to the fore in *King Arthur*, as are the themes of belonging, invasion and resistance – at one point Guinevere, a Woad, pointedly says to Arthur, a Roman military leader: 'I belong to this land. Where do you belong, Arthur?' It is ironic, then, that the film was made by an American production team, with an African-American director, Antoine Fuqua, and shot in Ireland. Ironic – but actually not unusual, in the sense that so many culturally English films are in some way or other transnational productions, with non-English directors at the helm.

Other films set in the English past are much less self-conscious about how they represent the nation or national identity, but they all still do so in one way or another. While *Elizabeth* and *King Arthur* are both biopics about monarchs, other biopics about monarchs, from *The Madness of King George* to *Young Victoria* to *The Queen*, still deal with national figureheads but no longer function as epics about the making or the remaking of the nation. Their engagement with established figures of national standing, ready-made icons of Englishness, is shared by other biopics about renowned and in many ways canonical English figures associated with the English cultural heritage, from *Shakespeare in Love* and *Becoming Jane* to *Topsy-Turvy* (about Gilbert and Sullivan) and *Chaplin*.

The protagonists of many other costume dramas of the modern past, from *Sense and Sensibility* to *Howards End* to *Ladies in Lavender* (2004), are no longer national figureheads presented in a mythic light, like the Arthurs or the Elizabeths; nor are they real historical characters with a known relationship to the national. The narratives of such films rarely deal with events of established national historical significance; they are instead generally small-scale and intimate, their settings and characters often localised and specific. But for all the banal, localising features of such films, they have still readily been taken up in critical debate as poignant representations of the nation, since the class of people with which they deal is still relatively powerful, since their morality, principles and values are deemed the 'proper' values of an English inheritance, since the literature from which they are adapted is often canonical, a part of the national cultural heritage, since their *mise-en-scène* is heavily associated with a sort of official heritage England through organisations like the National Trust – and since representations of this nature have for long been seen as 'true' representations of the nation. The class-specificity, the cultural status and the very local settings of these films thus command national attention.

In some films there is a perceived threat to a local community, and therefore by implication to the nation and to Englishness, when an outsider enters the community, or when the English are abroad, or when there is a national crisis of some sort. In *Ladies in Lavender*, for instance, a remote but ostensibly typical English community in the late 1930s is momentarily threatened by two German-speaking central Europeans who arrive unheralded. In other films the threat comes from an enemy within, an interloper from another class, who challenges the class-bound vision of ideal Englishness; this is the effect of Fanny in *Mansfield Park*, of Leonard Bast in *Howards End*, and Robbie, the housekeeper's son, in *Atonement*.

All of these films, from *King Arthur* to *Atonement*, explore what the 2007 Cultural Test identifies as Britain's cultural heritage. The test does not, however, simply promote films about the national heritage, but also encourages two other ways of engaging with the past. First, there is an emphasis on a genuinely creative approach to filmmaking, with filmmakers encouraged to develop 'unique interpretations of stories of British cultural heritage'.[39] Second, there is an emphasis on representing the UK as 'a culturally diverse nation',[40] with the implication being that a worthy approach to representing the past on film would be one that reflected and indeed celebrated such diversity in a historical context.

The range of stories told, and the ways in which they were presented on screen, suggests a degree of creativity in approaching history, yet clearly filmmakers were also working with well-established generic conventions for representing past times. In films about the past, England is often a strange and distant place, another country where they do things differently; but it is almost always at the same time presented as familiar, any otherness offset by the conventionality and predictability of generic representations, and the effort to make the past seem relevant to present-day audiences. The radical formal developments of certain films and filmmakers clearly stretch the boundaries of representation, as in the postmodernist aesthetics of Derek Jarman's *Edward II*, Sally Potter's *Orlando* and Michael Winterbottom's *A Cock and Bull Story*. A realist aesthetic is more typical of representations of the English past – but that aesthetic too can generate what is recognised within the film business as creative achievement, as demonstrated by the numerous awards given to the production designers and costume designers of films with a historical setting.

In various ways, too, it can be said that filmmakers were already, prior to the emergence of the Cultural Test, exploring the English past in terms of diversity. Thus a number of films focused on women as protagonists, and/or explored the plight of women in patriarchal historical settings. Rather fewer adopted ordinary or underprivileged people as their central characters, but there clearly are such films, ranging from *Anchoress* and the Robin Hood films in the Middle Ages, via *Moll Flanders* (1996) and *Plunkett & Macleane* in the early modern period, to *Nicholas Nickleby* and *Oliver Twist* in the nineteenth century and the gamekeeper of *Lady Chatterley* (2006) and the housekeeper's son in *Atonement* in the early twentieth century. There were, however, many more films focused on the privileged and the powerful.

Ethnic diversity is even less visible in films about the English past. Native Americans visit England in *Elizabeth: The Golden Age* and *The New World* (2005), Jewishness becomes an issue in *The Governess* (1998),

Indian culture is confronted in *Vanity Fair* (2004), there are occasional black servants visible in the background in various palaces, country houses and stately homes – and on just one or two occasions in the foreground, as in *The Tichborne Claimant* (1998). But these are rare examples indeed, and *King Arthur* is probably more self-conscious about the ethnic diversity of British history than most other films. *Amazing Grace* (2006), meanwhile, dealt with William Wilberforce's campaign to end the slave trade in the early nineteenth century, but was berated by some for 'belittling the contribution of black abolitionists'.[41]

As noted above, England does however become a far more culturally and socially diverse space in representations of the very recent past. In effect, such films present a new, more democratic vision of England, with their narratives more frequently placing poor, working-class or underprivileged characters in the foreground, and giving room to ethnicities beyond the white Anglo-Saxon. The ordinary protagonists of films like *Let Him Have It* (1991), *The Land Girls* (1998), *East Is East* (1999), *Billy Elliot* (2000), *Anita and Me* (2002), *Vera Drake* (2004), *This Is England* (2006) and *Control* (2007) are a far cry from the monarchs, aristocrats and upper-class protagonists of so many films set in earlier English pasts. As noted in chapter 1, such films share a great deal with social dramas set in the present. Thus the emphasis on inter-ethnic friendships and tensions in *East Is East* and *Anita and Me*, both set in the 1970s, is very similar to the relationships in *Bend It Like Beckham* (2002), set in the present; the community of working-class black Londoners of the 1970s in *Young Soul Rebels* (1991) shares much with the contemporary drama of *Bullet Boy* (2004); and the working-class milieu of *This Is England* and *Billy Elliot*, set in the early 1980s, is close to that represented in the present-day narratives of *Brassed Off* (1996) and *The Full Monty* (1997).

While many of the films about the pre-modern or the modern English past work as national cinema, mythologising the nation, the national heritage and national identity, this is much less true of films about the very recent English past. Most of the representations of the very recent past occur in small-scale, low-budget films; most of them focus on ordinary Englishness rather than the culture and identity of the privileged; and most of them again are highly localised in terms of setting and subject matter. As a result, films such as *East Is East*, about a mixed-race working-class family in Salford, *Vera Drake*, about a white working-class Londoner who performs illegal abortions, and *Billy Elliot*, about a white working-class boy growing up in a mining community

Vera Drake: representing ordinary Englishness in the recent past.

and becoming a dancer, refuse any such mythologizing tendencies; indeed, in their focus on the unheralded and their democratic extension of the range of social types represented on the big screen, they effectively demythologise England and Englishness.

Events of national significance will occasionally play out in the background of the drama, as the calamitous miner's strike of 1984 does in *Billy Elliot*. Such films will also occasionally be taken up as trenchant depictions of the condition of England. *This Is England*, for instance, about a motley group of working-class youths in the early 1980s, clearly gestures towards the national in its title, and in its exploration of far-right National Front politics and flag-waving, but even this film remains as much a dissection of a very specific local working-class community as a state-of-the-nation film. In most of the films about the very recent past, the local dimension will remain just that; the very specific, localised Englishness of the setting and the subject matter will thus remain at a banal, mundane level, unremarked and unremarkable (even if much effort has been put into creating this mundane historical setting). Language, accent and *mise-en-scène* may establish the films as culturally English, but because the social types represented on screen are from different class, ethnic and cultural milieux to those familiar from so many films set in earlier English pasts, because the protagonists are rarely well-established historical figures, and because the stories have not emerged from the pages of canonical literature, it is an Englishness that depends much less on established myths of nationhood and national identity.

Conclusion

An official government document declared in 2005 that 'British films are an important part of our cultural heritage and a significant channel for the continuing expression and dissemination of British culture.'[1] The document, discussed in chapter 2, laid the groundwork for tax incentives designed to enable 'the sustainable production of culturally British films'.[2] While the scope of this study has been culturally *English* film-making, it is clear that such nation-specific filmmaking has only been possible in the 1990s and 2000s thanks to transnational production arrangements and the possibility and sometimes the actuality of global distribution and exhibition. What the UK government calls *our* cultural heritage is of interest in various ways to financiers, producers, distributors and audiences well beyond the national borders. Paradoxically, 'the continuing expression and dissemination of British culture' has in large part become dependent on foreign capital and global enterprise, with foreign actors performing English identities in culturally English films directed by foreign filmmakers.

Such arrangements do not always result in films providing new visions of Englishness; on the contrary, in order to be successful in the global marketplace, culturally English filmmaking will at times rely on the most familiar, established traditions and identities. But alongside such films are others, usually of more modest means, that do often provide new visions of England and Englishness. *Young Soul Rebels* (1991) looked back to a moment of national celebration, the Queen's Silver Jubilee in 1977, but depicted black and gay working-class youths making their own cultural statement very much at odds with the mainstream. *Bend It Like Beckham* (2002) took one of England's national sports, football, but looked at it through the lens of teenage girls and the British-Asian experience. *This Is England* (2006) suggested that the nation might be understood from the perspective of young working-class kids trying to reconcile their own inter-ethnic friendships with the politics of far-right groups like the National Front.

Such low-budget films tend to circulate within niche markets, although just occasionally, as with *Bend It Like Beckham*, they cross over into the mainstream. But in fact culturally English filmmaking as a whole, whether it involves new or traditional English identities, should be understood as a niche practice within the global film business, a means of maintaining difference and distinctiveness in a market saturated with products. Of course, as the Austen, Bond and Harry Potter franchises demonstrate in their different ways, it is a well-developed niche, which can become surprisingly pervasive and indeed lucrative, thereby demonstrating once again the paradoxical relationship between national themes or subject matter, transnational production arrangements and international audiences.

For some filmmakers, England as a place, English history, English literature and the contemporary English scene are simply sources for film stories, characters and settings. But for many English filmmakers, there is a genuine commitment to telling stories that involve England, English characters and the English cultural heritage, a genuine commitment to telling stories about their homeland, a distinctive nation and its people. If this involves the expression and dissemination of English culture, it is still dependent on the possibility of raising production funds, which will often bring in foreign co-production partners and distributors, and involve addressing audiences in markets beyond the UK.

What the preceding chapters demonstrate is that across the 1990s and 2000s, various strategies were adopted by filmmakers and others to enable the production of culturally English films. The tax incentive scheme trailed by the government, for instance, was just one strand in a wider set of fiscal initiatives and cultural policies designed to enable such activities. Indeed, the period in question saw a gradual reinvention of national film policy and the mechanisms for putting that policy into practice, following the dismantling of the previous system in the 1980s. The allocation of Lottery funding for film production and the establishment of the UK Film Council were central planks of the new national policy, a policy that gradually came to be understood in terms of providing what the then Minister for Culture called a 'bulwark against the homogeneity of globalisation'.[3]

On the one hand, then, by the 2000s, UK film policy was intended as a means of ensuring cultural diversity: cinema was to be a space for creating and maintaining diverse representations of Englishness/Britishness, a space for creating distinctively British films – hence the Cultural Test, introduced in 2007. On the other hand, the response to globalisation was not simply about resisting it, or constructing it as a problem; on the contrary, national film policy was also designed to encourage inward investment from global Hollywood and to enable transnational cooperation. Paradoxically, transnational activity could both loosen national ties and reinforce them – as the European Commission did when it insisted on the strengthening of the Cultural Test.

Working in a context shaped in part by the globalisation of the film business and in part by national film policy, filmmakers adopted a variety of production strategies that involved creating culturally English films. Funding arrangements ranged from the big-budget blockbuster to the low-budget drama, with productions at all levels exploiting the fiscal opportunities made possible through government policy. Different types of production were intended for different markets and addressed to different audiences. A great many 'English' productions relied on foreign funding of one sort or another, especially from Hollywood; the economic circumstances of a film production will clearly have an effect on the cultural possibilities of a film, with investors and distributors inevitably anxious to see a return on their input. But it has to be accepted that American investment has in fact enabled a certain diversity of representations, including diverse representations of Englishness. Thus American investment made possible the global blockbusting Harry Potter franchise, the refined period Austen adaptations of *Sense and Sensibility* (1995) and *Emma* (1996), and the low-budget dramas of working-class Northern life *The Full Monty* (1997) and *Billy Elliot* (2000), both of which became major box-office successes thanks to the involvement of American distributors.

Production strategies designed to make possible the creation of culturally English films were not limited to funding arrangements. Also vital were the ways in which filmmakers worked with particular types of material, in many cases reworking subject matter or cultural products already strongly associated with England or Englishness. Hence the strategy of securing the rights to particular types of English fiction, from Jane Austen to J.K. Rowling, and from Ian Fleming to Ian McEwan. Another strategy was the identification of iconic English characters as subjects for biopics, from royalty and the aristocracy to pop stars and film stars, and from medieval heroes to literary figures. This was also a key means of tapping into some of the more familiar moments of English history.

What emerges from such strategies is a series of genres of filmic Englishness, which are at the same time regimes of taste, designed with particular markets and audiences in mind: the big-budget action-adventure film, the family film, the intimate costume drama, the romantic comedy, the social realist drama, and so on. None of these genres is unique to culturally English filmmaking, but all of them provided formal models, narrative structures and character types that proved amenable to making culturally English films that gained audience approval. And of course those genres could also be mixed together in different ways to create novel products and market crossovers.

What has been the outcome of these various strategies? In particular, to what extent can the range of films discussed here be identified as distinctively English? One way of identifying Englishness in films is by virtue of its difference from other national identities – but the forces of globalisation have meant that at some levels those differences are minimised. Thus contemporary Western clothing is not that different whether a film is set in the USA, England, Australia or western Europe – jeans, trainers, T-shirts and baseball caps are hardly markers of *national* identity. And while certain films seem English, or at least 'not-Hollywood', by virtue of their aesthetic differences from most Hollywood films, other culturally English films, like the Harry Potter films or the James Bond films, may well be identified by some non-English-speaking audiences as culturally Hollywood, by virtue of their production values and scale.

The question of identity is also complicated by foreign actors performing iconic versions of Englishness – and indeed by English actors playing American characters in American films. Then there is the problem of language, with English both a national language and a global one, but still a language that in some markets will be translated, via dubbing or subtitling, thereby reducing its potential as a marker of nationality. Thus Gwyneth Paltrow, the American star of the Miramax-backed period Austen adaptation *Emma*, no longer speaks in an English accent when the film is dubbed into German. Paradoxically, and in all sorts of ways, then, culturally English films are not necessarily distinctively English!

If it has become difficult in some respects to distinguish filmic Englishness on the basis of its difference from other filmic national identities, there are other ways in which Englishness does insist on its national distinctiveness. Thus the Englishness of *Emma* depends on cultural association or alignment as much as it does on cultural differentiation. That is to say that, in various ways, it taps into well-established traditions of English cultural identity that are indeed distinctive. Culturally English filmmaking thus depends to a great extent upon the exploitation of brands already identified and recognised as English, as part of the English cultural heritage. But certain established, iconic and canonical English brands also have a global presence, and in some ways therefore become global brands, as with Shakespeare, Austen and Rowling/Potter. There are for instance Jane Austen societies in Argentina, Australia, Brazil, Canada, Japan and the USA, as well as Austen websites in Chinese, German, Portuguese and Spanish, amongst others.

One of the most entrenched English brands is a particular image of the nation itself, as 'a country steeped in history'.[4] Hence the number of films set in the English past, most of which were designed with international audiences in mind, and many of which have been taken up by the tourism business. On the one hand, this maintains and reproduces the brand image of England as a country steeped in history; on the other hand, it is clear that there are many filmic versions of the English past, some of which resist the pleasures of tourism, nostalgia and the heritage industry. While the discourse of authenticity plays a major role in the reception of films about the English past, it is notable too that a Prague studio can provide the setting for Victorian London in *Oliver Twist* (2005), while the Irish countryside can stand in for Roman Britain (*King Arthur*, 2004) and Regency England (*Becoming Jane*, 2007).

Across historical and contemporary dramas, there is a great diversity of English characters, yet a Southern/Home Counties version of white, middle-class and upper-class Englishness remains dominant. In films, this is a character type with a distinctive accent, which resonates powerfully from the sixteenth century to the present. As a stereotype, it was inhabited with great effectiveness by Hugh Grant, playing a series of emotionally inhibited upper-middle-class Englishmen, in films from *Sense and Sensibility* in period costume, to the contemporary Richard Curtis-scripted dramas *Four Weddings and a Funeral* (1994), *Notting Hill* (1999) and *Love Actually* (2003). That he played the Prime Minister in the latter film indicates just how well-connected this character type tends to be. Yet alongside this abiding stereotype are a whole host of other

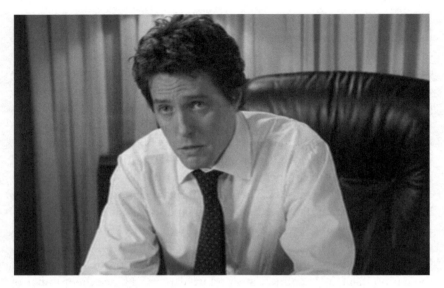

Hugh Grant as the Prime Minister in *Love Actually*: the dominance of southern, white, middle-class Englishness.

English characters from working-class backgrounds, from the Midlands and the North of England, from ethnic minority communities, and so on, displaying very different character attributes, with very different accents, and with a very different range of social connections, few of them granting access to the corridors of power. Collectively, such characters represent a culturally diverse England, an England that Labour government policy and Film Council practice in the 2000s were designed to promote.

Few culturally English films of the 1990s and 2000s have been explicitly patriotic celebrations of nationhood or national identity, yet through strategies such as those described here they remain recognisably English to many audiences, both domestic and foreign. A banal or mundane rather than explicitly patriotic sense of Englishness is established in part through voice, language and accent, and in part through *mise-en-scène*. In chapter 3, I identified three iconographies of Englishness that recur across films, from traditional heritage England to mundane urban modernity and monumental metropolitan modernity. At one level, these iconographies have become heavy with ideological meaning; as such they move beyond the banal and the everyday to become overdetermined stereotypes of Englishness – and, in the case of traditional heritage England and monumental metropolitan modernity, objects of the tourist gaze. But at another level, these iconographies are able to operate as indicative backdrops, subtly meaningful narrative spaces for the playing out of dramas that thereby become recognisably English.

Mundane urban modernity in particular frequently became the setting for highly localised narratives that were on the one hand identifiably English but on the other hand resisted incorporation into the processes of mythologizing nationalism. The local, in films like *Bullet Boy* (2004), could thus find a space within an overarching but still mundane, underplayed Englishness, alongside films that more self-consciously reworked established mythologies of the nation and the national cultural heritage, from *Elizabeth* (1998) to *Brideshead Revisited* (2008). Other films, like the globetrotting James Bond series, inserted Englishness into a global frame, while several of the family-friendly franchises, from Harry Potter (2001–10) and *The Lord of the Rings* (2001–3) to *The Chronicles of Narnia* (2005–10) and *The Golden Compass* (2007), explored a displaced form of Englishness situated in a fictional world.

Culturally English filmmaking is a local, a national, a transnational and a global enterprise. Within the complex world of film production, it is a niche practice, in which the representation of various versions of Englishness provides an element of diversity and difference within the global film business: that is one aspect of the cultural value of national cinema.

Notes

Introduction

1. Michael Billig, *Banal Nationalism*, London: Sage Publications, 1995.
2. See Mette Hjort, *Small Nation, Global Cinema: The New Danish Cinema*, Minneapolis/London: University of Minnesota Press, 2005.
3. James Christopher, 'An update deserving of an Oscar' (review of *The Ideal Husband*), *The Times*, 15 April 1999, p. 37.
4. Andrew Higson, *English Heritage, English Cinema: Costume Drama Since 1980*, Oxford: Oxford University Press, 2003.
5. Ian Christie, 'Will Lottery money assure the British film industry?', *New Statesman*, vol. 126, no. 4339, 20 June 1997, p. 38.

1 Film production in the UK in the 1990s and 2000s

1. For other accounts of aspects of the UK film business in the 1990s and 2000s, see Robert Murphy, ed., *British Cinema of the 90s*, London: British Film Institute, 2000; James Caterer and Andrew Higson, 'A indústria cinematográfica britânica', in Alessandra Meleiro, ed., *Cinema No Mundo: Indústria, Política e Mercado*, Vol. V: *Europa*, São Paulo: Escrituras Editora, 2007, pp. 59–85; and Andrew Higson, *English Heritage, English Cinema: Costume Drama Since 1980*, Oxford: Oxford University Press, 2003, pp. 86–145. The following also provide invaluable statistical information and overviews: the *BFI Film and Television Handbook* for the years 1990 to 2004, published annually by the British Film Institute, and the BFI's statistical website at www.bfi.org.uk/filmtvinfo/publications/pub-rep-brief/pdf/the-stats.pdf; and the *Statistical Yearbook* for the years 2002 to 2009, published annually by the UK Film Council, and the Film Council's website at www.ukfilmcouncil.org.uk. All web pages cited in this chapter were accessed in April 2009 unless otherwise indicated.

2. See e.g. UK Film Council (UKFC), *Statistical Yearbook 2008*, London: UKFC, 2008, p. 129.

3. Margaret Dickinson and Sylvia Harvey, 'Public policy and public funding for film: some recent UK developments', *Screen*, vol. 46, no. 1, spring 2005, p. 91.

4. www.bfi.org.uk/filmtvinfo/publications/pub-rep-brief/pdf/the-stats.pdf.

5. www.bfi.org.uk/filmtvinfo/publications/pub-rep-brief/pdf/the-stats.pdf.

6. www.bfi.org.uk/filmtvinfo/publications/pub-rep-brief/pdf/the-stats.pdf.

7. www.bfi.org.uk/filmtvinfo/publications/pub-rep-brief/pdf/the-stats.pdf.

8. www.bfi.org.uk/filmtvinfo/publications/pub-rep-brief/pdf/the-stats.pdf, p. 55; www.boxofficemojo.com/movies/?id=four weddingsandafuneral.htm.

9. 'UK Film Council at a glance', UKFC website, www.ukfilmcouncil.org.uk/glance, accessed 12 January 2009.

10. 'What we fund', UKFC website, www.ukfilmcouncil.org.uk/fund, accessed 25 March 2009.

11. UK Film Council Awards Database, UKFC website, www.ukfilmcouncil.org.uk/awards, accessed 17 March 2009.

12. Leo Hickman, 'The UK Film Industry', *The Guardian*, G2 section, 14 November 2005, p. 5.

13. UKFC, *Statistical Yearbook 2008*, p. 143.

14. UKFC, *Statistical Yearbook 2009*, London: UKFC, 2009, p. 144.

15. UKFC, *Statistical Yearbook 2008*, pp. 136–45.

16. Adam Dawtry, 'Channel 4 confirms FilmFour closure', www.variety.com, 9 July 2002, at www.variety.com/article/VR1117869446.html?c=19, accessed 9 May 2007.

17. UKFC, *Statistical Yearbook 2008*, p. 121.

18. UKFC, *Statistical Yearbook 2008*, pp. 6–23.

19. UKFC, *Statistical Yearbook 2008*, p. 29.

20. Mark Brown, 'Boomtime for British film industry thanks to Austen, Mr Bean and Gordon Brown', *The Guardian*, 15 January 2007, p. 3.

21. UKFC, *Statistical Yearbook 2008*, pp. 6–23.

22. Tim de Lisle, 'Home box office', *The Guardian*, G2 section, 14 January 2005, p. 5.

23. UKFC, *Statistical Yearbook 2008*, pp. 79–85.

24. Tim de Lisle, 'Home box office', p. 4.
25. HM Revenue and Customs, 'Film production companies: overview and general definitions: meaning of "limited-budget film"', *Film Production Company Manual*, section FPC10160, at www.hmrc.gov.uk/manuals/fpcmanual/fpc10160.htm, accessed 14 January 2009.
26. Charles Gant, 'Arthouse defeats naysayers', *Sight and Sound*, vol. 19, no. 2, February 2009, p. 9.
27. See UKFC website, especially www.ukfilmcouncil.org.uk/media/pdf/e/l/Definition_of_Specialised_Film.pdf, accessed 17 March 2009.
28. Compare Mette Hjort, *Small Nation, Global Cinema: The New Danish Cinema*, Minneapolis/London: University of Minnesota Press, 2005.
29. Gareth McLean, 'Hogwarts and all', *The Guardian*, *Review* section, 19 October 2001, p. 2.
30. Steve Norris, quoted in McLean, 'Hogwarts and all', p. 2.
31. For a more thorough discussion of English romantic comedy, see Nigel Mather, *Tears of Laughter: Comedy-Drama in 1990s British Cinema*, Manchester: Manchester University Press, 2006.
32. See Higson, *English Heritage, English Cinema*.
33. Compare Mette Hjort, 'Themes of nation', in Mette Hjort and Scott Mackenzie, eds, *Cinema and Nation*, London and New York: Routledge, 2000, pp. 103–18.
34. Narval Media/Birkbeck College/Media Consulting Group, *Stories We Tell Ourselves: The Cultural Impact of UK Film 1946–2006. A Study for the UK Film Council*, London: UKFC, June 2009, at www.ukfilmcouncil.org.uk/media/pdf/c/g/Cultural_Impact_Report_FINAL.pdf, p. 64 (accessed 30 June 2009).

2 Film policy and national cinema: cultural value and economic value

1. John Hill, 'UK film policy, cultural capital and social exclusion', *Cultural Trends*, vol. 13 (2), no. 50, June 2004, p. 32.
2. See the UK Film Council (UKFC) website, www.ukfilmcouncil.org.uk; for a useful overview of government policy and British film production in the 1990s and early 2000s, see Margaret Dickinson and Sylvia Harvey, 'Public policy and public funding for film: some recent UK developments', *Screen*, vol. 46, no. 1, spring 2005, pp. 87–95.
3. UKFC, *Our Second Three-Year Plan*, London: UKFC, 2004, p. 52, at www.ukfilmcouncil.org.uk/media/pdf/d/r/Our_Second_Three_Year_Plan.pdf, accessed 14 January 2009.

4. See Hill, 'UK film policy'.
5. UK government, *Films Act 1985*, Schedule 1, at www.opsi.gov. uk/RevisedStatutes/Acts/ukpga/1985/cukpga_19850021_en_2, accessed 14 January 2009.
6. Terry Ilott, 'Overview of film, television and video in the UK', in David Leafe and Terry Ilott, eds, *Film and Television Handbook 1994*, London: British Film Institute, 1993, p. 19.
7. Ilott, 'Overview of film, television and video in the UK', p. 19; emphasis added.
8. All definitions taken from Terry Ilott, 'UK film, television and video: overview', in Eddie Dyja, ed., *Film and Television Handbook 1997*, London: British Film Institute, 1996, pp. 24–7.
9. See e.g. UKFC, *Statistical Yearbook 2008*, London: UKFC, 2008, pp. 21–2.
10. John Hill, *British Cinema in the 1980s: Issues and Themes*, Oxford: Clarendon Press, 1999, p. 241.
11. See UKFC, 'Towards a sustainable UK film industry', London: UKFC, 2000, at www.ukfilmcouncil.org.uk/media/pdf/p/r/TASFI. pdf, accessed 14 January 2009.
12. 'UK Film Council at a glance', UKFC website, www.ukfilmcouncil. org.uk/glance, accessed 12 January 2009.
13. Preface to UKFC, *Statistical Yearbook 2008*, n.p.
14. Chris Smith, *Creative Britain*, London: Faber and Faber, 1998, p. 86; quoted in Peter Todd, 'The British film industry in the 1990s', in Robert Murphy, ed., *British Cinema of the 90s*, London: British Film Institute, 2000, p. 17.
15. Tessa Jowell, Minister for Culture, Media and Sport, 'Valuing culture', speech delivered on 17 June 2003, at www.culture.gov.uk/reference_ library/minister_speeches/2113.aspx, accessed 18 March 2009.
16. Department for Culture, Media and Sport, 'Chris Smith goes to Hollywood', M2 PressWIRE, 27 October 1997; quoted in Toby Miller, 'The Film Industry and the Government', in Murphy, ed., *British Cinema of the 90s*, p. 38.
17. Stephen Pratten and Simon Deakin, 'Competitiveness policy and economic organization: the case of the British film industry', *Screen*, vol. 41, no. 2, summer 2000, p. 222.
18. Pratten and Deakin, 'Competitiveness policy and economic organization', p. 223.
19. See e.g. UKFC, *Statistical Yearbook 2008*.

20. Oxford Economics, *The Economic Impact of the UK Film Industry*, Oxford: Oxford Economics, July 2007, all quotations from p. 1, at www.ukfilmcouncil.org.uk/media/pdf/5/8/FilmCouncilreport 190707.pdf, accessed 14 January 2009; a new edition of this report was issued in June 2010, when this book was in press.
21. Oxford Economics, *The Economic Impact of the UK Film Industry*, all quotations from p. 1.
22. Oxford Economics, *The Economic Impact of the UK Film Industry*, p. 49.
23. Oxford Economics, *The Economic Impact of the UK Film Industry*, p. 4.
24. Oxford Economics, *The Economic Impact of the UK Film Industry*, p. 47.
25. Oxford Economics, *The Economic Impact of the UK Film Industry*, p. 54.
26. Oxford Economics, *The Economic Impact of the UK Film Industry*, p. 55.
27. Oxford Economics, *The Economic Impact of the UK Film Industry*, all quotations from p. 1.
28. HM Treasury, 'Consultations and Legislation: The Reform of Film Tax Incentives: Promoting the sustainable production of culturally British films', 29 July 2005, at www.hm-treasury.gov.uk/filmtax, accessed 18 March 2009.
29. HM Treasury, 'Reform of film tax incentives: Promoting the sustainable production of culturally British films', July 2005, at www.hm-treasury.gov.uk/d/filmcondocv1.pdf, accessed 18 March 2009, para 1.1.
30. HM Treasury, 'Reform of film tax incentives', para 2.24.
31. HM Treasury, 'Reform of film tax incentives', para 2.1.
32. HM Treasury, 'Reform of film tax incentives', para 2.4.
33. See HM Treasury, 'Reform of film tax incentives', para 2.19.
34. HM Treasury, 'Reform of film tax incentives', Appendix B, p. 34.
35. Jowell, 'Valuing culture'.
36. HM Treasury, 'Reform of film tax incentives', para 2.3.
37. HM Treasury, 'Reform of film tax incentives', Appendix B, p. 34.
38. Mette Hjort and Duncan Petrie, 'Introduction', in Hjort and Petrie, eds, *The Cinema of Small Nations*, Edinburgh: Edinburgh University Press, 2007, p. 9.
39. HM Revenue and Customs, 'Film Production Companies: Overview and general definitions: Introduction', *Film Production Company Manual*, section FPC10010, at www.hmrc.gov.uk/manuals/fpc-manual/fpc10010.htm, accessed 14 January 2009.
40. Council of Europe, European Convention on Cinematographic Co-Production, 'Summary of the Treaty', at http://conventions.coe.int/Treaty/en/Summaries/Html/147.htm, accessed 9 January 2009.

41. HM Revenue and Customs, 'Film Tax Relief – Co-productions: Introduction', *Film Production Company Manual*, section FPC70010, at www.hmrc.gov.uk/manuals/fpcmanual/fpc70010.htm, accessed 14 January 2009.

42. Department for Culture, Media and Sport (DCMS), 'Guidance Notes – 1 January 2007, Schedule 1 to the Films Act 1985', p. 11, at www.culture.gov.uk/images/relevant_forms/culturaltest_260107. pdf, accessed 14 January 2009.

43. DCMS, 'Guidance Notes', p. 12.

44. DCMS, 'Guidance Notes', p. 11.

45. DCMS, 'Guidance Notes', p. 11.

46. DCMS, 'British film test gets the green light', 14 July 2006, at www. culture.gov.uk/reference_library/media_releases/2478.aspx, accessed 7 January 2009.

47. DCMS, 'Guidance Notes', pp. 12–13.

48. DCMS, 'Guidance Notes', pp. 13, 12.

49. DCMS, 'Guidance Notes', p. 13.

50. DCMS, 'Guidance Notes', p. 14.

51. DCMS, 'Guidance Notes', p. 14.

52. DCMS, 'Guidance Notes', p. 14.

53. DCMS, 'Guidance Notes', p. 14.

54. DCMS, 'Guidance Notes', p. 14.

55. DCMS, 'Guidance Notes', p. 14.

56. DCMS, 'Guidance Notes', p. 13.

57. DCMS, 'Guidance Notes', p. 13.

58. Michael Billig, *Banal Nationalism*, London: Sage Publications, 1995.

59. DCMS, 'Cultural test for British films: Final Framework', DCMS: Creative Industries, Film Branch, November 2005, p. 3.

60. BECTU, 'Cultural test for British films: BECTU response to DCMS consultation', 14 October 2005, at www.bectu.org.uk/policy/pol092. html, accessed 7 January 2009.

61. Shaun Woodward, quoted in DCMS, 'British film test gets the green light', 14 July 2006, at www.culture.gov.uk/reference_library/media_releases/2478.aspx, accessed 7 January 2009.

62. Geoffrey Macnab, 'The big exodus', *The Independent*, 5 June 2008, p. 14.

63. Andrea Calderwood, quoted in Salamander Davoudi, 'Film industry reeling from tax regime', *Financial Times*, 1 December 2008, p. 4.

64. Oxford Economics report, quoted in Davoudi, 'Film industry reeling from tax regime', p. 4. See also Macnab, 'The big exodus', p. 14;

Adam Dawtrey, 'Brit producers push gov't on tax credits', *Variety*, 26 November 2006, at www.variety.com, accessed 9 January 2009; Michael Gubbins, 'UK finance in sickness or in health', www.screendaily.com, 5 October 2007; Ben Fenton, 'Film tax overhaul proves box-office hit', www.ft.com, 21 July 2008; and Audrey Ward, 'Co-production report reopens debate over UK tax credit', www.screendaily.com, 4 December 2008; all websites accessed 9 January 2009.

65. Quoted in Davoudi, 'Film industry reeling from tax regime', p. 4.
66. Statistics from the UKFC website, at http://www.ukfilmcouncil. com/article/16909/Abolition-of-UK-Film-Council, accessed 28 July 2010; quotations from Ronan Bennett, 'Axing the Film Council: a move that impoverishes us all', *The Guardian*, 26 July 2010, online at http://www.guardian.co.uk/film/2010/jul/26/uk-film-council-abolished-reaction, accessed 28 July 2010.

3 English cinema, transnationalism and globalisation

1. Olsberg/SPI, 'Stately Attraction: How Film and Television Programmes Promote Tourism in the UK', report commissioned by the UK Film Council et al., 2007, at www.ukfilmcouncil.org.uk/media/pdf/a/6/ Final_Stately_Attraction_Report_to_UKFC_and_Partners_20.08.07. pdf, accessed 13 July 2009, pp. 19–20.
2. Eddie Dyja, 'UK film, television and video: overview', in Dyja, ed., *BFI Film and Television Handbook 2001*, London: British Film Institute, 2000, p. 41; and Box Office Mojo website, www.boxofficemojo.com/ movies/?id=nottinghill.htmworldwide, accessed 5 April 2009.
3. Box Office Mojo website, www.boxofficemojo.com/movies/?id= brideandprejudice.htm, and www.boxofficemojo.com/movies/?id= constantgardener.htm, accessed 5 April 2009.
4. See Andrew Higson, 'The concept of national cinema', *Screen*, vol. 30, no. 4, autumn 1989, pp. 36–46.
5. See Anthony D. Smith, *National Identity*, Harmondsworth: Penguin, 1991, pp. 8–11.
6. See e.g. David Bordwell, *Narration in the Fiction Film*, Madison: University of Wisconsin Press, 1985.
7. I discuss such films in more detail in *Waving the Flag: Constructing a National Cinema in Britain*, Oxford: Oxford University Press, 1995, pp. 212–71.
8. Seton Margrave, *Daily Mail*, no date, on *The Bells Go Down* microfiche in the British Film Institute National Library, London.

9. Diane Negra, 'Romance and/as tourism', in Matthew Tinkcom and Amy Villarejo, eds, *Keyframes: Popular Cinema and Cultural Studies*, London: Routledge, 2001, p. 82.
10. Negra, 'Romance and/as tourism', p. 90.
11. Negra, 'Romance and/as tourism', p. 91.
12. Negra, 'Romance and/as tourism', p. 92.
13. Andy Medhurst, 'Dressing the part', *Sight and Sound*, vol. 6, no. 6, June 1996, p. 30; and Charlotte Brunsdon, 'The poignancy of place: London and the cinema', *Visual Culture in Britain*, vol. 5, no. 1, 2004, p. 59.
14. Brunsdon, 'The poignancy of place', p. 64; and Charlotte Brunsdon, *London in Cinema: The Cinematic City Since 1945*, Basingstoke: Palgrave Macmillan, 2007.
15. Michael Billig, *Banal Nationalism*, London: Sage Publications, 1995.
16. Olsberg/SPI, 'Stately Attraction', p. 11.
17. Olsberg/SPI, 'Stately Attraction', p. 14.
18. See Olsberg/SPI, 'Stately Attraction', pp. 11, 14 and 15–16.
19. Oxford Economics, *The Economic Impact of the UK Film Industry*, Oxford: Oxford Economics, July 2007, p. 6.
20. Roland Robertson, 'Glocalization: time-space and homogeneity-heterogeneity', in Mike Featherstone, Scott Lash and Robert Robertson, eds, *Global Modernities*, London: Sage, 1995, p. 40.
21. Robertson, 'Glocalization', p. 28.
22. Robertson, 'Glocalization', p. 29.
23. Katie Allen, 'Magic Kingdom woos China with tale of an enchanted vegetable', *The Guardian*, 11 June 2007, p. 27; the quotation is from Thomas Staggs.
24. Mike Featherstone, 'Global Culture: An Introduction', *Theory, Culture & Society*, 7 (2–3), 1990, p. 2.
25. Colin Hoskins and Stuart McFadyen, 'Guest Editors' Introduction', *Canadian Journal of Communications* 16 (2), 1991, at www.cjc-online.ca, accessed 5 April 2009.
26. Andrew Pulver, 'Bard to worse at the multiplex', *The Guardian*, 5 February 1999, p. 19.
27. David Harvey, *The Condition of Postmodernity: An Enquiry into the Origins of Cultural Change*, Oxford: Blackwell, 1990.

4   English literature, the contemporary novel and the cinema

1. UK Film Council, *Statistical Yearbook 2008*, London: UK Film Council, 2008, pp. 29–31, esp. section 5.1.

2. See table on Box Office Mojo website, at www.boxofficemojo.com/alltime/world/, accessed 10 April 2009.

3. Information here and subsequently about adaptations of English novels is from a database compiled for this book and based on a thorough trawl through the film reviews in *Monthly Film Bulletin* (January 1990–April 1991) and *Sight and Sound* (May 1991–August 2009), supplemented with searches on the Internet Movie Database (www.imdb.com), inter alia; my thanks to Jon Stubbs, Jane Bryan and Pierluigi Ercole for compiling the database.

4. Statistics on British film production are drawn from the British Film Institute website at www.bfi.org.uk, and the UK Film Council website at www.ukfilmcouncil.org.uk; statistics on adaptations are drawn from the database referred to in note 3 above.

5. Christopher Tookey, 'Once more unto the breach', *Sunday Telegraph*, 8 October 1989, p. 44.

6. Philip French, 'Be-all and end-all for triumph', *The Observer*, 3 May 1992, p. 52; Julie Salamon, 'Film: Merchant Ivory's "Howards End"', *Wall Street Journal*, 12 March 1992, cutting – no page number; Tom Crow, 'Regarding *Howards End*', *Village View*, 17–23 April 1992, cutting – no page number.

7. Rex Reed, 'Something nice happened...', *The New York Observer*, 23 September 2004, cutting – no page number.

8. Philip French, *The Observer*, quoted on Samuelson Entertainment's website for *Wilde*, at www.oscarwilde.com/newrev5.html, accessed 10 April 2009.

9. Mike Goodridge, 'Shakespeare in Love', *Screen International*, 18 December 1998, p. 19.

10. Owen Gleiberman, *Entertainment Weekly*, quoted in Miramax advertisement in *Screen International*, 11 December 1998, p. 7.

11. Paul Howlett, 'Film choice: Gosford Park', *The Guardian Guide*, 21 March 2009, p. 53; Derek Elley, 'Quite a royal send-off', *Variety*, 19–25 May 2003, p. 27.

12. David Rooney, 'Stage Beauty', *Variety*, 10–16 May 2004, p. 50.

13. *Mail on Sunday, Night & Day Magazine*, quoted on the official website for *Stage Beauty*, at www.radiotimes.com/stagebeauty/pressquotes.html, accessed 31 August 2005.

14. Telephone interview by the author with PolyGram Film Entertainment staff, 23 November 1998.

15. John Calley, quoted in Joseph Steuer, 'Sony's Classic trio inks, plans to get aggressive', *Hollywood Reporter*, 31 January–2 February 1997.

16. Information here and subsequently about best-selling fiction is drawn from John Sutherland, *Reading the Decades: Fifty Years of the Nation's Bestselling Books*, London: BBC, 2002; the website of *The Bookseller* (www.thebookseller.com); Cader Books' US bestsellers website (www.caderbooks.com/best80.html); and Alex Hamilton's and latterly John Dugdale's annual 'Fastsellers' survey in *The Guardian* (see e.g. Alex Hamilton, 'Fastsellers '99', *The Guardian*, 8 January 2000, p. 10; and John Dugdale, 'Sofa, so good', *The Guardian*, Review section, 30 December 2006, p. 18).

17. Alex Hamilton, 'Fastsellers 2001: hot paperbacks', *The Guardian*, 29 December 2001, at http://books.guardian.co.uk/news/articles/0,6109,625340,00.html, accessed 10 April 2009.

18. Alex Hamilton, 'Fastsellers of 1998', *The Guardian*, 9 January 1999, p. 10; Sutherland, *Reading the Decades*, p. 166.

19. Dan Franklin, 'Commissioning and editing modern fiction', in Zachary Leader, ed., *On Modern British Fiction*, Oxford: Oxford University Press, 2002, p. 275.

20. For more detailed discussions of the process of literary adaptation, see e.g. Deborah Cartmell, I.Q. Hunter, Heidi Kaye and Imelda Whelehan, eds, *Pulping Fictions: Consuming Culture across the Literature/Media Divide*, London: Pluto Press, 1996; Deborah Cartmell and Imelda Whelehan, eds, *Adaptations: From Text to Screen, Screen to Text*, London: Routledge, 1999; Brian McFarlane, *Novel to Film: An Introduction to the Theory of Adaptation*, Oxford: Clarendon Press, 1996; Robert Stam, *Literature Through Film: Realism, Magic and the Art of Adaptation*, Oxford: Blackwell Publishing, 2004; Robert Stam and Alessandra Raengo, eds, *A Companion to Literature and Film*, Oxford: Blackwell Publishing, 2004; Robert Stam and Alessandra Raengo, eds, *Literature and Film: A Guide to the Theory and Practice of Film Adaptation*, Oxford: Blackwell Publishing, 2004; and Christine Geraghty, *Now a Major Motion Picture: Film Adaptations of Literature and Drama*, Lanham: Rowman and Littlefield, 2008.

21. Neil LaBute, 'Commentary by Director Neil LaBute', special feature on *Possession* DVD, Warner Home Video, 2003.

22. A.S. Byatt, *Possession: A Romance*, London: Vintage, 1991 (1st publ. 1990), p. 508.

23. LaBute, 'Commentary'.

24. LaBute, 'Commentary'.
25. LaBute, 'Commentary'.
26. LaBute, 'Commentary'.

5   Jane Austen: 'the hottest scriptwriter in Hollywood'

1. David Furnish of Rocket Pictures, quoted in Charles Gant, 'Mash up: how mixing and matching genres can pay', *The Observer Film Quarterly*, March 2009, p. 49, issued with *The Observer*, 22 March 2009.
2. Ami Angelowicz, 'Natalie Portman to conquer "Zombies"', www. cnn.com, 12 December 2009, at www.cnn.com/2009/SHOWBIZ/ Movies/12/11/natalie.portman.prejudice.zombies/index.html, accessed 12 December 2009.
3. www.pemberley.com/, accessed 2 December 2008.
4. Arielle Eckstut, *Pride and Promiscuity: The Lost Sex Scenes of Jane Austen*, New York: Fireside, 2001.
5. All details and quotations from Steven Morris, 'A literary sensibility that makes solid financial sense', *The Guardian*, 3 September 2005, p. 9.
6. See e.g. Ros Ballaster, 'Adapting Jane Austen', *The English Review*, September 1996; Julianne Pidduck, 'Of windows and country walks: frames of space and movement in 1990s Austen adaptations', *Screen*, vol. 39, no. 4, winter 1998; Julian North, 'Conservative Austen, radical Austen: *Sense and Sensibility* from text to screen', and Esther Sonnet, 'From *Emma* to *Clueless*: taste, pleasure and the scene of history', both in Deborah Cartmell and Imelda Whelehan, eds, *Adaptations: From Text to Screen, Screen to Text*, London: Routledge, 1999; Roger Sales, 'In Face of All the Servants: Spectators and Spies in Austen', in Deidre Lynch, ed., *Janeites: Austen's Disciples and Devotees*, Princeton: Princeton University Press, 2000; John Wiltshire, *Recreating Jane Austen*, Cambridge: Cambridge University Press, 2001; Linda Troost and Sayre Greenfield, eds, *Jane Austen in Hollywood*, Kentucky: The University Press of Kentucky, 2001, 2nd edn; Sue Parrill, *Jane Austen on Film and Television: A Critical Study of the Adaptations*, Jefferson, NC: McFarland, 2002; Gina and Andrew F. MacDonald, eds, *Jane Austen on Screen*, Cambridge: Cambridge University Press, 2003; Suzanne R. Pucci and James Thompson, eds, *Jane Austen and Co.: Remaking the Past in Contemporary Culture*, New York: SUNY Press, 2003; Eckart Voigts-Virchow, *Janespotting and Beyond: British Heritage Retrovisions since the Mid-1990s*, Tübingen: Gunter Narr Verlag Tübingen, 2004;

Kathryn Sutherland, *Jane Austen's Textual Lives: From Aeschylus to Bollywood*, Oxford: Oxford University Press, 2007; Marc Edward DiPaolo, *Emma Adapted: Jane Austen's Heroine from Book to Film*, New York: Peter Lang, 2007; David Monaghan, Ariane Hudelet and John Wiltshire, eds, *The Cinematic Jane Austen: Essays on the Filmic Sensibility of the Novels*, Jefferson, NC, and London: McFarland, 2009.

7. Norman Oder, 'Sensible Tie-ins', *Publisher's Weekly*, 1 January 1996 (page number unknown).

8. Emma Thompson, *Jane Austen's Sense and Sensibility: The Screenplay and Diaries*, London: Bloomsbury, 1995; and Emma Thompson, *Sense and Sensibility: The Diaries*, London: Bloomsbury, 1996; Oder, 'Sensible Tie-ins', page number unknown.

9. See e.g. Louis Menand, 'What Jane Austen doesn't tell us', *New York Review of Books*, vol. 43, no. 2, 1 February 1996, pp. 13–15; Lindsay Duguid, 'Love and money', *Times Literary Supplement*, 1 March 1996, p. 21.

10. See note 5 above.

11. The phrase was used in publicity for the video and DVD in the USA – see e.g. the official Miramax website for *Emma*, at www.miramax.com/emma/, accessed 10 April 2009.

12. Deborah Brown, 'Sense and Sensibility', *Empire*, March 1996, p. 33.

13. Linda Troost and Sayre Greenfield, 'Watching Ourselves Watching', in Troost and Greenfield, eds, *Jane Austen in Hollywood*, p. 9.

14. Deborah Kaplan, 'Mass marketing Jane Austen: men, women and courtship in two film adaptations', in Troost and Greenfield, eds, *Jane Austen in Hollywood*, p. 178.

15. Wiltshire, *Recreating Jane Austen*, passim.

16. Ang Lee, quoted in Michael Tunison, 'A sense of balance', *Entertainment Today*, 15–21 December 1995, p. 6.

17. See e.g. the advertisement for *Pride and Prejudice* in *Picturegoer*, 16 November 1940, p. 2; and the poster for the film reproduced at http://factualimagining.wordpress.com/2008/09/21/pride-prejudice-1940/, accessed 10 April 2009.

18. Laura Jacobs, 'Playing Jane', *Vanity Fair*, January 1996, p. 74.

19. Richard A. Blake, 'Plain Jane', *America*, 9 March 1996, p. 20.

20. Jack Kroll, 'Jane Austen does lunch', *Newsweek*, 18 December 1995, pp. 67–8.

21. Evan Thomas, 'Hooray for hypocrisy', *Newsweek*, 29 January 1996, p. 61.

22. Janet Maslin, 'Sense and Sensibility', *New York Times*, 13 December 1995, p. C15.

23. Rex Weiner, 'More Jane mania: Orion buys Austen's Sanditon', www.variety.com, 17 January 1997.
24. James Collins, 'Jane reaction', *Vogue*, January 1996, p. 70.
25. Andrew Higson, *English Heritage, English Cinema: Costume Drama Since 1980*, Oxford: Oxford University Press, 2003.
26. These statistics are drawn from a database compiled for this book and based on a thorough trawl through the film reviews in *Monthly Film Bulletin* (January 1990–April 1991) and *Sight and Sound* (May 1991–August 2009), supplemented with searches on the Internet Movie Database (www.imdb.com), inter alia; and on the table in Eddie Dyja, *BFI Film and Television Handbook*, London: British Film Institute, 2002, p. 34.
27. See e.g. Claire Monk, 'Sense and Sensibility', *Sight and Sound*, vol. 6, no. 3, March 1996.
28. Higson, *English Heritage, English Cinema*, pp. 101–6.
29. Wendy Wasserstein, 'The Premiere Review', *Premiere*, February 1996, p. 17.
30. Thompson, *Sense and Sensibility: The Diaries*, p. 56.
31. Todd McCarthy, 'Sense and Sensibility', *Variety*, 4 December 1995, p. 51.
32. Thompson, *Jane Austen's Sense and Sensibility*, p. 11.
33. 'Production information', in the Press Pack (UK version) for *Sense and Sensibility*, Columbia Films/Corbett and Keane Ltd., 1995, p. 1.
34. Monk, 'Sense and Sensibility', p. 51.
35. Juliann Garey, 'Movies', *Glamour*, February 1996, p. 120.
36. Janet Maslin, 'Sense and Sensibility', p. C15; Allison Pearson, 'Television: the fine art of Persuasion', *The Independent on Sunday*, *The Critics* section, 23 April 1995, p. 20.
37. Fiona Finlay, quoted in Tristan Davies, 'To kiss or not to kiss', *Daily Telegraph*, 7 January 1995, p. 12.
38. Fiona Finlay, quoted on the official website for *Persuasion*, at www.sonypictures.com/classics/persuasion/credits/finlay.html, accessed 7 July 2003.
39. For the poster, see the Sony Classics website, at www.sonypictures.com/classics/persuasion/persuasion.html; Davies, 'To kiss or not to kiss', p. 12.
40. Anon., 'Hot Austen', *The Times*, T2 section, 29 May 1996, p. 22.
41. Thompson, *Sense and Sensibility: The Diaries*, p. 32.
42. Roger Michell, quoted on the official website for *Persuasion*.
43. Ila Stanger, 'Jane Austen's England', *Town and Country*, January 1996.

44. Stanger, 'Jane Austen's England', pp. 78–9.
45. Stanger, 'Jane Austen's England', pp. 78–9, 82, 81.
46. Press Pack for *Sense and Sensibility*; Thompson, *Sense and Sensibility: The Diaries*, pp. 120–3.
47. David Gritten, 'Plymouth, England', *LA Times*, 24 March 1996, pp. 87–8.
48. James Meikle, 'Movies redraw the tourist map: visits to locations featured in popular films provide profitable new dimension in the travel business', *The Guardian*, 16 June 1999, p. 12.
49. Andrew Culf, 'Pride wins over tourist prejudice', *The Guardian*, 13 March 1996, p. 9.
50. Terrence Rafferty, 'Fidelity and infidelity', *The New Yorker*, 18 December 1995, p. 124.
51. McCarthy, 'Sense and Sensibility', p. 51.
52. Kroll, 'Jane Austen does lunch', p. 66.
53. Blake, 'Plain Jane', p. 21.
54. Jacobs, 'Playing Jane', p. 122.
55. Duguid, 'Love and money', p. 21.
56. Anon, *Video Hound's Golden Movie Retriever*, Detroit: Visible Ink Press, 1997, p. 663.
57. Rafferty, 'Fidelity and infidelity', p. 124.
58. Richard Alleva, 'Emma can read, too', *Commonweal*, 8 March 1996, p. 16.
59. Alleva, 'Emma can read, too', p. 17.
60. Ballaster, 'Adapting Jane Austen'; Pidduck, 'Of windows and country walks'; the quotation is on p. 386.
61. Roger Michell, quoted in Davies, 'To kiss or not to kiss', p. 12.
62. Stanger, 'Jane Austen's England', p. 82.
63. In this case, a reference to *Sense and Sensibility*: Judy Sloane, 'Emma makes sense', *Film Review*, March 1996, p. 30.
64. Michell, quoted in Davies, 'To kiss or not to kiss', p. 12.
65. Michell, quoted in Davies, 'To kiss or not to kiss', p. 12.
66. Fiona Finlay, quoted on the official website for *Persuasion*.
67. Ken Eisner, 'Emma', *Variety*, 17 June 1996, p. 52; Janet Maslin, 'Emma', *New York Times*, 2 August 1996, p. C1.
68. See e.g. Donald Lyons, 'Passionate precision', *Film Comment*, January–February 1996, p. 41.
69. Andy Medhurst, 'Dressing the part', *Sight and Sound*, vol. 6, no. 6, June 1996, p. 30.
70. Angela Krewani, 'Heritage as international film format', in Voigts-Virchow, *Janespotting and Beyond*, pp. 161–6.

71. Higson, *English Heritage, English Cinema*, pp. 262–7.
72. Higson, *English Heritage, English Cinema*, pp. 119–45.
73. Derek Elley, 'Persuasion', *Variety*, 29 May 1995, p. 60.
74. Doran, quoted in Oscar Moore, 'Sense and sensibility', *Screen International*, 7 July 1995, p. 18.
75. Louis Menand, 'What Jane Austen doesn't tell us', *New York Review of Books*, vol. 43, no. 2, 1 February 1996; Jacobs, 'Playing Jane'; Lyons, 'Passionate precision'.
76. James Bowman, 'Nonsense and insensibility', *The American Spectator*, February 1996, p. 61; 'The best of 1995', *Time*, no. 26, vol. 146, 25 December 1995, at www.time.com/time/magazine/article/0,9171,983896,00.html, accessed 19 December 1998.
77. Monica Roman, 'Arthouse, haunted house buoy Miramax', www.variety.com, 9 January 1997, accessed 10 May 2005.
78. Eisner, 'Emma', p. 52.
79. Maslin, 'Emma', p. C1.
80. Eisner, 'Emma', p. 52.
81. See the weekly box-office charts in *Variety*, December 1995 to May 1996; the *Sense and Sensibility* page on Box Office Mojo, at www.box-officemojo.com/movies/?id=senseandsensibility.htm, accessed 10 April 2009; and Eddie Dyja, ed., *BFI Film and Television Handbook 1997* (London: British Film Institute, 1996), p. 27.
82. See the weekly box-office charts in *Variety*, August–October 1996; the *Emma* page on Box Office Mojo, at www.boxofficemojo.com/movies/?id=emma.htm, accessed 10 April 2009; and Eddie Dyja, ed., *BFI Film and Television Handbook 1997* (London: British Film Institute, 1996), p. 27.
83. Jon Anderson, quoted in Mike Goodridge, 'Sense and marketability', *Screen International*, 29 March 1996, p. 34.
84. Goodridge, 'Sense and marketability', p. 34.
85. Mike Goodridge, 'Executive suite – Lindsay Doran', *Screen International*, 9 February 1996, p. 42; and Goodridge, 'Sense and marketability', p. 34.
86. Kenneth Turan, 'An Austen-tatious year', *Los Angeles Times*, 13 December 1995, p. F1.

6 The Austen screen franchise in the 2000s

1. Poster tagline, quoted in Jonathan Romney, 'Jane Austen's Spice Girl', *New Statesman*, 3 April 2000, p. 46.

2. www.bfi.org.uk/filmtvinfo/publications/pub-rep-brief/pdf/the-stats.pdf; and www.box-officemojo.com.
3. See e.g. Claudia L. Johnson, 'Run mad, but do not faint', *Times Literary Supplement*, 31 December 1999, pp. 16–17; Romney, 'Jane Austen's Spice Girl'. See also Pamela Church Gibson, 'Otherness, transgression and the post-colonial perspective: Patricia Rozema's *Mansfield Park*', in Eckart Voigts-Virchow, ed., *Janespotting and Beyond: British Heritage Retrovisions Since the Mid-1990s*, Tübingen: Gunter Narr Verlag Tübingen, 2004, pp. 51–64; Roger Sales, 'Paying the price for the party: Patricia Rozema's 1999 version of *Mansfield Park*', in Beatrice Battaglia and Diego Saglia, eds, *Re-drawing Austen: Picturesque Travels in Austenland*, Naples: Liguori, 2004, pp. 177–94.
4. Back-cover blurb on the British retail video sleeve (Miramax Home Entertainment/Buena Vista Home Entertainment).
5. 'CW', 'Mansfield Park', *Empire*, no. 136, October 2000, p. 126.
6. Brendan Kelly, 'Mansfield opens Montreal fest', www.variety.com, 30 September 1999, accessed 30 May 2003.
7. Andy Richards, 'Mansfield Park', *Sight and Sound*, vol. 10, no. 4, April 2000, p. 59.
8. Unnamed source, quoted in Tom Leonard, 'Jane Austen is censored for young audiences', *Daily Telegraph*, 16 November 1999, p. 14.
9. David Aukin, quoted in Adam Dawtrey, 'Hail Britannia', www.variety.com, 19 May 1998, accessed 30 May 2003.
10. Quoted in Carol Midgley, ' "Sexy" Austen film offends US sensibilities', *The Times*, 16 November 1999, p. 7.
11. Pamela Cuthbert, 'Mansfield Park', *Screen International*, 1 October 1999, p. 32.
12. Andrew O'Hagan, 'Sexual politics take over Jane Austen', *Daily Telegraph*, 31 March 2000, p. 27.
13. Leonard, 'Jane Austen is censored for young audiences', p. 14.
14. See Midgley, ' "Sexy" Austen film offends US sensibilities', p. 7; Sarah Shannon, 'No sex please, we're American', *Evening Standard*, 15 November 1999, p. 3; and Fiachra Gibbons, 'Film sets Mansfield Park alight with passion', *The Guardian*, 16 November 1999, p. 5.
15. Angie Errigo, 'Mansfield Park', *Empire*, no. 130, April 2000, p. 26.
16. Alexander Walker, 'Not the girl we once knew', *Evening Standard*, 30 March 2000, p. 30.
17. Quoted in Gibbons, 'Film sets Mansfield Park alight', p. 5.
18. Johnson, 'Run mad, but do not faint', p. 16.

19. See weekly box-office charts in *Variety*, November 1999 to March 2000.

20. See *Variety* online, at www.variety.com, 30 March 2000, accessed 30 May 2003.

21. See www.bbc.co.uk/arts/bigread/top100.shtml, accessed 14 July 2009; Jenny Colgan, 'Is this the book that changed your life?', *The Guardian*, G2 section, 9 December 2004, p. 11; and John Ezard, 'Pride and Prejudice the most precious as modern readers turn over an old leaf', at www.guardian.co.uk/uk/2007/mar/01/topstories3.books, accessed 14 July 2009.

22. See the user comments of Cindy S. and Brittany W. on the Metacritic web page for the film, at www.metacritic.com/film/titles/prideandprejudicealatterdaycomedy/, accessed 8 December 2008; *Salt Lake Tribune*, quoted on the official DVD website for *Pride and Prejudice – A Latter-Day Comedy*, at www.prideandprejudice.com, accessed 8 December 2008.

23. Anon., *Screen International*, 5 December 2003, p. 6.

24. Chadha, quoted in 'Chadha takes Austen to Bollywood', BBC News website, 1 October 2004, at http://news.bbc.co.uk/1/hi/entertainment/film/3706698, accessed 12 October 2004.

25. Chadha, quoted in Ziya Us Salam, 'All pride, no prejudice', *The Hindu*, 27 September 2004, at www.hinduonnet.com/thehindu/thscrip/print.pl?file=2004092702400300.htm, accessed 4 November 2004.

26. Chadha, quoted in 'Bollywood news', BBC website, 24 January 2003, at www.bbc.net.uk/manchester/masti/2003/01/24/bollywood_news.shtml, accessed 12 October 2004.

27. Chadha, quoted in Amit Roy, 'Never mind the fur, Ash does a Cruise', *The Telegraph* (Calcutta, India), 6 October 2004, at www.telegraphindia.com/1041006/asp/frontpage/story_3847747.asp, accessed 12 October 2004.

28. Chadha, quoted in Emma Brockes, 'Laughing all the way to the box-office', *The Guardian*, G2 section, 19 July 2004, p. 8.

29. See the BLM agency's case study of the prize-winning marketing campaign, at www.arenablm.co.uk/work/Pathé-bride-and-prejudice/, accessed 15 September 2007; also the official website for the film, at www.brideandprejudicethemovie.com, accessed 15 September 2007.

30. Quoted in 'Production Notes', on the Working Title website for *Pride and Prejudice*, at www.workingtitlefilms.com/downloads/PridePrejudice_ProductionNotes.pdf.

31. Judy Silkoff, 'Mad for MacFadyen', *Jane Austen's Regency World*, no. 18, November 2005, p. 7.
32. Will Hodgkinson, 'Bodice ripper', *The Guardian*, G2 section, 9 September 2005, p. 7.
33. Peter Bradshaw, 'Sweet Jane', *The Guardian*, Film and Music section, 16 September 2005, p. 9.
34. Bradshaw, 'Sweet Jane', p. 9.
35. Natasha Walter, 'Unrealistic, but undeniably real', *The Guardian*, 6 September 2005, p. 22.
36. Fionnuola Halligan, 'Pride and Prejudice', www.screendaily com, 12 September 2005, at www.screendaily.com/pride-and-prejudice/4024282.article, accessed 13 July 2009.
37. Wright quoted in Liz Hoggard, 'Meet the puppet master', *The Observer*, Review section, 1 September 2005, p. 5; and Silkoff, 'Mad for MacFadyen', p. 8.
38. Chris Ayres and Jack Malvern, 'Why new Pride and Prejudice is abridged in Britain', Times Online, 15 November 2005, at www.times-online.co.uk/tol/news/uk/article590309.ece, accessed 29 November 2008.
39. 'Top 10 UK Films', *The Guardian*, Film and Music section, 23 September 2005, p. 18; Charles Gant, 'Yesterday's heroes', *Sight and Sound*, vol. 16, no. 2, February 2006, p. 8; and Anon., 'Box-office Film History', www.variety.com, accessed 21 August 2006.
40. Steven Morris, 'A literary sensibility that makes solid financial sense', *The Guardian*, 3 September 2005, p. 9.
41. See www.visitbritain.com/VB3-en-GB/experiences/Tour/inspirational_landscapes/prideandprejudice; and www.visitprideandprejudice.com; both accessed 31 January 2007.
42. 'Jane Austen film and TV' page on the National Trust website, at www.nationaltrust.org.uk/main/w-vh/w-daysout/w-daysout-themed/w-daysout-themed-jane_austen_film_tv.htm, accessed 23 July 2009.
43. Olsberg/SPI, 'Stately Attraction: How Film and Television Programmes Promote Tourism in the UK', report commissioned by the UK Film Council et al., 2007, at www.ukfilmcouncil.org.uk/media/pdf/a/6/Final_Stately_Attraction_Report_to_UKFC_and_Partners_20.08.07.pdf, accessed 13 July 2009, p. 102.
44. Robert McCrum, 'Austen powers', *The Observer*, Review section, 1 September 2005, p. 5.

45. Ayres and Malvern, 'Why new Pride and Prejudice is abridged'.
46. Anon., 'Emma', *Radio Times*, 17–23 March 2007, p. 47.
47. For a survey of YouTube material, see Caryn James, 'Austen on YouTube', *New York Times*, 29 July 2007, at www.nytimes.com/2007/07/29/movies/29webjame.html?_r=1, accessed 10 December 2008.
48. Richard Woods, 'Austen mania', *The Sunday Times*, 11 March 2007, at www.timesonline.co.uk, accessed 13 March 2007.
49. See e.g. *Radio Times*, 17–23 March 2007, p. 1; *TV Quick*, 17–23 March 2007, p. 18; and *TV & Satellite Week*, 17–23 March 2007, p. 4.
50. Anon., 'Emma', *TV Times*, 17–23 March 2007, p. 30.
51. *Radio Times*, 17–23 March 2007.
52. *TV Quick*, 17–23 March 2007, p. 18.
53. Marie-Anne Hamilton, 'Corsets galore!', *TV Choice*, no. 12, 17–23 March 2007, p. 5.
54. Gill Hudson, 'Editor's letter: a brave new world for Miss Austen', *Radio Times*, 17–23 March 2007, p. 3.
55. Woods, 'Austen mania'.
56. Chris Hastings, Beth Jones and Stephanie Plemtl, 'Jane Austen to be the latest teenage sensation', *The Sunday Telegraph*, 4 February 2007, at www.telegraph.co.uk, accessed 12 March 2007.
57. Hastings, Jones and Plemtl, 'Jane Austen to be the latest teenage sensation'.
58. Quoted in Hastings, Jones and Plemtl, 'Jane Austen to be the latest teenage sensation'.
59. E. Jane Dickson, 'Revved-up Austen', *Radio Times*, 17–23 March 2007, p. 15.
60. Dickson, 'Revved-up Austen', p. 15.
61. 'Mansfield Park', *TV Times*, 17–23 March 2007, p. 45.
62. Dickson, 'Revved-up Austen', p. 15.
63. Quoted in Dickson, 'Revved-up Austen', p. 15.
64. 'Austen power', *TV & Satellite Week*, 17–23 March 2007, p. 4.
65. Marie-Anne Hamilton, 'Austen powers', *TV Quick*, 17–23 March 2007, p. 18.
66. Quoted in Dickson, 'Revved-up Austen', p. 16.
67. *TV Quick*, 17–23 March 2007, p. 19.
68. Dickson, 'Revved-up Austen', pp. 15–16.
69. Dickson, 'Revved-up Austen', p. 16.
70. Quoted in Woods, 'Austen mania'.

71. All quotations from the PBS press release for the Masterpiece 'Complete Jane Austen' season, at http://pressroom.pbs.org/documents/masterpiece_theatre_complete_jane_austen_rls, accessed 10 December 2008.

72. Adam Dawtrey, 'World in motion', *Variety*, 25 July 2004, at www.variety.com, accessed 19 March 2007.

73. See e.g. Nigel Reynolds, 'I could only become Jane by reading all her letters, admits star', *Daily Telegraph*, 7 March 2007, at www.telegraph.co.uk, accessed 14 March 2007; the Internet Movie Database, at www.imdb.com/title/tt0416508/business, accessed 10 December 2008; Anon., 'Brits jump to Jane, Outlaw', *Variety*, 9 March 2007, at www.variety.com, accessed 19 March 2007; quotation from Dade Hayes, 'Hollywood eyes new platforms', *Variety*, 21 January 2007, at www.variety.com, accessed 19 March 2007.

74. Allan Hunter, 'Becoming Jane', www.screendaily.com, 8 March 2007, accessed 12 March 2007.

75. Hunter, 'Becoming Jane'.

76. Steven Zeitchik, ' "Queen" energizes Miramax', *Variety*, 17 December 2006, at www.variety.com, accessed 19 March 2007.

77. Hayes, 'Hollywood eyes new platforms'.

78. Steven Friedlander, quoted in Hayes, 'Hollywood eyes new platforms'.

79. Archie Thomas, 'Italian audiences love "I Want You" ', *Variety*, 13 March 2007, at www.variety.com, accessed 19 March 2007.

80. www.boxofficemojo.com/movies/?id=becomingjane.htm; www.imdb.com/title/tt0416508/business; www.the-numbers.com/movies/ 2007/BJANE.php.

81. *Becoming Jane Reader Kit*, Miramax/YMI, 2007, available as a download on the official *Becoming Jane* website, at http://video.movies.go.com/becomingjane/, accessed 10 December 2008.

82. *Becoming Jane Reader Kit*.

83. Robert Bernstein, co-producer, quoted in Hugh Davies, 'Jane Austen at 19: the real life love story', www.telegraph.co.uk, 6 April 2006, accessed 14 March 2007.

84. Jon Spence, *Becoming Jane Austen: A Life*, London: Continuum, 2003.

85. See e.g. Reynolds, 'I could only become Jane'.

86. Quoted in Craig McLean, ' "Sexing up" Jane Austen', *The Daily Telegraph*, 2 March 2007, at www.telegraph.co.uk, accessed 14 March 2007.

87. Nigel Reynolds, 'City whizzkids drive out Jane Austen', *Daily Telegraph*, 3 March 2007, at www.telegraph.co.uk, accessed 14 March 2007.

88. Quoted in Sally Williams, 'Not so plain Jane', *Telegraph Magazine*, 17 February 2007, at www.telegraph.co.uk, accessed 14 March 2007.

89. Quoted in Williams, 'Not so plain Jane'.

90. Robert Bernstein, quoted in Davies, 'Jane Austen at 19'.

91. Jarrold, quoted in Wendy Ide, 'Breathing passionate life into the nation's favourite spinster', *The Times*, 8 March 2007, at www.times-online.co.uk, accessed 13 March 2007.

92. Quoted in Williams, 'Not so plain Jane'.

93. Douglas Rae, quoted in Jack Malvern, 'Austen's movie "a fanciful affair"', Times Online, 18 March 2006, at www.timesonline.co.uk, accessed 13 March 2007.

94. Quoted in Williams, 'Not so plain Jane'.

95. Jarrold, quoted in Ide, 'Breathing passionate life'.

96. Julian Jarrold, in 'Behind the scenes', special feature on *Becoming Jane* DVD, 2Entertain Video Ltd., 2007.

97. Hastings, Jones and Plemtl, 'Jane Austen to be the latest teenage sensation'.

98. Leo Benedictus, 'Calamity Jane?', at www.guardian.co.uk, accessed 14 March 2007; on Janeite concern on the internet, see especially the copious material on www.austenblog.com.

99. Craig McLean, ' "Sexing up" Jane Austen', *The Daily Telegraph*, 2 March 2007, at www.telegraph.co.uk, accessed 14 March 2007; Liz Beardsworth, 'Becoming Jane', *Empire*, April 2007, p. 56.

100. Anon., 'Brits jump to Jane, Outlaw'.

101. Trevor Johnston, 'Becoming Jane', *Time Out*, 7–13 March 2007, p. 59.

102. Hunter, 'Becoming Jane'.

103. Hunter, 'Becoming Jane'.

104. Allan Hunter, 'Tender truth of Jane's lost love', *Daily Express*, 17 March 2007, at www.express.co.uk, accessed 27 March 2007.

105. Williams, 'Not so plain Jane'.

106. Hunter, 'Becoming Jane'.

107. Hunter, 'Becoming Jane'.

108. C.S. Strowbridge, 'DVD releases for February 12, 2008', 12 February 2008, at www.the-numbers.com/interactive/newsStory.php? newsID= 3190, accessed 10 April 2009.

109. Tookey, 'Perfectly pleasant'.

110. Lisa Mullen, 'Becoming Jane', *Sight and Sound*, vol. 17, no. 4, April 2007, p. 49.

111. Peter Bradshaw, 'Becoming Jane', *The Guardian*, 9 March 2007, at www.guardian.co.uk, accessed 12 March 2007.
112. Strowbridge, 'DVD releases for February 12, 2008'.
113. Nicholas Barber, 'Becoming Jane', *The Independent*, 11 March 2007, at www.independent.co.uk, accessed 12 March 2007.
114. Nev Pierce, 'Becoming Jane', *Total Film*, no. 126, April 2007, p. 36.
115. Rosamund Witcher, *Grazia*, quoted on Ecosse Films website, www.ecossefilms.com/film_becoming.aspx, accessed 8 December 2008.
116. Pierce, 'Becoming Jane', p. 36.
117. Jeffrey Lyons, on NBC's *Reel Talk*, quoted on the official *Becoming Jane* DVD website, at http://video.movies.go.com/becomingjane/.
118. Advertisement for *Becoming Jane*, *The Guardian*, 16 March 2007, p. 5.
119. McLean, ' "Sexing up" Jane Austen'.
120. Hunter, 'Becoming Jane'; see also the same reviewer in another publication: Hunter, 'Tender truth of Jane's lost love'.
121. Tim Robey, 'A touching tribute to Austen's power', *Daily Telegraph*, 9 March 2007, at www.telegraph.co.uk, accessed 14 March 2007.
122. Williams, 'Not so plain Jane'.
123. See e.g. 'Becoming Jane', *The Daily Mirror*, 9 March 2007, at www.mirror.co.uk, accessed 27 March 2007.
124. Ide, 'Becoming Jane'.

7 Intimate and epic versions of the English past

1. Statistical information about numbers of period films released since 1990 is drawn from the database compiled for this book and based on a thorough trawl through the film reviews in *Monthly Film Bulletin* (January 1990–April 1991) and *Sight and Sound* (May 1991–August 2009), supplemented with searches on the Internet Movie Database (www.imdb.com), inter alia.
2. Ian George, Managing Director of Pathé Distribution, quoted in Nick Hunt, 'Case Study: *To Kill a King*', *Screen International*, 21–7 March 2003, p. 13.
3. David Rooney, 'Stage Beauty', *Variety*, 10–16 May 2004, p. 49.
4. *Mail on Sunday, Night & Day Magazine*, quoted on the official website for *Stage Beauty*, at www.radiotimes.com/stagebeauty/pressquotes.html, accessed 31 August 2005.
5. All box-office figures and budgets from www.variety.com; accessed 31 August 2006.

6. All box-office figures and budgets from www.variety.com; accessed 31 August 2006 and 14 July 2009.

7. Andrew Higson, *English Heritage, English Cinema: Costume Drama Since 1980*, Oxford: Oxford University Press, 2003.

8. 'Sound Bites: Charles Dance', special feature on *Ladies in Lavender* DVD, Entertainment in Video, 2005.

9. Nick James, 'Restoration', *Sight and Sound*, vol. 6, no. 4, April 1996, p. 52.

10. Lizzie Francke, 'Orlando', *Sight and Sound*, vol. 3, no. 3, March 1993, p. 48.

11. Andrew Wilson, 'All the Queen's castles', *Mail on Sunday Magazine*, 10 October 1998, p. 20.

12. Wilson, 'All the Queen's castles', p. 20.

13. Gerald Kaufman, 'Royal Flush', *New Statesman*, 2 October 1998, pp. 36–7.

14. Andy Medhurst, 'Dressing the part', *Sight and Sound*, vol. 6, no. 6, June 1996, p. 30.

15. Allan Hunter, 'To Kill a King', *Screen International*, 2–8 May 2003, p. 28.

16. Derek Elley, 'To Kill a King', *Variety*, 19–25 May 2003, p. 27.

17. Philip Kemp, 'Anazapta', *Sight and Sound*, vol. 14, no. 6, June 2004, p. 44.

18. Kemp, 'Anazapta', p. 44.

19. Leo McKinstry, 'Dumbing down? Rubbish. Britain is braining up', *Daily Mail*, 10 February 1999, p. 10.

20. McKinstry, 'Dumbing down?', p. 10.

8   Blurring boundaries: historical myopia and period authenticity

1. All release details and box-office figures from www.variety.com; accessed 31 August 2006.

2. Eddie Dyja, ed., *BFI Film and Television Handbook 2000*, London: British Film Institute, 1999, p. 22; and entry for *Shakespeare in Love* on Box Office Mojo website, at www.boxofficemojo.com/movies/?id=shakespeareinlove.htm, accessed 10 April 2009.

3. Mike Goodridge, 'Shakespeare in Love', *Screen International*, 18 December 1998, p. 19.

4. Mariella Frostrup, 'The good, the Bard and the lovely', *News of the World*, 31 January 1999, p. 60.

5. Emma Forrest, 'To be a hit or not to be...', *The Observer*, 24 January 1999, p. 25.
6. Quoted in 'Production Notes', on the Working Title website for *Pride and Prejudice*, at www.workingtitlefilms.com/downloads/ PridePrejudice_ProductionNotes.pdf, accessed 10 April 2009.
7. Pawel Edelman, Director of Photography, in 'The Best of Twist', special feature documentary on the *Oliver Twist* DVD, Pathé, 2005; see also 'Twist by Polanski', another special feature documentary on the same DVD.
8. Nick Hunt, 'Case Study: *To Kill a King*', *Screen International*, 21–7 March 2003, p. 13.
9. See *King Arthur: Director's Cut* DVD, Touchstone Home Entertainment, n.d.; the quotation is from the back cover blurb.
10. Back cover blurb, *King Arthur: Director's Cut*.
11. Front cover banner, *King Arthur: Director's Cut*.
12. I am indebted to Jon Stubbs for suggesting this way of thinking about changing representations of the past.
13. Dan Glaister, 'The romance continues as American and UK audiences fall in love with Shakespeare', *The Guardian*, 3 February 1999, p. 3.
14. Bob Davis of *Spin* magazine, quoted in Michael Ellison, 'Bard battles for Oscars against Private Ryan', *The Guardian*, 10 February 1999, p. 5.
15. Anthony Holden, 'Will's secret history', *The Observer Review*, 3 January 1999, p. 5.
16. Jonathan Romney, 'A bard day's night', *The Guardian, Friday Review*, 29 January 1999, p. 8.
17. Lael Lowenstein, '*Shakespeare in Love*', *Variety*, 6 December 1998, at www.variety.com, accessed 30 May 2003.
18. Forrest, 'To be a hit'.
19. Todd McCarthy, 'A Knight's Tale', www.variety.com, 19 April 2001, accessed 30 May 2003.
20. Quoted on the official website for *Elizabeth*, at www.elizabeth.the-movie.com, accessed 20 November 2000.
21. Richard Eyre, in 'Setting the stage: behind the scenes of *Stage Beauty*', featurette on *Stage Beauty* DVD, Momentum Pictures, 2004.
22. Geoffrey Macnab, 'Stage Beauty', www.screendaily.com, 9 July 2004, accessed 7 December 2004.
23. Speaking to camera in 'Setting the stage: behind the scenes of *Stage Beauty*'.

24. Jenny McCartney, 'His beauty is her curse', *Sunday Telegraph*, 5 September 2004, p. 6.

25. Andy Medhurst, 'Dressing the part', *Sight and Sound*, vol. 6, no. 6, June 1996, p. 28.

26. Quoted in Adam Sherwin, 'Civil War re-enacted in battle for viewers', *The Times*, 22 December 2001, p. 9.

27. Derek Elley, 'To Kill a King', *Variety*, 19–25 May 2003, p. 27.

28. Philip Kemp, 'Love of the common people', *Sight and Sound*, vol. 13, no. 6, June 2003, p. 34.

29. Allan Hunter, 'Troubled feature keeps its head but lacks focus', *Screen International*, 2–8 May 2003, p. 28.

30. Loader quoted in Hunt, 'Case Study: *To Kill a King*', p. 13.

31. Peter Bradshaw, 'Twist again', *The Guardian*, G2 section, 7 October 2005, p. 7; see also Philip French, 'This Oliver needs more', *The Observer*, 9 October 2005, p. 9.

32. Rose, quoted in Martyn Palmer, 'Blood, sweat and spears', *The Times*, *Magazine* section, 24 July 2004, p. 37.

33. McCarthy, 'A Knight's Tale'.

34. Ridley Scott, 'When worlds collide', *The Guardian*, *Review* section, 29 April 2005, p. 7.

35. See Cahal Milmo, 'A wound that has lasted 900 years', *The Independent*, 3 May 2005, pp. 12–13.

36. See Robert Spencer, 'Crusading against history', www.frontpage-mag.com, 3 May 2005, accessed 25 October 2007.

37. 'Interview with Alberto Sciamma (director/co-writer)', special feature on *Anazapta* DVD, Guerilla Films, 2004.

38. Department for Culture, Media and Sport (DCMS), 'Guidance Notes – 1 January 2007, Schedule 1 to the Films Act 1985', p. 12.

39. DCMS, 'Guidance Notes', p. 13.

40. DCMS, 'Guidance Notes', p. 14.

41. See James Langton and Chris Hastings, 'Slave film turns Wilberforce into a US hero', 25 February 2007, at www.telegraph.co.uk/news/worldnews/1543807/Slave-film-turns-Wilberforce-into-a-US-hero.html, accessed 20 July 2009.

Conclusion

1. HM Treasury, 'Reform of film tax incentives: Promoting the sustainable production of culturally British films', July 2005, at www.hm-treasury.gov.uk/d/filmcondocv1.pdf, accessed 18 March 2009, para 2.3.

2. HM Treasury, 'Reform of film tax incentives'.

3. Tessa Jowell, Minister for Culture, Media and Sport, 'Valuing culture', speech delivered on 17 June 2003, at www.culture.gov.uk/reference_library/minister_speeches/2113.aspx, accessed 18 March 2009.

4. Olsberg/SPI, 'Stately Attraction: How Film and Television Programmes Promote Tourism in the UK', report commissioned by the UK Film Council et al., 2007, at www.ukfilmcouncil.org.uk/media/pdf/a/6/Final_Stately_Attraction_Report_to_UKFC_and_Partners_20.08.07.pdf, accessed 13 July 2009, p. 14.

Select Bibliography

Books and journals

Ballaster, Ros, 'Adapting Jane Austen', *The English Review*, September 1996.

Billig, Michael, *Banal Nationalism*, London: Sage Publications, 1995.

Bordwell, David, *Narration in the Fiction Film*, Madison: University of Wisconsin Press, 1985.

Brunsdon, Charlotte, 'The poignancy of place: London and the cinema', *Visual Culture in Britain*, vol. 5, no. 1, 2004, p. 59.

——— *London in Cinema: The Cinematic City Since 1945*, Basingstoke: Palgrave Macmillan, 2007.

Byatt, A.S., *Possession: A Romance*, London: Vintage, 1991 (1st publ. 1990).

Cartmell, Deborah, I.Q. Hunter, Heidi Kaye and Imelda Whelehan, eds, *Pulping Fictions: Consuming Culture across the Literature/Media Divide*, London: Pluto Press, 1996.

Cartmell, Deborah, and Imelda Whelehan, eds, *Adaptations: From Text to Screen, Screen to Text*, London: Routledge, 1999.

Caterer, James, and Andrew Higson, 'A indústria cinematográfica britânica', in Alessandra Meleiro, ed., *Cinema No Mundo: Indústria, Política e Mercado*, Vol. V: *Europa*, São Paulo: Escrituras Editora, 2007, pp. 59–85.

Church Gibson, Pamela, 'Otherness, transgression and the post-colonial perspective: Patricia Rozema's *Mansfield Park*', in Voigts-Virchow, ed., *Janespotting and Beyond: British Heritage Retrovisions Since the Mid-1990s*, pp. 51–64.

Dickinson, Margaret, and Sylvia Harvey, 'Public policy and public funding for film: some recent UK developments', *Screen*, vol. 46, no. 1, spring 2005, pp. 87–95.

DiPaolo, Marc Edward, *Emma Adapted: Jane Austen's Heroine from Book to Film*, New York: Peter Lang, 2007.

Eckstut, Arielle, *Pride and Promiscuity: The Lost Sex Scenes of Jane Austen*, New York: Fireside, 2001.

Featherstone, Mike, 'Global Culture: An Introduction', *Theory, Culture & Society*, 7 (2–3), 1990, p. 2.

Franklin, Dan, 'Commissioning and editing modern fiction', in Zachary Leader, ed., *On Modern British Fiction*, Oxford: Oxford University Press, 2002, pp. 270–83.

Geraghty, Christine, *Now a Major Motion Picture: Film Adaptations of Literature and Drama*, Lanham: Rowman and Littlefield, 2008.

Harvey, David, *The Condition of Postmodernity: An Enquiry into the Origins of Cultural Change*, Oxford: Blackwell, 1990.

Higson, Andrew, 'The concept of national cinema', *Screen*, vol. 30, no. 4, autumn 1989, pp. 36–46.

—— *Waving the Flag: Constructing a National Cinema in Britain*, Oxford: Oxford University Press, 1995, 212–71.

—— *English Heritage, English Cinema: Costume Drama Since 1980*, Oxford: Oxford University Press, 2003.

Hill, John, *British Cinema in the 1980s: Issues and Themes*, Oxford: Clarendon Press, 1999.

—— 'UK film policy, cultural capital and social exclusion', *Cultural Trends*, vol. 13 (2), no. 50, June 2004, p. 32.

Hjort, Mette, 'Themes of nation', in Mette Hjort and Scott Mackenzie, eds, *Cinema and Nation*, London and New York: Routledge, 2000, pp. 103–18.

—— *Small Nation, Global Cinema: The New Danish Cinema*, Minneapolis/London: University of Minnesota Press, 2005.

Hjort, Mette and Duncan Petrie, 'Introduction', in Hjort and Petrie, eds, *The Cinema of Small Nations*, Edinburgh: Edinburgh University Press, 2007, pp. 1–22.

Hoskins, Colin, and Stuart McFadyen, 'Guest Editors' Introduction', *Canadian Journal of Communications*, 16 (2), 1991, at www.cjc-online.ca, accessed 5 April 2009.

Kaplan, Deborah, 'Mass marketing Jane Austen: men, women and courtship in two film adaptations', in Troost and Greenfield, eds, *Jane Austen in Hollywood*, pp. 177–87.

Krewani, Angela, 'Heritage as international film format', in Voigts-Virchow, *Janespotting and Beyond*, pp. 161–6.

MacDonald, Gina and Andrew F., eds, *Jane Austen on Screen*, Cambridge: Cambridge University Press, 2003.

McFarlane, Brian, *Novel to Film: An Introduction to the Theory of Adaptation*, Oxford: Clarendon Press, 1996.

Mather, Nigel, *Tears of Laughter: Comedy-Drama in 1990s British Cinema*, Manchester: Manchester University Press, 2006.

Medhurst, Andy, 'Dressing the part', *Sight and Sound*, vol. 6, no. 6, June 1996, p. 30.

Miller, Toby, 'The Film Industry and the Government', in Murphy, ed., *British Cinema of the 90s*, pp. 37–47.

Monaghan, David, Ariane Hudelet and John Wiltshire, eds, *The Cinematic Jane Austen: Essays on the Filmic Sensibility of the Novels*, Jefferson, NC, and London: McFarland, 2009.

Murphy, Robert, ed., *British Cinema of the 90s*, London: British Film Institute, 2000.

Negra, Diane, 'Romance and/as tourism', in Matthew Tinkcom and Amy Villarejo, eds, *Keyframes: Popular Cinema and Cultural Studies*, London: Routledge, 2001, pp. 98–114.

North, Julian, 'Conservative Austen, radical Austen: *Sense and Sensibility* from text to screen', in Cartmell and Whelehan, eds, *Adaptations: From Text to Screen, Screen to Text*, pp. 38–50.

Parrill, Sue, *Jane Austen on Film and Television: A Critical Study of the Adaptations*, Jefferson, NC: McFarland, 2002.

Pidduck, Julianne, 'Of windows and country walks: frames of space and movement in 1990s Austen adaptations', *Screen*, vol. 39, no. 4, winter 1998.

Pratten, Stephen, and Simon Deakin, 'Competitiveness policy and economic organization: the case of the British film industry', *Screen*, vol. 41, no. 2, summer 2000, pp. 217–37.

Pucci, Suzanne R., and James Thompson, eds, *Jane Austen and Co.: Remaking the Past in Contemporary Culture*, New York: SUNY Press, 2003.

Robertson, Roland, 'Glocalization: time-space and homogeneity-heterogeneity', in Mike Featherstone, Scott Lash and Robert Robertson, eds, *Global Modernities*, London: Sage, 1995, pp. 25–44.

Sales, Roger, 'In Face of All the Servants: Spectators and Spies in Austen', in Deidre Lynch, ed., *Janeites: Austen's Disciples and Devotees*, Princeton: Princeton University Press, 2000.

——— 'Paying the price for the party: Patricia Rozema's 1999 version of *Mansfield Park*', in Beatrice Battaglia and Diego Saglia, eds, *Re-drawing Austen: Picturesque Travels in Austenland*, Naples: Liguori, 2004, pp. 177–94.

Smith, Anthony D., *National Identity*, Harmondsworth: Penguin, 1991, pp. 8–11.

Smith, Chris, *Creative Britain*, London: Faber and Faber, 1998.

Sonnet, Esther, 'From *Emma* to *Clueless*: taste, pleasure and the scene of history', in Cartmell and Whelehan, eds, *Adaptations: From Text to Screen, Screen to Text*, pp. 51–62.

Spence, Jon, *Becoming Jane Austen: A Life*, London: Continuum, 2003.

Stam, Robert, *Literature Through Film: Realism, Magic and the Art of Adaptation*, Oxford: Blackwell Publishing, 2004.

Stam, Robert, and Alessandra Raengo, eds, *A Companion to Literature and Film*, Oxford: Blackwell Publishing, 2004.

——— *Literature and Film: A Guide to the Theory and Practice of Film Adaptation*, Oxford: Blackwell Publishing, 2004.

Sutherland, John, *Reading the Decades: Fifty Years of the Nation's Bestselling Books*, London: BBC, 2002.

Sutherland, Kathryn, *Jane Austen's Textual Lives: From Aeschylus to Bollywood*, Oxford: Oxford University Press, 2007.

Thompson, Emma, *Jane Austen's Sense and Sensibility: The Screenplay and Diaries*, London: Bloomsbury, 1995.

——— *Sense and Sensibility: The Diaries*, London: Bloomsbury, 1996.

Todd, Peter, 'The British film industry in the 1990s', in Murphy, ed., *British Cinema of the 90s*, pp. 17–26.

Troost, Linda, and Sayre Greenfield, 'Watching Ourselves Watching', in Troost and Greenfield, eds, *Jane Austen in Hollywood*, pp. 1–12.

Troost, Linda, and Sayre Greenfield, eds, *Jane Austen in Hollywood*, Kentucky: The University Press of Kentucky, 2001, 2nd edn.

Voigts-Virchow, Eckart, *Janespotting and Beyond: British Heritage Retrovisions since the Mid-1990s*, Tübingen: Gunter Narr Verlag Tübingen, 2004.

Wiltshire, John, *Recreating Jane Austen*, Cambridge: Cambridge University Press, 2001.

Reports, yearbooks, official publications, etc.

British Film Institute, *BFI Film and Television Handbook*, published annually for the period 1990–2004, edited by David Leafe (1990–3, and co-ed., 1994), Terry Ilott (co-ed., 1994), Nick Thomas (1995–6) and Eddie Dyja (1997–2004), London: British Film Institute.

——— 'The Stats: an overview of the film, television, video and DVD industries in the UK 1990–2003', www.bfi.org.uk/filmtvinfo/publications/pub-rep-brief/pdf/the-stats.pdf.

HM Revenue and Customs, *Film Production Company Manual*, section FPC10160, at www.hmrc.gov.uk/manuals/fpcmanual.htm, accessed 14 January 2009.

Narval Media/Birkbeck College/Media Consulting Group, *Stories We Tell Ourselves: The Cultural Impact of UK Film 1946–2006. A Study for the UK Film Council*, London: UKFC, June 2009, at www.ukfilmcouncil.org.uk/media/pdf/c/g/Cultural_Impact_Report_FINAL.pdf, accessed 30 June 2009.

Olsberg/SPI, 'Stately Attraction: How Film and Television Programmes Promote Tourism in the UK', report commissioned by the UK Film Council et al., 2007, at www.ukfilmcouncil.org.uk/media/pdf/a/6/Final_Stately_Attraction_Report_to_UKFC_and_Partners_20.08.07.pdf, accessed 13 July 2009.

Oxford Economics, *The Economic Impact of the UK Film Industry*, Oxford: Oxford Economics, July 2007, at www.ukfilmcouncil.org.uk/media/pdf/5/8/FilmCouncilreport190707.pdf, accessed 14 January 2009.

UK Film Council, *Our Second Three-Year Plan*, London: UKFC, 2004, at www.ukfilmcouncil.org.uk/media/pdf/d/r/Our_Second_Three_Year_Plan.pdf, accessed 14 January 2009.

——— *Statistical Yearbook*, published annually for the period 2002–9, London: UKFC.

——— 'Towards a sustainable UK film industry', London: UKFC, 2000, at www.ukfilmcouncil.org.uk/media/pdf/p/r/TASFI.pdf, accessed 14 January 2009.

UK government, *Films Act 1985*, Schedule 1, at www.opsi.gov.uk/RevisedStatutes/Acts/ukpga/1985/cukpga_19850021_en_2, accessed 14 January 2009.

Websites

Box Office Mojo, www.boxofficemojo.com.
UK Film Council, www.ukfilmcouncil.org.uk.
Variety, www.variety.com.
Internet Movie Database, www.imdb.com.

Index

Entries in bold indicate substantive discussions